"*Onward & Upward* is the memoir of a rare and v̖
extraordinary life. It's filled with Michael Wiese's adventures, his incredible journeys,
and his interactions with amazing people. I consider myself very privileged to know
Michael. Read this book, and you'll understand why."

  — John Robbins, author: *Diet for a New America*, co-founder: Food
   Revolution Network

"Michael Wiese is a modern shaman whose lifelong quest has been to discover what is
possible in the physical, intellectual, and spiritual worlds. But who could have imagined
that he would become the publisher of more books on film in English than anyone
else in the world? While other shamans may meditate and gaze inward for revelation,
Wiese follows The GOYA Principle (Get Off Your Ass....) and he does. From Bali to
the jungles of Peru and New York, Wiese's search for an ethical existence filled with
meaning has constantly pushed him on. Reading *Onward & Upward* is a joyous, often
humorous, and moving experience."

  — Howard Suber, professor for 48 years in the UCLA film school, founder
   of the UCLA Film and Television Producers Program, author: *The Power
   of Film*

"Like some of the best things in life, *Onward & Upward* was a joy I wasn't expecting. An
autobiography of author, filmmaker, producer, and entrepreneur Michael Wiese, this
book craftily outlines a life well lived, weaving in wide-angle historical sketches with
intimate close-ups on the moviemaking and distribution business. The cast is studded
with luminaries like Salvador Dalí, Buckminster Fuller, Shirley MacLaine, and a host of
Hollywood movers-and-shakers, as well as Wiese's family and teachers. But the real star
is Wiese himself, and the strange, intoxicating journey of his own spiritual path — from
Bali to the jungles of the Amazon. Wiese peels back theme and story to remind us why
we make films, and books, and love — and like Balinese shadow puppets, he reveals the
hand of something greater in the drama of life."

  — Rak Razam, author: *Aya: A Shamanic Odyssey*

"Michael Wiese has written a unique memoir, the inspiring story of a courageous individual born at a time of huge cultural change who has followed his heart and made a
genuine contribution to consciousness. From small-town America, to Haight-Ashbury
at its peak, to the world of New York and Hollywood media, to deep spiritual exploration in the jungles of Peru and beyond, Michael has trusted his inner being and taken
risks that would have daunted a lesser person. His book is an emotionally honest,

entirely unpredictable adventure. It tells the compelling tale of a gifted and resourceful person who stays true to his values, always chooses the spiritual and the compassionate, never forsakes his deepest values, and is often willing to head into the unknown. The result has been a joyful life, permeated increasingly by spiritual wisdom. This is a book that readers will cherish. It imparts the immense value of staying true to one's convictions and visions, and demonstrates the inwardly rich life that results when integrity is maintained despite the circumstances. One puts this book down with a sense of a life well lived, and a feeling of gratitude that the author has chosen to give us such a candid record of his impressive journey to wholeness."

> — Ralph White, Co-Founder and Creative Director, New York Open Center

"A kaleidoscope of the human spirit and soul. Deceptively simple to read, yet transcendent for its inner journey. Michael Wiese's life memoir takes us traveling to myriad countries and life explorations, growing up in the arts in the real world — as his many experiences in the spiritual realm gently reflect off our own consciousness. We find ourselves spending time with luminous people like Buckminster Fuller, shadow puppet masters in Bali, and members of Michael's own fascinating family, all feeling like warm old friends one hasn't met yet. Inspirational, revealing, and at times, valuably poignant."

> — Pen Densham, filmmaker, author: *Riding the Alligator: Strategies for a Career in Screenplay Writing*

"A love letter to life, and Michael Wiese's gift to the artists of the future. A loving autobiography of a successful filmmaker, writer, and artist, whose life is devoted to achieving artistic integrity, loving relationships, and spiritual awareness. Wiese shows how it is possible to live a fulfilling and artistically satisfying life in the post-industrial world. His global path to spiritual awakening and success as a filmmaker and publisher holds lessons for all artists of the 21st century and beyond."

> — Tony Levelle, editor: *The Psychedelic Explorer's Guide*

"*Onward & Upward* is an incredible journey and adventurous ride through the 65 years of Michael Wiese's life as a filmmaker, from his hometown of Champaign, Illinois, to San Francisco, Japan, Los Angeles, Bali, India, Africa, Peru, Bahamas, New York, and Europe. His spiritual and filmmaking quest is told with candor, humor, passion, and enlightenment. By far, one of the most intriguing stories I've read; I couldn't put it down."

> — Ann Baldwin, screenwriter, author: *The Power of Dreams*

"Seeker, pilgrim, moviemaker, producer, Michael Wiese opens up his heart in this joyous celebration of creativity, imagination, and the wonderful, nutty people who make movies. What a half century of moviemaking! What a funny, knowing, joy-inspiring book!"

> — Robert Gerst, author: *Make Film History: Rewrite, Reshoot, and Recut the World's Greatest Films*

"A statement about writing goes something like this: Writing is easy — you just open a vein and bleed onto the page. If that's true, then writing a memoir is like cutting open your chest without benefit of anesthesia and slicing off a piece of your heart. That's what Michael Wiese does in his book *Onward & Upward*. Enhanced by lovingly recorded photographs of people and stories of years gone by, this book surgically examines Wiese's DNA. The prognosis is excellent. He has a lot of loving, living, and writing to do."

> — Mary J. Schirmer, writer, teacher

"Michael Wiese balances a life's journey on the page in a brisk, vivid, self-effacing style, making *Onward & Upward* not simply the story of himself, but of everyone and every-thing he encounters, with the reader always included on the journey. Remarkable."

> — Matthew Barber, playwright: *Enchanted April*

"Michael Wiese is one of the most unique individuals I have ever met — and I've known a lot of creative people! Simply put, inquisitive and decent, it's difficult to imagine someone spending time in Michael's company without feeling better for it."

> — D.W. Brown, author: *2500 Years of Wisdom: Sayings of the Great Masters*

"*Onward & Upward* was a pleasure from start to finish — a genuinely engaging auto-biography. The fact that Michael Wiese is the only person I've ever heard of who was thrown out of school for not sleeping with a girl, that he was pivotal in bringing the first underwater concert to dolphins, and that the most successful years of his career was when he was most lost, gives his narrative enough twists and turns to have kept my attention to the very magical end. I'm so glad that he wrote it. You will be too."

> — James Fadiman, Ph.D., author: *The Psychedelic Explorer's Guide*

"My students became accustomed to my expressions of concern for their screenplays to be a 'good story well told,' and over time they became energized to do just that, tell their stories well! *Onward & Upward* is the story of a 'good life well lived,' without a doubt. Like Emerson, who defined the success in a life he perceived as well-lived, Michael Wiese forged the connections that sustained him throughout his life to feed his creative forces, no matter how difficult and challenged that life often became. Fascinating!"

— Fred G. Thorne, writer, producer, director, professor

"'The journey of a thousand miles begins beneath one's feet,' wrote Lao Tzu. Although the last three words of this popular quote are frequently written as 'with a single step,' the Chinese philosopher's original version more aptly captures the globetrekking adventures of author Michael Wiese in his new book, *Onward & Upward: Reflections of a Joyful Life*. To reach one's geographical and spiritual destinations requires not only the ability to have well grounded values to begin with but also the vision to look to the stars and say with unabashed confidence, 'Why not?' Michael Wiese may be halfway through his sixth decade, but the evocative cover art of youthfulness and determination affirms that his globetrekking adventures and his unabashed passions for film, divine enlightenment, and cultural awareness are far from over. He writes that each unscripted chapter of existence is a lesson whose takeaway value is often unknown until the next challenge presents itself. The photographs sprinkled throughout the text are an engaging time-capsule of life in the past lane (how *did* we survive the '70s?), on the shores of exotic realms, and amidst the tranquility of the Cornwall setting Wiese and his family call home. The tone is as conversational as if he were sitting across a table from the reader and having a cup of tea. For that matter, it would likely be the same conversation if the person in his company were Lao Tzu himself, pausing thoughtfully between sips to remark, 'Yes, Michael. You understand the journey.'"

— Christina Hamlett, script consultant, playwright, author: *Screenwriting for Teens*

"You'll be propelled 'onward and upward' by this mesmerizing account of a true spiritual explorer's quest to find all that's beautiful, positive, and true in every corner of our planet, plus side-trips to some places not of this world! You'll discover courage and inspiration in this journey of an artist whose true art form, it seems, is empowering others (including me!) to express themselves. Every page overflows with Michael's awed appreciation for the wonder of life, and it will fill you with the desire to explore on your own."

— Christopher Vogler, author: *The Writer's Journey*

Onward &
UPWARD

REFLECTIONS *of* A JOYFUL LIFE

MICHAEL WIESE

Published by Michael Wiese Productions
12400 Ventura Blvd. #1111
Studio City, CA 91604
(818) 379-8799, (818) 986-3408 (FAX)
mw@mwp.com
www.mwp.com

Copy Editor/Photo Editor: Geraldine Overton
Cover Design: Johnny Ink
Proofreader: Matt Barber
Printed by McNaughton & Gunn

Manufactured in the United States of America
Copyright 2013 by Michael Wiese

Library of Congress Cataloging-in-Publication Data

Wiese, Michael, 1947-
 Onward & upward : reflections of a joyful life / Michael Wiese.
    pages cm
 ISBN 978-1-61593-139-2
1. Wiese, Michael, 1947- 2. Motion picture producers and directors--United States--Biography. I. Title.
II. Title: Onward and upward.
 PN1998.3.W548A3 2013
 791.4302'33092--dc23
 [B]
                            2013006159

Printed on Recycled Stock
Publisher plants 10 trees for every one tree used to produce this book.

Dedicated to:

Geraldine Overton
Wife, Soul Partner, Adventurer, and Muse
She who brings Beauty and Perfection to everything she touches

Julia Bronwyn Wiese
My brave, questing, jewel of a daughter
The book is my past
The future is all yours

My Teachers
Each and every one of you
Whether you appear in this book or not
Whether we can see you or not

Table
of Contents

Prologue

Before sleep comes and as you recall the passing day, you'll find that it's made up of stories, many stories, some free floating, some interconnected, some strands of other stories, some complete, and some incomplete. Some will carry great urgency but no clue to content, like the one-sentence postcard home to my parents that I sent after my first week at summer camp: "Dear Mom & Dad, I was almost killed twice yesterday."

This book contains stories that hold meaning for me. These are stories I tell about myself. The stories may honor teachers, lovers, or friends who traveled with me for so brief a moment before our stories veered off into divergent directions. These are stories that make up a life, but are not that life. They may make up my becoming, but they are not who I've become. They are beautiful snake skins left behind as my spirit passes through them and then vanishes.

The stories do, for a moment, make someone real. That eight-year-old Michael still exists, trying to build a wooden raft that will carry him, like Huck Finn, down a great river. I honor him, acknowledge who he was and what he was learning, and send him along, not to follow me into adulthood, but to live out his eight-year old life in another dimension of time. In these fragments of stories, like the brooms in *The Sorcerer's Apprentice*, I send out a myriad of Michaels, each one struggling to find the "secret of life" that I so hoped my Rabbi would tell me, but didn't.

Our stories weave and criss-cross like the crust on Grandma Wiese's rhubarb pie. They carry personal remembrances, teachings, insights, and transmissions about what it means to be human. From these infinite lives I've selected some that I've been storing in a silver box, waiting for the right time to tell them.

As a human being, now in my 65th year, I turn and suddenly I've become an elder, and it's my responsibility, and perhaps even my duty, to share my experiences on earth. May they bring some enjoyment and inspiration for you in a celebration of life.

Onward and Upward,

Michael Wiese
Cornwall, August 2012

Observing
Champaign

1947  *1965*

"A little boy was asked how he learned to skate. 'By getting up every time I fell down,' he answered."

— David Seabury

....

Time exposure self-portrait with City of New Orleans train.

BRIGHT LIGHTS

My skin presses on a metal slab. It's very cold. I shiver. Eyes peer down at me. Rough meaty hands poke me. Something big carries me and sets me down with a clunk on a hard surface and wraps me in something scratchy. Bright lights. There is much space. Soft forms move around and shade me from the light. I am glad to be out. I am ready to start my mission. It's then I notice that my arms and legs don't work yet.

I am new born... with double pneumonia. It's a miracle I survive.

TOES

Every night Mom and Dad fool around with my feet. They wrap gauze around my overlapping toes to force them apart. It doesn't hurt. I enjoy the attention. This is always fun for me. I can walk.

BABY JEFF

No longer do my feet need wrapping. But someone else is in a crib in my room. It's baby Jeff. He fusses and everybody gathers round him. What about me? I forget how to go potty.

WABBITS

In first grade I have special classes with Mrs. Meeker, a speech therapist. She's pretty and kind. Those dern R's. I can't make that sound. I stare at the printed yellow flowers on her dress as I practice pushing air by curling my tongue. "Wun, wabbit, wun." "Wun, wabbit, wun." After many months I learn to do it! Christmas comes and with my new-found confidence I belt out my favorite song, "Wudolph da wed-nose waindee."

DOUGH BOY

I am four. Mother is out for lunch. Dad is at the store. Maddie, a once-a-week maid, watches after me and Jeff. She is down in the basement ironing and smoking Kools, the ones with the penguin cartoon on them. I carry Jeff, who is almost two, and put him gently on the changing table as I'd seen my mother do. I lock the door to the room. I am going to change the baby all by myself.

Jeff sits there like a little naked Buddha, I rub baby oil all over him. I finish him off with a heavy sprinkle of talcum powder. He looks funny, like the Pillsbury Doughboy or a small snowman.

Maddie bangs on the door. I ignore her. She calls my Dad because soon I see his face through the window. He is huffing and puffing. His face is red. He pounds on the locked door shouting, "Michael! Michael! Let me in!" I reply, "Not by the hair of my chinny chin chin!"

ELM STREET

We live at 1108 S. Elm Street in Champaign, Illinois. It's a two-bedroom, one-bath, pre-fabricated house popular with returning WWII vets. It costs $7,000. It's like a trailer, only better. It's rectangular with concrete steps that lead up to it. Open the door and you walk immediately into the living room, which is connected to a dining room. Straight ahead, past a small bathroom, are two bedrooms.

Some days a horse-drawn white wagon brings us cold bottles of milk packed in ice. I run outside to see the horse or to see the ice cream man who rides a bicycle with a big white box in front filled with dry ice and cold treats. His handlebar has a row of silver bells that I can hear from many blocks away. Someday when I am bigger I want to be an ice cream man.

Lots of friends live in my neighborhood. During the warm summer nights we run wild under huge elm trees chasing lightning bugs as they magically blink on and off. I catch them and keep them in jars with holes punched in the lids. They die by morning and leave a funny smell. Now when I catch them, I let them go.

ENCOUNTER WITH DEATH

We have a parakeet. He's "Keety," my favorite pet. He's a beautiful blue. One day I am home sick with not much to do. I think I'll go hunting. I take the rubber end off the arrow and sharpen it in a pencil sharpener. I sneak up on my prey with my bow and arrow. I put the arrow through the slots of the cage and let loose. I don't think about what will happen until it's too late. I am terrified when the arrow pins Keety to the back of the cage. He flutters and dies quickly. I throw up.

THE PADDLE

One afternoon Jeff and I build our own swimming pool in front of the driveway. We dig a big hole. Then we put down newspaper and fill the hole to the top with lots of water, just in time to show Dad as he drives up. He's not happy. He sends us inside while he fills up the hole and cleans up the mess.

When we got older and pulled these kinds of stunts we would get "the paddle." The number of solid, well-connected swats to the backside depended on the severity of the crime and the anger of the paddler. Once I saw it coming, so I grabbed a Golden Book and crammed it down my pants. The first whack didn't hurt, but the book was quickly discovered and it just made Dad even madder. Better to take it like a man.

BIG CHIEF AL'S

The best time is summer. Hot, muggy Illinois summer. The heat drifts into Champaign from the surrounding cornfields. During the day Jeff and I go to Big Chief Al's Indian Day Camp where we play games and then cool off in the over-chlorinated pool. At night we run around our neighbor's house playing war or hide-and-seek. For a real treat, Dad would drive Mom and us boys out on the new highway to the Dairy Queen for butterscotch sundaes. We'd wear our pyjamas. Magic times.

JOHNNY DISAPPEARS

My best friend is Johnny Mercer. He lives a block away. In his backyard is a huge willow tree where we hide and hold club meetings until our parents ring bells and strike triangles to signal dinner time. One day I hear whispers, "He has leukemia." I don't know what that is, but it must be real bad because I never see him again.

FIRST GRADE CANDY

Mom walks me the three blocks to South Side School, which is a large red brick building on a hill. At the bottom of the hill is a baseball diamond and a little store across the street. I pinch nickels and pennies from my Mom's purse. She has plenty. I buy erasers and tiny wax bottles filled with brightly colored sugar water. One afternoon she catches me red-handed. No paddle, but a very serious talk about right and wrong.

THE CHEATER

One warm summer evening Dad takes Jeff and me to the County Fair. This is a very big deal for kids in Champaign. There is something dangerous and edgy about the whole atmosphere. Hundreds of farm families drift up and down the rows of the carnival midway. There is a tent with a freak show: a bearded lady and a snake-man with two heads. I am not allowed to see them. I bet they aren't real. Dad gives us our choice to play "just one" game of chance, so we look at them all. Most are run by greasy looking guys with gold teeth and lots of tattoos who shout "Hurry, hurry! Everyone's a winner!"

I pick a game with the mouse and the roulette wheel. Dad holds Jeff up to watch and I stand on my tiptoes to see the spinning wheel and the numbered holes. We bet on 6 because that's how old I am. The man drops a little mouse onto the spinning wheel. Drunkenly, it spins around, then runs right into hole number 6. "We won! We won!" I scream. But the fairground man with the lazy eye says "Nope" as he tucks Dad's money into the pocket of his torn shirt. "No, we did win, we did, I saw it!" The man leers at Dad as I start shouting louder and louder. Dad looks at the man then back at us, and then says, "Let's go, boys." I can't believe it. My Dad backs down! The man cheated us. "That's not fair, Dad!"

A CLOSE ONE

That summer we drive to Kentucky Lake. Dad gets a special deal in a hotel across from an amusement park. I can hear the music and noise in my room. It's exciting. Outside our window you can see the games of chance and hear people scream as the rusty roller coaster ratchets up and down. Jeff and I wear ourselves out playing miniature golf and trying to get nickels to land on slippery plates so we can win a big stuffed bear. Jeff falls asleep before he even gets into bed. In the middle of the night, Dad shakes me awake and carries me through the halls of the hotel that are filling with smoke. Everyone is coughing. Outside, we shiver in our pyjamas and watch as the flames eat the old wooden hotel. The fire, cracking and popping, casts shadows on the darkened amusement park. Someone had been smoking in bed.

MIAMI

It's Christmas school break. We go to Miami Beach. I am six. We play on the beach and chase crabs into their sandy holes. When it's too hot, I stay in the room with Mom and we read books. Once, when Jeff and I wake up from our naps, Mom and Dad are gone. We look on the beach and at the side of the pool, but they are really gone. I decide to take Jeff back home. We get dressed and I find some money in the top dresser drawer. But before we look for the train station, Jeff gets hungry and wants to eat. I take him to the café and get him a peanut butter and jelly sandwich. I spend all the money except for a few pennies. We wander out into the parking lot next to a busy highway. The asphalt under my shoes is hot. This isn't going to be easy. Just then Mom and Dad run up to us and hug us. We are happy to be together again.

When we really do leave Miami we catch a taxi back to the train station. On the way we cross one of the many drawbridges. I see a sparkle from a ring on the side of the bridge. I start screaming, "Stop! Stop! I see a ring!" They don't believe me, so I yell louder, "Stop! Stop! There's a ring!" Dad gets out. "Sure enough, just like I said." He picks up a Masonic ring, encrusted with twelve cut diamonds. Probably a fisherman took it off and forgot it. Dad scours the newspapers and even calls the Florida police but never finds the owner. A year later he designs a ring for my mother. He buys the diamonds from me and the money goes into my savings account. Years later I use it to buy my first drum set. Today, my wife Geraldine wears the ring.

READING CLUB

By the second grade I am a pretty good student. I love reading *The Weekly Reader*. I start a Reading Club with Jeff and four or five of the kids in the neighborhood. Of course, I appoint myself president and make it official by writing it on the front of the Club's notebook. I make each member read a page from a storybook just like we do in school. Everyone except Jeff as he is too young, but he is allowed to sit there. The club meets only once.

KING OF THE WILD FRONTIER

We are the second people on our block to get a television set. It has a tiny circular black-and-white screen. My parents watch variety shows. I watch Davy Crockett. All us kids watch Davy Crockett. It's a big craze. He is a great explorer and "King of the wild frontier." He is always fighting Indians and he "Killed him a b'ar when he was only three." I crave a Davy Crockett coon-skin cap. It has magic powers to make you strong. And I like the word "Coon" because my middle name, Kuhn, sounds the same. Maybe we are related. I can feel there is a great hero lurking somewhere inside of me too. I renew my campaign of endless begging and eventually get a coon-skin cap. It has a raccoon tail running down the back that tickles my neck when I run or have to fight Indians. Sometimes I wear it with the tail on the side. I also have the official Davy Crockett shirt. I imagine what it feels like to be Davy Crockett — strong, brave, and loved by all. I want to sleep in the cap, but mom won't let me.

One day some workmen are laying a new concrete driveway across the street. I go over to watch. Before they can pour the concrete, they have to unroll and hammer down a heavy wire mesh. As they cut a section from a huge roll, the end springs up and a sharp metal rod about the size of a pencil penetrates my temple. It doesn't hurt. The workmen look at me in horror. From their faces I know something very bad has happened. I say, "Bye. I have to go now," and walk across the street, brave as I can, blood spilling everywhere.

I knock on our door and wait. I know if I go in the living room all messy I will get told off. I hear Mom's footsteps. "Michael is that you?" She opens the screen door and then freezes as the color drains from her face. Then she quickly kneels and throws her arms around me. The blood ruins my Davy Crockett shirt but I knew from somewhere deep down that wearing the shirt magically saved my life. I didn't play Davy Crockett any more after that. Someone else can be "King of the wild frontier."

LAKE OF THE WEEDS

During the summer Dad drives us across the tracks to Grandma and Granddad Wiese's house on the North side of town. Grandma always makes us lunch and then gives Dad and Jeff rhubarb pie. I don't like it so she gives me my special plate of just pie crust with sugar and cinnamon. Then just "us men" would drive the ten miles or so to The Lake of the Woods (we call it "Lake of the Weeds"). It takes forever. When I had grown up and returned for a look around, the place was small and tacky but as kids it was a magic jungle filled with adventure. Dad rents a rowboat and Jeff and I row until we roast or get tired, which isn't very long. We sneak up on painted turtles as they sun themselves on lily pads. Grandad shows us how to put worms on the hooks. Yuck. It's easy to catch blue-gills, a feisty little fish, which once caught we'd throw back, 'cause I don't think you can eat them. Once I catch a catfish with long whiskers. They are scary. We take the turtles home and keep them until the end of summer in an aluminium tub with a rock island in the center and then return the turtles to the lake in the fall.

KILLING

It's freezing cold. The ground is frozen solid in the farm fields. My Dad takes me pheasant hunting. Jeff's too little. Dad shows me how to use a small-gauge shotgun. He was in the Navy during the war. Maybe that's how he learned. When a pheasant flies out of the hedge, I swing around and blast it, nearly getting knocked over by the recoil. We run up to the pheasant flapping on the ground. It doesn't die immediately. I don't like killing and never go again.

COMEDY

Fourth grade has the best teacher ever. Mrs. Clifford gets my humor. She thinks I am very funny. The principal, Mr. Hollingshead ("Mr. Hollow Head") doesn't. I love Mrs. Clifford's lively classes. She makes learning fun and encourages me. I participate in everything and get straight A's. She says I should be a comedian when I grow up. They think everything is funny, just like me. I am sorry when fourth grade ends.

TREASURE

I study an ad for a metal detector on the back of a Quaker Oats cereal box. There's a drawing of a man finding treasure in the sand. I get Mom to order one for my birthday. I dream about traveling all over the world finding treasure.

It takes forever to arrive. I tear open the box and Dad sets it up. Nothing happens. It doesn't work. I put nickels and dimes under it and there is no sound or flashing light. My dream career as a treasure hunter comes to an abrupt end before it starts.

SOFTIES

Mary lives next door. I stretch a string from my bedroom window to hers with a tin can at each end. We shout "Hello" to each other and it works. She is twelve, about four years older than me. One afternoon she crawls under her bed so I can't see her, takes my hand and has me touch her breasts. That, I think, is a weird thing to do.

NEW HOUSE

It won't be long before we move to a new house that is being built for us in Mayfair, a subdivision a few miles out of town near the Champaign County Country Club. It's nothing yet, but Dad says it will be. Fields that just a year ago grew corn are divided and paved with curvy concrete lanes waiting for houses to be built. Ours, at 1205 Waverly Drive, is the second house being built there. It's fun going out to the house. Jeff and I explore the framed rooms without walls and climb all around and imagine what it will be like when it's finished.

We move in when I am in the fifth grade. I change schools to Westview, which is only a few blocks away. In the beginning of the school year there are cows in some of the fields and corn and alfalfa in others, but soon there are new houses springing up like wooden mushrooms everywhere. Even during school I can hear the hammering and sawing. Once the workers leave, Jeff and I explore every new house and climb on the tractors. We know when it's dinner time: Mom rings a bell.

The Champaign County Country Club borders Mayfair. My folks join so they can play golf and party with their wide circle of friends. We swim in the pool and eat sticky buns in the formal dining room on special occasions. Black waiters in white jackets serve the food. They are especially polite. On the fourth of July, the Dads throw silver dollars in the pool and us kids almost drown each other trying to snatch the coins from the bottom.

Melissa is my first love but no one knows. I fall in love with her when I spot her on the diving board dripping wet in her black silk bathing suit. She looks like a mermaid with long blonde hair turned green by the chlorine in the pool. She is on the swimming team and is always winning ribbons. I am an okay swimmer but nowhere as good as Melissa. But it doesn't stop me from fantasizing that one day I will save Melissa from drowning and, in my arms, she will fall in love with me. But maybe she won't because the other kids tease me about having a big nose.

THE BIG BANG

I am ten when I get a chemistry set for Christmas. Perfect timing because I'd just found a book at the library on how to make fireworks. The chemistry set doesn't have the good stuff I need for explosives, so on Saturday I go to the pharmacy and buy saltpeter, sulphur, charcoal, potassium chlorate, and metal filings. I set up a secret lab in the basement. With the book propped open, I mix the chemicals, make a fuse and light it. It fizzes, then ignites, then explodes, burning a big hole in the ping-pong table and filling the basement with toxic smoke. Out comes the paddle.

Another time, on a school field trip to *The News-Gazette*'s printing press, I collect cold type lead letters. I get a saucepan and melt down the lead and pour it into a mold that I have for making lead soldiers. I spill the hot lead accidentally on the new kitchen Formica workspace. Another meeting with the paddle.

Bikes, archery sets, and BB guns are just some of the treasures pictured on the backs of comic books. All you have to do is sell some corny greeting cards from the American Youth Association and you can win it all. I fill out the form and in a few weeks boxes of greeting cards arrive. I immediately canvas the neighborhood knocking on doors and selling boxes of cards. It goes really well. "I am Michael from down the street and I am selling cards for the American Yow-th Association," I proudly declare. Big smiles all around as hands reach into their purses and wallets. The boxes sell quickly. This is easy. When I get home the neighbors have already reported in to my Mom. She lovingly tells me, you pronounce it "yoo-th" not "yow-th."

I've got to get a go-cart! I have turned down the pages in all the magazines with pictures of the best ones. Dad finally caves and buys one. But I see right away that he didn't buy a fast one. It has a governor on the engine so its top speed is only two miles an hour. "Heck, Dad, I can walk faster than that. The good ones go 60 mph." I drive it in wimpy baby circles around the driveway. Bor-ing. One day I get out the toolbox and figure out how to take the governor off. I also take off the muffler so it roars like a real go-cart. I ROAR down Waverly Drive at 10 mph. The need for speed! Yes, the paddle. But worth it.

When I got older (and bigger) and Mom came at me with the paddle, I just grab it out of her hand. (I don't mean to suggest that we were beaten or abused because we weren't. But back in the day, before political correctness and children's rights, this is how kids were raised in Central Illinois.)

THE SECRET OF LIFE

I am twelve years old. I go to Sinai Temple on Sunday mornings, then afterwards Sunday school. I study Hebrew and Jewish history. We are reformed Jewish and since Dad is Methodist we celebrate Christmas and Easter; just the presents bit and egg hunting, not the going to church bit. We go to temple instead.

I don't mind the Sunday School but sometimes the teacher's feelings show when they talk about the Holocaust. It makes me feel uneasy or even guilty but I don't know why. I didn't do anything. I wasn't even there. Worse is the scratchy woollen suit which is almost too much to bear. What I like about going to the Jewish High Holy Days at temple is the canting, that magical and mysterious voice that comes from an ancient past. The adults sit so straight in the wooden pews. Each family has its own section and always sits there. I am sure that adults know the secret of life and if I can just stick it out — both the study and woollen suit — until confirmation, I too will learn what life is all about.

Confirmation Day arrives. I recite the prayers in Hebrew and do all the things I am suppose to do. All us kids stand facing the congregation. The jewel-encrusted cover is taken off the Torah. I stand behind the Rabbi and can see the hand-written holy Hebrew letters on the scroll. I am terribly excited. Today's the day everything is going to fall into place and be clear. I'll become an adult. The Rabbi makes his way to each child, one at a time. As a "W" "Wiese" I am the very last. Each child is handed a rolled-up certificate and then the Rabbi whispers something. The tension is unbearable. I am minutes away from learning the secret of life! He stands before me, hands me a certificate, shakes my hand, then bends down to ear level. Here it comes! "Good luck, Mike," he says. He turns to leave. I grab his arm. "What? That's it? That's it?!" I plead. I am not going to learn the secret of life here. I quit going to temple. I never go back.

ALL-DAY PARKING

My first job is selling programs at the Illini football games. Parking lots on all sides of the stadium are already full. I stand alongside an empty farmer's field and sell programs to the drivers of cars who are creeping along looking for a place to park. One of the drivers asks me if he can park in the field. I say, "Sure, why not?" He hands me a dollar and turns in. All the cars behind follow him, stopping only briefly to hand me a dollar. In about twenty minutes I am holding nearly $200 in dollar bills!! Dad does not celebrate my victory. I get a lecture.

The next weekend I sneak back to the field but the farmer has put up a temporary fence and is standing nearby. So I find another location to sell my programs. It's November and brutally cold. It starts to snow. I have a blanket with me. It's near game time and people are rushing by, anxious to get in the stadium for the kickoff. I am selling programs like crazy. I drop a fifty-cent piece and kneel down to find it, all the while selling programs. People grab programs off the stack and throw money on the blanket that I've wrapped around my waist and knees. After it's all over and I count up the money, I have about $100 more than I expect. I count it again. I can't figure it out... unless... no?!... They don't think I am crippled, do they?! I don't tell Dad this story.

THE KUHNS AND THE WIESES

My Dad is the general manager at Joseph Kuhn and Co. at 45 Main Street in downtown Champaign. It's owned by the Kuhns, my mother's side of the family, and named after my great grandfather who founded the business in 1865. My Granddad Kuhn joined the business in 1888 and now my Dad is the boss. It's one of the longest continuously operated businesses in all of Central Illinois. It's the best men's clothing store — "unmatched in 118-½ miles." I know this because it is printed on the store's promotional matchboxes and glass ashtrays and on the outside wall of the store in big letters. But what is better and 118-½ miles away? There is a bigger clothing store in Indianapolis.

The store is across the street from *The News-Gazette* and about 100 yards from the train station. Kuhns is four stories high, has 35,000 square feet, and has an atrium that extends from the first to the fourth floor. I can stand in the shoe department on the first floor and look up past the men's and ladies' floors to a stained glass ceiling. It's like a great cathedral. Looking up is always the first thing I do when dragged to the store to buy new clothes the week before school starts. All those reds, blues, and golds. I almost have a religious experience. Years later the store is remodelled and the atrium boarded over to make more floor space. The stained glass dome is moved to the new store at the shopping center. Dad gives me a few pieces of stained glass as a souvenir, but it's not the same. Nothing can make up for the loss of that magnificent stained glass ceiling.

My whole universe is this little town in Illinois. I don't know how people get in or out of the town, or if they ever did. I hear some people talk about the big city, Chicago. I think, if there is any escape, it must be north to Chicago on the tracks that shuttle the train called "The City of New Orleans" from New Orleans to Chicago. At night I lay in bed and hear the train's horn announce its brief passing as it comes out of the surrounding cornfields, slips through Champaign-Urbana, and then disappears out through the other side, like a snake in tall grass. There is something mysterious about it. The train to me is as magical as the Orient Express I'd read about in my boy's adventure books. I imagine the wonderful places the train must go. Our little town is an oasis in a sea of cornfields and the train is the only escape. But only a few trains ever stop in Champaign.

When I become a teenager, I set up a camera on a time exposure, lean against a post, and make a self-portrait as "The City of New Orleans" streaks past. You can see my silhouette and the train passing through my transparent body. It's one of my most treasured photographs as it is loaded with meaning for me.

It's like an image in a crystal ball that suggests escape, flight, spirits, and other dimensions — a portent of my future.

Grandfather (Isaac) and Grandmother (Rose) Kuhn are highly respected in the community. Grandfather carries on his father's retail clothing business, gives scholarships to foreign students at the University of Illinois, and contributes to building Sinai Temple. They live in one of the grand Victorian houses on University Avenue, which was lined with big elm trees before elm disease killed most of them. Grandfather is much older than Grandmother. She is his second wife. He dies when I am six. I was in awe of him, maybe because all the adults around him treated him with such reverence. I remember eating a bowl of vanilla ice cream with him and he told me not to eat too fast. I still wrap his favorite blanket around me when I meditate on cold days. He warmed himself with it when he wrote letters in the sitting room. I can still hear the scratchy sounds his ink pen made.

Grandma (Marie) and Granddad (Ellis) Wiese live on the other side of the tracks in a rambling, creaky old clapboard house. Grandma is a big jovial woman with several prominent moles and beauty marks on her face. I love to follow her up the two flights of stairs to the attic where she thrills me and Jeff by opening cigar boxes full of Dad's old treasures: war medals, foreign coins, bottle openers, and carved *netsuke* that Dad brought back from his wartime tour of Yokohama. (Today, on my meditation altar, I have a Buddhist bracelet made of twenty-one tiny hand-carved ivory skulls from that cherished cigar box.)

Granddad is the strong silent type. He had been a motorcycle policeman and received newspaper headlines for apprehending some Chicago bootleggers. He is a hero. Now he is retired. He murmurs "Hi boys" when we come to the house and then dozes off in front of a TV Western undisturbed by the shooting, yelling, and clomping of hooves. It's Grandma Wiese, with her big blue Irish eyes, who likes to play with us boys and make us laugh.

Going to Grandmother and Grandfather Kuhn's (we never called them Grandma or Grandpa) is a more formal affair. Their Victorian house is large, the stairs squeak, and the closets smell of cedar. Everything is antique and very clean and has its exact place. I am not allowed to touch anything. We always have to wear our very best clothes when we visit them, which means something itchy.

My mother is always tense and nervous during those infrequent times when both grandparents come to a holiday dinner at our house. The Wieses are farm people, simple, unpretentious, and uneducated. You could imagine Grandma Wiese on a farm. Grandmother Kuhn is more like the Queen. She wears white gloves at the dinner table, when she drives her Buick, and at the store when she goes to inspect it. The sets of grandparents never really had much to say to each other. Grandma and Grandpa Wiese were very poor. They never went beyond the 7th grade and their parents were not educated at all except by hard work on the farm. While Grandmother Kuhn wears a string of pearls, Grandma Wiese wears her one party dress. I poke my fork between the small oil bubbles in the gravy so they will make one big oil bubble.

MAGIC IN THE DARK

One afternoon my dentist, Ford Hausermann, takes me into a dark room illuminated by only a red light. In front of him is an enlarger on a metal stand and three trays filled with smelly chemicals. He puts a negative in the enlarger, takes out a piece of photographic paper, puts it in a frame under the enlarger, turns on its light for a few seconds, then immerses the paper in the first tray of developing solution. In a minute an image starts to emerge, faint at first, then darker. Wow! It's magical. It's a picture of a fence in a snowdrift. It's beautiful. That moment, right there, hooks me forever on photography.

A DIME A DANCE

Dad's passion is his trumpet. He would occasionally open the storage closet, reach up to a top shelf and pull down an old battered case and take out a faded golden trumpet. He'd played in big bands. A dime a dance. He lights up when he plays and looks like a different person with no worries. As he gets older he plays less. He encourages me to take up an instrument.

Okay — drums. Drums are cool. No, my folks want me to select a "musical" instrument. I like Bill Haley's "Yakety Sax" and pick the saxophone. For a year I take lessons and play it in band, but I don't like the squeaky sound I get from it or the way the reed feels in my mouth. Next I take piano lessons, but the piano teacher gives me such awful songs to play that I abandon it. I eventually get my way: drums. I play in several school bands. It's horrible. We read sheet music and about every eight bars I get to wallop a kettledrum or tap a triangle. Bor-ing.

PUNY UNI

My mother says that I should take the entrance exam to see if I can get into the University of Illinois High School. It's a small experimental laboratory school for the brainy sons and daughters of the University professors. I am not very interested until I hear that if I go to Uni I can graduate in five years instead of the usual six because 7th and 8th grades are combined. I like that. It means I can graduate at sixteen! My escape plans from Champaign are already being hatched. The entrance exam is really tough, so I am surprised when I am offered a place to enter the school as a sub-freshman.

There are only 50 kids in our year, 250 in the whole school. They are very eccentric. Nerds. You know how you see some kids and their 12-year-old faces look like fully formed adults? These kids may be socially immature, but mentally they are intellectual giants. They are very competitive and can easily handle mountains of advanced homework assignments. I am an outsider, and a "Townie" besides. My grade average — for the five years I was there — must have been at the bottom of the bell-shaped curve. Later I discover that I was at the top of the lower third and there were actually sixteen kids below me! All through high school I felt intellectually inferior and hence developed outside interests.

Moving to Uni High put a greater distance between Jeff and me. From then on we lived in very different worlds. The year I skip a grade is the year he is held back. He has dyslexia, but no one calls it that at the time. Although we are only two years apart by age our social groups are now four years apart and we are at different schools. People can't understand how we are so different. We don't even look like brothers. Mom and Dad treat us exactly alike. Whatever birthday or Christmas gift I get, Jeff gets the exact same thing. Until I leave high school we share the same bedroom. I try to get attention by being clever or seeking approval for my photographs. Jeff gets his attention through failing at school.

I like English class but the exercises are usually monotonous. The tables in the room are put in a big square. We each take turns reading a stanza of some romantic poet. I count ahead to see what I will read. I notice the word "bosom" a few stanzas before my turn. Everyone else has picked up on this too. We all know <u>exactly</u> whose turn it will fall on: Helen Manner's. The tension in the room mounts as the countdown begins. Her face turning bright red, she reads it: "...*bosom*." The class explodes with laughter.

But mostly it's dull and I don't really enjoy school that much. I prefer my extra-curricular activities, drumming and photography, which I practice every day. I also like writing reports. I don't know why. Maybe the act of bringing something from nothing onto a blank page and then having someone read it and react. I like researching and going to the huge University of Illinois library as if on a treasure hunt, finding quotes of what people said. Plus I can type fast and that's a plus.

I use the *World Book* encyclopedia and research King John of England and the Magna Carta. I find out that he is left-handed, but an illustration shows him signing with his right hand. I write *World Book*, "What gives?" Two months later a big envelope arrives from the *World Book* editorial office. It's extensive research on my question. They apologize for the oversight and promise to fix it in the next edition. Yes!

I write a biography on World War II correspondent Ernie Pyle, whose life fascinates me. He is from Dana, Indiana, just on the other side of the Illinois border. He had a real folksy writing style, and a huge readership. I put months into this project and am really proud when I hand it in. My teacher gives me a "D." Although she can't prove it, she says it is "too good" to be my work. I "must have copied it from someone else." This is devastating for me.

In shop class we learn to use table saws, drills, and lathes. All the boys are making shelves or pencil holders or coat racks. Bor-ing. I take some clay and make a prehistoric Venus with large breasts and hips. I don't know why. I hadn't even seen a Venus before. It just seems to come to me. The shop teacher grabs it and holds it up. "What the hell do you think you're doing?" "I am making a paperweight."

What I do like about the school is that there are kids from India and Kenya in our class. They fascinate me with their musical accents and stories of their homelands. I still remember their magical sounding names: Chandra Rajaratnam and Joel Otieno.

The school takes pride in introducing us to new people and ideas. One Saturday our music class takes a field trip to Harry Partch's studio above the Co-Ed Theater on Green Street, a block from the Champaign-Urbana border. We go into a room filled with overturned artillery shells, weird harps, and big glass bowls which hang from the ceiling. Percussive instruments tuned to ancient Greek scales? The other kids are too intimidated to say anything, but I am a drummer so I ask a lot of questions. Harry enthusiastically shows me each instrument and lets me bang on them endlessly. A few weeks later, on my own, I go back and climb the stairs into that fascinating world of sound. Harry is a very kind man. I learn later that he is a great and innovative composer who builds all of his own instruments. It's a fortuitous meeting. I have no idea until years later how much this brief encounter with a supportive mentor would influence me. Here was a portal for me to non-Western forms of musical percussion.

The first day of typing class I sit next to Gregory T. White, a tall, alert black boy. Being a drummer I can't resist tapping out a rhythm when I type. Tak-a-tak-a, tak-a-tak-a, ritditdit, DING (as the manual carriage comes to its end and the bell rings). Greg responds with his own riff. We keep this up throughout the class and through every class for a whole year. The teacher can't make us stop because we hardly make any errors. This class becomes a great joy. Greg becomes one of my best friends as well as the fastest typist in the universe. Because he plays organ for his Baptist church choir, he can play snappy gospel piano like Ray Charles. I persuade him a few times to play in our band, but he only performs in public with us a few times and even then he keeps his back turned to the audience. I think he's just shy, but years later he laughed and told me he felt that he was betraying his religious upbringing by playing "the Devil's music."

Gregory comes to our house to practice with our band. My mom is completely open to our friendship and serves cookies or sandwiches whenever he comes over. It's a great gift that she gave me because at the time there was more racism in Champaign than I ever imagined. Years later, Greg told me that the white "Townies" would harass him when he walked home from school through the park. He was my friend throughout my life and the last time I saw him he told me he always appreciated me for defending and protecting him. This came as a surprise because I don't remember ever doing this.

When he grew up Greg joined the Peace Corps in Africa and learned Swahili. Then he took a job with *The San Francisco Chronicle* that he held for several decades. He worked three days a week taking down personal ads over the phone and helping people compose their requests. ("Buffed Tarzan Seeks Adventuresome Jane.") The short work week gave him time to pursue his passion, which was translating archaic poetry. Greg lived in a tiny apartment and kept his needs simple. He was the most contented person I've ever known. When he died unexpectedly a few years ago, I discovered he had hundreds of close friends who all cherished him as much as I did.

INITIATION

It's February. We just had a huge ice storm. I ride the bus across town from Uni High in Urbana and get dropped off near the Country Club. I decide to take a shortcut across the golf course. The snow crunches under my feet. It's freezing and the light is fading fast. I still have a ways to go and won't get home until dark. I walk down the fairways and then head for a cluster of fir trees. I walk into a clearing surrounded by the trees. It's very quiet except for my crunching. I get a chill and feel like I am being watched. I look up and in every tree is an owl! A dozen of them. It feels like I interrupted a conference of elders. Yellow eyes glare down at me. I run like hell, making a crunchy racket, and don't stop until I get home. Today I recognize this as an initiation in the spirit world.

FIRST JOBS

I land a lunchtime job at Mooney's Café, which is only two blocks from Uni High. It's a true "greasy spoon" and the Mooneys are obese people who dish out hamburgers, fries, and Cokes to workmen and U. of I. students. I am a waiter. I want to save enough money to buy a ring for Laura, a girl who I hope to make my girlfriend. But by the time I save enough money we'd broken up, so I buy a drum.

I don't participate in school clubs like Chess, Latin, Greek, or Calculus, but instead form a band, The Corvairs — "The Compact Group with the Impact Sound" — with my best friend Don Kennedy and some others from Champaign High School. Don's father is a well-known abstract painter. He has a big sandbox in an upstairs bedroom where he props up chicken bones and drapes them with colored crepe paper. From this, he paints abstract and fantasy landscapes. Don's father gives us old tubes of oil paint, which we smear to make paintings and write titles to match what they look like. We fight over who gets to keep the best paintings.

Forming a band with Champaign High kids is difficult because the Champaign kids hate the kids from "Puny Uni" and, conversely, the brainy Uni students have no respect for my dumb friends from Champaign High. People from Champaign put down those from Urbana, and vice versa. University people snub the townies. Blacks vs. whites. Everything is so polarized. Lemme outta here!

The Corvairs' first gig is at the YMCA. We know about five songs, sort of. We are really scared. Rack Jack, an older, tougher, and scar-faced drummer from the best band in town, The Sterlings, comes to our gig. He stands over me, inches from my cymbal, and stares me down as if I am less than nothing. I sweat so much I can barely hang onto the sticks. After playing a ten-minute extended version of "Wipeout," we quickly run out of songs, so we disguise "Yellow Bird" by playing it three times at different speeds: as a rock number, a cha-cha, and a slow dance. Nobody notices. Everyone is too busy making out.

We feel we have entered the big time and are about to get our big break when we play our first out-of-town talent contest at a county fair. A sausage-shaped blonde girl in a homemade sparkly-pink leotard goes on before us. She confidently throws a flaming baton high into the air. We bounce on stage as the newly-named Torquettes and play a blazing guitar rendition of a Ventures' surf song. The judges dramatically pause, then announce, "And the first place prize... goes to... The Torquettes!" We jump to our feet and are almost on stage when he announces "Oh wait, sorry, read that wrong, The Torquettes are second, the first place winner is... Betty May and her Flaming Baton." We are crushed. I swear, at the next talent contest, I'm going to set my drums on fire!

Bands are what keep me from going stark raving mad throughout high school. Beating on drums lets out a lot of the frustration and anger from being in that uncomfortable netherworld between adolescence and adulthood. I hurry home from school and rush to the basement to practice with Bo Diddley, Little Richard, Ray Charles, and James Brown. Mom turns on and off the basement lights when it's time for dinner.

Besides making money in the bands, my Dad gives me a job making boxes at Kuhns. "Everyone starts at the bottom," he reassures me. Ancestral eyes peer down from the huge oil paintings of Joseph and Isaac Kuhn, which to this day have the place of honor on the first floor landing. My workstation is below the ancestral altar, down in the Dickens-dark and musty basement where I hopelessly try to avoid slow death by paper cut. After a week I quit. A few summers later Dad tries again to engage my talents and find a place for me in the family store. This time he shows me how to do newspaper layouts for the store's Florsheim shoe advertisements in *The News-Gazette* and *The Courier*. I am pretty good at it and very proud when I see my first layout in print. I am an ad man. My brother Jeff, having much more stick-to-it-ness than I have, starts at the bottom making boxes, then works his way up to shoe salesmen, then manager of the new Joseph Kuhn out in the mall off the new Interstate. Today the mall store is long gone, but the original Kuhn's by the railroad tracks, a faint shadow of its former self, carries on for the Big and Tall.

MY FIRST DEAL

Summer is coming to an end in two weeks and I have a plan. I make an appointment to meet with the directors of the Champaign High School Board after their monthly meeting. I tell them I have a great band (we know dozens of songs now) and we want to play "The Howdy Hop." This is Champaign High's first dance of the new school year. If we can play at that event, everyone will know who we are. The School Board asks our price. I say, "$75." They negotiate by saying that this is too much. I say, "That's our standard rate." They rebut, "Anyway, we don't expect a big turnout." I say, "All right then, we'll play for free and if anyone shows up we'll take 75% of the gate." They agree. My Dad, who has a law degree but never practiced, always says to "write it down." So I get their promise in writing.

On the night of "The Howdy Hop" the gymnasium is jammed packed with 1,000 kids, so many that the fire marshall will not let everyone in. The gym is like a sauna. After a killer rendition of a Beach Boys song, we take a break. I am dripping with sweat. I go into the cafeteria, grab a drink, and go over to meet with the School Board. They hand me an envelope. In it is $75. Shaking, I hand it back to them. "That's not our deal." They say, "Take it or leave it." I hold my ground, pulling the crinkled "contract" from my dress pants. The trio of very large men stare me down. I am not going to back down because I know I have the last card. I play it. "Maybe you want to go out and explain to the kids why the band is going home? Or do you want to honor our deal?" Out comes the cash box and they count out our 75% share which is nearly $700. After the gig the band members are expecting the usual $10 or maybe $20. I give them $150 each! They can't believe it. After that, I am like Champaign's Nelson Riddle or Benny Goodman — everyone wants to play in my band. I'd successfully negotiated my first percentage deal.

When Uni High's "Vice-Versa Dance" rolls around, pretty Sally Smith invites me to be her date. I agree, but then a few days before the dance I get a call from The Sterlings! Wow. The Sterlings! They called me. They are the best band in town. They want me to fill in for Rack Jack, their drummer, who has once again mysteriously gone missing. It's a gig playing for a big fraternity party at the U. of I. I call Sally and break the news. She's very unhappy. Of course, I invite her to come to the gig instead. Her father grabs the phone and gives me a piece of his mind. Her mother has made her a new dress and I had better show up. I am sorry, Sally, please understand. This could be my big break.

THE STERLINGS

The Sterlings are hands-down the hottest local band and I had desperately wanted to play with them for years. The musicians are mostly eight years older than me. I can't even drive yet! They are a six- to ten-member blues band depending on who shows up. Besides Mike Stoner, the singer, there is the basic four (two guitars, bass, and drum), there is a three-piece horn section, a Wurlitzer organist, and Paula and Nancy, two ya-ya girl backup singers. I am fifteen and they are ancient: maybe mid-twenties. I have a serious crush on Paula, the thin blonde backup singer, whose microphone is right in front of my drums. Once she invited me to her apartment. Imagine the fantasies going through my mind as I rode my bike to her apartment deep in Urbana. But the only thing that ever happens stayed in my mind.

Rack Jack is a much better drummer. His roll is tight: cool. As much as I practice, I am never able to fully master it. But he is slightly crazy and impulsive and completely irresponsible, which results in me eventually replacing him. One thing I do well — which he doesn't — is show up. My Dad has to drive me out to Route 45 when we play the roadhouses. (It's remarkable to think about it now: a fifteen-year-old playing in these dives with country drunks whose main source of fun is starting fistfights and throwing beer at the band. Watching adults behave like this is probably what turned me off forever from drinking.) I never asked him, but I suppose my Dad understood the music world and felt it okay for me to be initiated in this way. After all, drumming was a real passion of mine. I am underage to be in these roadside bars, but then I am pretty hidden behind massive Zildjian cymbals and my oversized Roy Orbison-inspired sunglasses. The band does covers of all the best Rhythm & Blues tunes and each night I get a real workout.

The older guys all have developed signature ways to be cool. Gary Wright, the bass player, is closest to me in age. He is missing an upper front tooth. This is where he sticks his cigarette when he plays. When he smiles at the girls, he waves the cigarette through his teeth. He is the wildest kid I know. Imagine my surprise when years later he becomes a detective in Champaign's police department in charge of narcotics investigations! He shows me a cabinet full of guns and knives he has confiscated. "Mike, you wouldn't believe how many criminals there are in Champaign and how many I've put away," he boasts. His fifteen minutes of fame come in an interview on national news. He witnesses, "I was in the examining room at the morgue when this corpse comes to life. It sat up!" He tells *The New York Times*, "I've seen dead people a hundred times in my life. She was friggin' dead. What I saw was a resurrection, a miracle, man."

Tim Stillwell (school teacher by day, Sterling's lead guitarist by night) has a mahogany Gibson and plays sweet jazz riffs like Kenny Burrell. He is far too good to be in this band. He is lightning fast. His signature look is to play without moving his head so that his cigarette ash will burn out an inch or two. How cool is that? Should I tire during a fast number, or not play slightly ahead of the driving beat for even a second, he'll turn back at me and scowl. And that hurts. But if that ash should fall, I will be in deep shit the entire night.

Francis is a smooth, handsome black guy who coaxes silky sounds from his tenor sax. Between sets (we play five a night), I go out back to get some fresh air. He is sharing a strange smelling cigarette with Dennis, another horn player. They both get all weird and put their hands behind their backs when I walk over.

Unlike most of the local drummers, I do show up, so it's easy to get jobs with one band or another every weekend. Fine with me, because I don't play basketball or have any interest in engaging in other Uni High activities.

When I am about sixteen, I get a job with a real R&B band, not just a bunch of white guys playing the blues. I forget the band's name, but its lead guitarist's real name is James Brown. True. I am the only white guy in the band and am excited to be "touring" to an out-of-state gig in Missouri. I ride in James' big old Cadillac which pulls a trailer with our sparkly suits and guitar amps. The rest of the guys follow in a station wagon. By late afternoon we enter a very poor farming town. It's like going back in time or entering a Faulkner novel: dusty roads, cotton fields, bib overalls, and wooden shacks. About a mile before we find the town hall we start seeing the posters that our shady promoter has plastered on barns along the road announcing "ONE NIGHT ONLY: JAMES BROWN & HIS BAND." This makes our James Brown very nervous.

We go in, set up, and start to play. There are a few hundred people inside, but outside hundreds more. We can hear them cheering and yelling. Everyone has already cashed and spent their welfare checks three days earlier. Few are buying tickets, so most crowd around outside. On the stage, behind my drum kit, is a window. I can see them running around, jumping and dancing through bonfires, kicking up sparks and waving whiskey bottles in the air. We play some James Brown instrumentals which are part of our repertoire, but that only gets people outside shouting, "James Brown!! James Brown!!"

We take a break to figure out what to do. We can't keep the charade going. It's only a matter of time. Do they really, for a moment, think we are James Brown's band? Maybe we haven't been strung up yet because most people are outside. We go backstage during a break. Our James Brown has gone AWOL. Bluesman Junior Wells appears in our dressing room. As fate would have it, he is in town for a funeral. We tell him what has happened and he has a good laugh. A gold-capped tooth shines as he says, "Yeah, that's some bad luck."

We go back on stage. Junior Wells steps up to the mike. People start shouting because they recognize him. He says, "You know you can't trust nobody these days. These boys had a bad-ass promoter telling ya'll James Brown is coming. Don't matter. These boys gonna play real good and ya'll going to have a good time." He counts down, "1, 2, 3..." and brings a harmonica to his mouth.

When it's time to pack up, the trailer is gone. James Brown has taken his Cadillac and the trailer and headed for the hills. No one ever heard from him again.

BAD ART

If I am not rehearsing or playing in a band, I am photographing everything. I had a plastic Kodak box camera when I was six but now have saved enough to buy a Miranda C 35mm single lens reflex. I love that camera and polish the lens incessantly. I show the principal of Uni High my photos and he asks me to join the school yearbook called *The Gargoyle* to document every boring thing that occurs in that medieval school. That is until I extended my role to include art critic.

I am on the third floor of the school in the art room. Lined up against the open windows are some really bad plaster sculptures. I mean really bad. I can't stand bad art. Hmm, just a little nudge would cleanse the world of bad art. I make sure no one is walking three stories below. Then... Crash! Crash! Crash! White plaster explosions everywhere. That stunt gets me thrown off the yearbook for a year.

Since I am not taking photos at school anymore I set up a studio in my basement. I buy a seamless roll and some cheap lights. I start with still-lifes of gears and shadows, then graduate to dressing up a friend like a beatnik and photographing him with a beret and a painted-on moustache. Then I try some fancy lighting and shoot portraits of anyone I can get to sit for me. I shoot a model's portfolio for one girl. I get another older girl to pose nude by telling her that "the Greeks sculpted everybody naked." My hands are shaking when she takes off her clothes and strikes a pose in front of me while my mother vacuums upstairs. I can hardly work the camera. The photos? They are dreadful.

FASTER AND FASTER

I finally get a drivers license. The first place I drive to is my girlfriend Marcia's house. Marcia tells her parents that she doesn't want to go out with them to dinner because she doesn't feel well. Then she calls me as soon as they are gone. I park a few houses away. We are in her bedroom listening to Johnny Mathis and making out when we hear the key in the front door. Her parents! I am out the back window in milliseconds and into my mom's Rambler Convertible, the one with the push-button gears. (Can you believe my mom actually traded her bright yellow 1957 Chevy convertible for a Rambler?!) I speed along a county road bordered by cornfields. When I look in the rear-view mirror a car is gaining on me. Her dad?! I go faster and faster. I come to a T-junction and make a hard left, skidding out of control in the gravel. The car veers off the road, down a five-foot embankment, rolls over and crashes to a stop in a cornfield. My face hits the steering wheel, glass flies everywhere, and the steering wheel crushes my leg.

I crawl out of the car and climb up onto the road above. I am bleeding from my mouth, face, head, and shoulder, but feel no pain. I know I need to get to a hospital. I try to flag down a car but no one will stop. I guess they don't want to get their seats bloody. Finally some servicemen from the local airbase stop and drop me off at a phone booth in a near-by gas station. "Dad, I've good news and bad news: I am not dead but Mom's car is totalled."

THE NEWS-GAZETTE

That summer I get a job at *The News-Gazette*, across Main Street from Joseph Kuhn & Co. I work there for two summers, first as a darkroom assistant (goodbye bright summer days) and later as a photographer. I get the assignments that the other photographers don't want to do, like women's club meetings or elderly citizen awards. Roger Ebert is also there as a cub reporter. We cover the county fair together and the 4-H awards. I take a picture of the fat girl with the fat heifer and then he interviews her before we move on to the skinny girl with the scrawny chicken. After we complete our assignment, we are magnetically drawn to the carnival midway, to the forbidden fruit: the striptease tent. We try to peek into the tent when the curtain is pulled back, but as Roger reminded me recently, "We felt the eyes of the church elders upon us."

The next day I am back at the county fair to photograph the stock car races. I stand in the middle of the circular course with my heavy 3¼ x 4¼ Speed Graphic press camera. I have to anticipate when the cars would crash into each other so I can get the ultimate shot. Two cars spin out of control in front of me. No matter which way I try to run, they skid closer to me. The crowds in the stands cheer in the hopes that I'll be run over. They want to see blood.

After the stock car races, I photograph country singer Roy Orbison, who sings "Oh, Pretty Woman." My first celebrity portrait.

CAPTIONS

Today is the hottest day in Illinois history. I break an egg on the sidewalk so I can take a picture. I've already written the caption: "So hot you can fry an egg on the sidewalk." The editor is always encouraging me to write captions for my photos. Only it wasn't hot enough on the sidewalk and the egg made a real mess. Somebody told me that it would be hotter on something black. So I broke an egg over a black car hood. It fried up real fast and I got my shot, but the editor wouldn't publish it.

A few weeks later, Illinois has a cricket invasion. The biggest cricket invasion since the 1880s. So I find some dead crickets, line them up, make a little flag, and caption it, "Onward Cricket Soldiers." I am sure this will garner a front-page photo and by-line: "Photo by Mike Wiese." Nope. Every time I walk by the editor's desk, the picture is still languishing in his "In" box. I can't bug him anymore about it, but I can feel my hot story getting cold. Realizing this is a fast-breaking story, I take the photo over to *The Courier*, the competing news-paper in town. The next day they publish it with my name and address, so there would be no mistake, knowing full well that I work for *The Gazette*. Suddenly I get a lot of attention from the editor. "And who writes your pay check?" Can't they understand? Publish or perish.

One afternoon I walk through the park and see a boxer dog standing up on two legs taking a drink from a drinking fountain. I shoot it and caption it, "The Paws That Refreshes" (a pun on Coca-Cola's tag line — "The Pause That Refreshes" — for those too young to remember). My paper in all their wisdom did publish it. But it's a really great shot and deserves wider exposure.

One of my jobs is to run the Associated Press wire photo machine. We receive images but never send them. I develop a fascination for John Glenn, who is the third person to go into space and the first American to orbit the Earth. Whenever any news photos about Glenn or NASA come out of the machine, I paste them into a scrapbook. I know history is being made. I want to make history too — with my dog shot.

The wire photo machine looks like a lathe and has a red hot needle that burns dots across a piece of blue plastic, resulting in a photo plate that is inked and put on the press. It takes about thirty minutes to receive one photo. (Think of it as a really slow fax machine.) The machine can only send one photo to newspapers throughout the whole country at a time. You call the operator's number that is written on a scrap of paper near the machine, and then you schedule your send so as to not interfere with another send. I have never sent one before so I didn't know this when I put my dog photo on the machine and hit "send." On hundreds of wire photo machines in large and small newspapers all over

America, a dog at a water fountain appears instead of a NASA missile launch. Sor-ry.

I enter the Illinois Press High School Photographer of the Year contest. My portfolio consists of a portrait of a young woman, a clown putting on make up, a rotting wooden boat, my paws-that-refreshes dog, and some other *Popular Photography* inspired clichés. I win second place. Yes! (My mother frames each photo and hangs them down the long hallway in our house. They hang there in their glory for nearly forty years.)

FILM BUG

Back at Uni High I am selected to be in a "New Math" class conducted by its creator, the formidable Max Beberman. The government has given Max a grant of $2 million to create a series of films to teach educators how to introduce New Math. Our class is filmed every day for nearly a year in a specially built studio/classroom. I can see the microphone that hangs over my head. I can see the red light that signals that "we are rolling." There is a camera booth a few feet above the blackboard, another off to the side, and another behind me. At the end of the class, I persuade the cameraman to let me look through the zoom lens. That does it for me. I am hooked on filming.

New math gave me super mental powers and intellectual confidence. My pal Rich Leng and I go to a nearby drug store where they have a "guess how many pills" contest going. A tall glass canister is crammed full of pills, all colors and sizes. We are currently studying how to calculate volumes so we each take measurements and try to figure out the volume of the canister and the volume of the average pill and subtract the volume of air where the pills are not touching. We promise each other that if either of us wins, we'll split the prize with the other. Well, we did win. This time not second place, but first place. My luck is changing. I am coming up in the world.

First place is a 200-cup coffee percolator! What are two teenagers going to do with a 200-cup coffee percolator? I don't even know 200 people. It's about the size of a small grain silo! We couldn't split it, so we try to give it to a church, but the pastor lectures us about stealing things. "You boys won that thing? Sure ya did." So we take it to another church that were believers. Hallelujah. I feel good.

DOCUMENTARY UNIT

A few years after learning New Math I get a summer job at the University of Illinois documentary unit. One of my first tasks is to throw away some films they had shot in order to liberate the expensive metal reels. There are a dozen reels of exposed 16mm film they want removed. Since I already have mounted them on rewinds, I thought I'd better see what's on these babies. I run them through a viewer. Hey, that's our math class! Hey, that's me! Can't throw these out. This is valuable historical stuff. All 47 hours of film are archived at the University of Texas Austin in the Max Beberman Film Collection. Anyone up for a New Math Film Festival?

My next assignment is a "shoot." Well, sort of. I shoot animated cells of concentric circles, one frame at a time, resulting in a kind of vortexing bull's-eye. It takes weeks to shoot. The two-minute film is part of a navigation experiment and will only be shown to pigeons. My first film is for the birds! This'll look good on my résumé.

I love filmmaking. The images move, and breathe, and are more engaging than stills. I find that my sense of timing from playing drums informs how to edit moving images. All summer, whenever I can, I work at night on my own little films.

That same summer I discover foreign films at The Art Theater. (This theatre, formerly called The Park, was for a brief time owned by my grandfather Isaac Kuhn, who helped finance it in 1913.) The films are mostly "new wave" French and Italian films. They open me up to the sights and sounds of other cultures, and different lifestyles that I'd not imagined. They are shot in a more intimate and realistic way than Hollywood films and are about life, not fantasy. The mere fact that films made in other parts of the world can be about something meaningful makes a very powerful impact on me.

My summer is jam-packed. I go into the newspaper's darkroom at 7 a.m., work until 4 or 5, catch a foreign film at 7, then hurry to a band gig at 9 and play until midnight. I do this all summer long. The hard part is that after a gig my ears keep ringing. I can't get to sleep until I go through the entire evening in my mind. I hear all the songs in order, the mistakes and even the breaks. It's like listening to a tape played back except it's my brain. Weird. I don't fall asleep until 3 or 4 in the morning.

ROCHESTER

High school has been five gruelling, miserable, confusing, and repressive years. I'm glad it's over. I know exactly what I want to do. I want to be a fashion photographer like Richard Avedon because I'd seen his iconic model and elephant photo and loved it. I figured being a fashion photographer would be a good way to meet beautiful women.

At last I catapult off to Rochester Institute of Technology to study photography. My Mom and Dad fill up the station wagon with my stuff and drive me up. When I arrive, the school registrar says I may have my choice to study Illustration, Professional, or Science. I say "Illustration. I'll do fine art photography." He says, "You should have registered earlier, all filled up." "Okay, Professional, I'll shoot for weddings or magazines." "Filled up." He says, "You can either be a Scientist or go home."

Being a Scientist means I have to study the physics of light and lenses, densitometry, calculus, chemistry, photo science, and laboratory. No picture taking. Our instructor is one of the inventors of the photographic emulsion that was used in a camera in the first moon shot. They don't let me take real pictures. Instead it's all pictures of test tubes and grey scales in order to measure the gamma of the image. Snore.

R.I.T. doesn't have a single class in filmmaking. I befriend a producer at the local TV station who lets me use their editing room after class to edit a short film I shoot on the weekends. It's called *The Gift* and is a simple Zen study. (Not that I knew what Zen is, but it seemed like it could be a Zen film.) A young bearded man sits under a tree that has just one leaf. He waits for it to fall. We hear the melody of a flute. The leaf falls, he jumps up and, in slow motion, catches it in mid-air in his teeth and, landing, he smiles. I am very proud of that little film, but I can't get any of my teachers to let me show it in class. "Remember, we're Scientists here." But Kodak likes it and awards it a prize in their Student Film Competition and encourages me by sending me two new rolls of film.

At Thanksgiving I fly home for the holiday. Dad gives me the family station wagon so I can drive back with my drums. I join Rochester's most popular band, The Invictas. (Not my fault that all bands in those days are named after cars.) They too had an unreliable drummer. They are a greasy gang that wears Beatles boots. I put a micro-switch under the foot pedal so every time I hit the bass drum a light flashes inside. Who's cool now? The band records an original tune that becomes a local hit. It's called "The Hump" and starts a dirty-dancing dance craze.

Rochester, New York, is cold, dark, and gloomy. The word "depressing" was invented here. Everyone on the street has pale green skin, or maybe it's just all that fluorescent lighting. The school is very institutional and located in the Third Ward ghetto (it has since moved) where race riots break out later that summer of '65.

I share a dorm room with four other guys. Jake, from Schenectady, disappears from the room around midnight and does not return for hours. A few weeks later the police show up and go through his chest of drawers. It's filled with stolen car parts. We'd been living with a professional thief stealing his way through photography school.

I join Sigma Pi fraternity after enduring weeks of sadistic freshmen razing. Humiliating stuff. I wasn't really that into it, but I put up with it because I figure this is what you do if you want a social life. Besides, they promised security for my future: I'd have sixty fraternity brothers who'd give me jobs for the rest of my life.

I survive the first year at R.I.T. and am finally able to transfer into Illustration. I have classes in portraiture, lighting, graphic design, and the more aesthetic aspects of photography. I meet a whole different kind of student: artists. I encounter freer ways of thinking. I like that.

I am walking down the hall in the photography department. A classroom door is ajar. Inside graduate students are sitting on the floor with their eyes closed, meditating. They are taught by Minor White, creator of the Zone System, a technique for previsualizing the grey tones in a scene before making a photograph. I hope someday to study with him. Something is going on here that intrigues me.

One day I catch a glimpse of someone, maybe an apparition or a spirit, walking through a wooded area on campus. A petite woman with long dark blonde hair that falls below her waist, turns and looks back at me. She has big, koala bear eyes best suited for night vision, and an extraordinarily beautiful mouth. She speaks in whispers, if at all. Looking at her you wouldn't think she is a big fan of Blind Lemon Jefferson, Lead Belly, or John Lee Hooker. I am captivated. Bonnie is a weaver in R.I.T.'s School for American Crafts — the exclusive domain of the real artists. She is light years ahead of me in everything: music (Miles Davis, Robert Johnson, Bob Dylan), art, religious studies, and psychology (Carl Jung). Whenever I spend time with her she turns me on to something new. Quickly I realize that I don't know zip.

But by now I am deeply entrenched in my classes, the fraternity, and my greaser band, which Bonnie calls "the hoods." Well, she's right. Everything in my world is well beneath her and she keeps no secret of it. Somehow she tolerates me, but very soon I have to put all that behind me and prove myself to her as an artist, a photographer, a musician, an awake human being, anything. I start by buying some retro gold-frame glasses, thinking this might help. I also enter a poetry contest and win second prize. She is not impressed. I am in the shallow end of the pool in this relationship.

Another weekend arrives, which can only mean another fraternity beer blast party. This one is off-campus at a private house rented by one of the brothers. It's my second date with Pat. A week earlier we'd rolled in the hay on a slow, horse-drawn hayride. Boy, did things start to heat up. The brothers say she has a reputation for being "fast" and give me winks. Pat and I are in the back bedroom and within five minutes she has stripped off all her clothes and emerges like Botticelli's *The Birth of Venus*. She wants me. I stumble backward like a frightened deer. Whoa, this is happening way too very fast. What about Bonnie? Shouldn't I save myself for someone I really care about? It's fish or cut bait time. I panic and head for the exit. She comes after me and presses herself against me. I don't know what to do. I kick open the door and throw her out. Suddenly my "brothers" are all over me, punching and screaming. I nearly fall down a flight of stairs. Someone shoves me into a snow drift.

The next day I tell Bonnie what has happened. She comforts me. But this is not the end of it by any means. To my "forever loyal" fraternity brothers I become an untouchable. Only Paul LaBarbera, an art student, stays my friend. Worse yet, word of the incident spreads like wildfire. I am called in to see the school psychiatrist who is convinced I am on drugs. I've never touched drugs. I can't explain it. "I just freaked, okay? Please tell Pat I'm sorry."

The school sets up its first student court and I am its first case. I am never called before the court to tell my side of the story. Justice comes quickly: I am expelled. My parents come and pack me up. It's a very long and silent drive back to Illinois.

Back in Champaign I apply to Southern Illinois University, which at the time had a good film program. (Somewhere in the back of my brain I knew Buckminster Fuller taught and lived there.) My application is rejected. They don't want any troublemakers. I apply to a dozen other schools, but once they read the report of my expulsion they quickly reject me. Every place except The San Francisco Art Institute. I tell them about what has happened and they say "no problem, we have lots of crazy artists here, come on out!"

These childhood photos of Dad and Mom were my Dad's favorites and had the place of honor on his dresser for years.

Grandfather Joseph Kuhn's birthplace, Ort Sulz am Neckar, Germany.

Ellis and Marie Wiese in Champaign, Illinois.

The trio is my Dad with his father and grandmother.

Ellis was a motorcycle policeman and got front page attention in the local paper for arresting some bigtime bootleggers.

Jeff and I loved to follow Grandma Wiese up that creaky staircase to the attic to go through her boxes of treasure.

Dad told me my great grandparents lived on a farm and had a auto dealership.
My granddad worked there as a mechanic as a young man.

*Ancestral eyes peer down from the huge oil paintings
of Joseph and Isaac Kuhn, which to this day have
the place of honor on the first floor landing.*

Charles Webster

*Clockwise: Great-Grandfather Joseph Kuhn, Grandfather Isaac Kuhn,
Grandmother Rose Kuhn, and the family store.*

"Unmatched in 118-1/2 miles" Jos. Kuhn & Co. in its hey-day with stainglass window skylights before the floors were filled in to make more space for stock. As a boy, I marvelled at the colors streaking down from above.

*My parents, Helen Kuhn and Bill Wiese, when they were dating, then together
when Dad is on Navy leave during WWII. They knew how to have fun.*

Mom and Dad get married during one of Dad's Navy leaves in 1945 in Seattle. Michael arrives two years later.

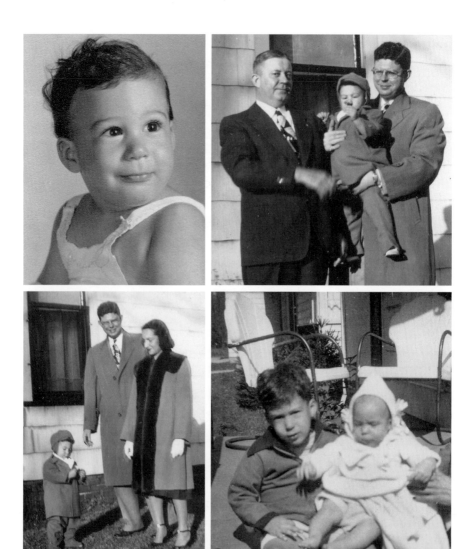

Clockwise from top: Michael, with Grandad Wiese and Dad, with new arrival brother Jeff, and with Mom and Dad.

In the pool in Miami when I was six years old. Later that day we thought we had been "deserted" and tried to make our way back to Champaign.

Jeff

Michael

Michael and Jeff at "Lake of the Weeds". We rowed around the lake catching sun-gills and painted turtles.

Jeff and Michael visit Grandmother and Grandfather Kuhn.
Mom models clothes for a Kuhn's store ad promoting the new women's department.

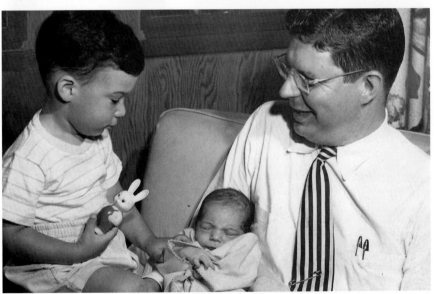

*Michael also models for Kuhn's newspaper ad, Michael and Jeff on the swing set
and dressed for success. Michael and newborn Jeff with Dad.*

Mike with Alberto VO-5 hair gel.

*Love those Buddy Holly glasses in
my senior yearbook photo.*

The University of Illinois High School (aka "Uni").

Michael Wiese

"Onward Cricket Soldiers" It was the summer of Champaign's worse cricket invasion. The photo got me into trouble when a competing newspaper ran it.

Michael Wiese

"The Paws That Refreshes"

Michael Wiese

As a cub photographer for The News-Gazette, *I photographed Roy Orbison and the demolition derby at the Champaign County Fair.*

Michael Wiese

Curt Beamer

L-R: The Torquettes - Don Kennedy, Denny Guy, Mike Wiese, Jim Zorns, and Gary Wright. We quickly run out of songs so we disguise "Yellow Bird" by playing it three times at different speeds. Nobody notices. Everyone is too busy making out.

The hottest band in Champaign-Urbana. The Sterlings L-R: Francis, Tim Stillwell, unknown, Mike Wiese, Mike Stoller, Gary Wright. I was the youngest in the band. I got the job not because I was a great drummer but because I was reliable and always showed up.

Two of the winning photos from
my portfolio which garnered a 2nd
Place award in the Illinois Press
Photographers' contest. The oyster
shed was shot in Wellfleet, Cape Cod,
and the clown backstage at a circus
in Champaign. I always thought the
clown was an escaped convict on the
lam hiding behind his make-up.

Opening *in*
San Francisco

1966  *1969*

"If your eyes are opened, you'll see things worth seeing."
— Rumi

....

Pat and Steven Arnold. Photo by Michael Wiese.

Looking back I see that carefree exploration seems to be naturally built into the fabric of one's being. A necessary component of learning. Like children of all time, we have to test the world, push on it, poke it, and see what's solid. Where are the limits? Should there be limits?

My young self was exploring and testing the world, not only to see what I can get away with, but to see just how far my imagination and subsequent actions can take me. It's an ongoing experiment drawn from a pure energy that I unconsciously ride until I become conscious. Now I step into a much bigger world to be tested again. How far can I take it?

I head West. I don't know if the Golden Gate Bridge is in Hollywood or San Francisco, but I'll find out soon enough. For the first few months I stay in a boarding house in Pacific Heights. Bonnie follows six months later and enrolls in The School of Arts and Crafts in Oakland. I arrive just in time for the first "Be-In" and "The Summer of Love." My education at R.I.T. gives me a technical edge over the other students, but definitely not an artistic one. I see quickly that creatively, I suck. Jerry Burchard, my photography teacher, has students doing very personal work. "Today we are going to do portraits of our own feet." My photographs are dark and mirror the dark mood of Rochester. Jerry shakes his head as he studies my photos, silently critiquing my perfectly printed but artistically impaired work. A big shift in perception is necessary. Desperate times, desperate measures.

That night Jerry invites me over to his apartment for some private mentoring. The flat is a short walk from the Art Institute and has Indian carpets on the floors, psychedelic art and his own photographs on the walls. Jerry wears his trademark rose-colored granny glasses, and with the self-satisfied smile of a Cheshire cat he holds up a sugar cube. Down the hatch. For the next six hours the walls melt, sounds become colors, colors have voices, time stretches, and my whole sense of who I am crumbles and then is revealed. I am light! I am an electromagnetic orgasm, I am energy manifest! All is love. Koo-koo-ka-choo.

I am still coming down as Jerry drives me back to Bonnie's flat near the Opera House. San Francisco's Victorian houses appear as a vast Hollywood cardboard set. And all the houses appear to be sliding up and down the hills, and enjoying it. When I first see Bonnie I can see through her body, blood rushing through her veins, her skin changing colors like a chameleon. We communicate telepathically and make love.

JADE MUSE

Summer is coming and I have a decision to make. I can either go back to Illinois and work with the documentary unit again or take a chance with some guy called Marty who asks me to audition for a new band he's putting together. I'd rather stay in San Francisco, but with no sure work here and another chance to work in film, I go back to Illinois. I cancel the audition. The band Marty Balin ends up forming is Jefferson Airplane.

When I return to San Francisco, Bonnie and I rent a place together near Union on Fillmore, not far from a Japanese movie theatre. I am a fiend for anything by Kurosawa, Misoguchi, or Teshigahara. I also see my first Ozu films (now my favorite), but at the time he was too slow for me. Bonnie sets up her silk screens in one room and I set up a darkroom in another.

I spend many evenings at the Matrix, a rock club two blocks down the street that has just opened. Marty Balin rented it so the Airplane would have a place to play. Every San Francisco band plays at the intimate club, including Janis Joplin and Big Brother, Country Joe and the Fish, Quicksilver Messenger Service, Dan Hicks and His Hot Licks, Steve Miller Band, Steppenwolf, The Doors, the Grateful Dead, and countless others, including my old bandmate Don Kennedy's band, The Buffum Tool Company. During the breaks the musicians come up to our apartment to get stoned.

I audition and am hired by Mark Spoelstra's new electric band, Jade Muse. Once again everyone is older, including Mark, who is seven years older than me. This is very exciting. I am in a band with a true recording legend. Mark had been a folkie in New York and had shown Bob Dylan the ropes when he arrived. ("How can you stumble when you got no place to fall" and other lyrics were written by Mark and made famous by Dylan. He had a falling out with Dylan, which I only read about recently in a Dylan biography. Mark was a gentleman and never bad-mouthed Dylan, but he must have been very hurt.) Mark plays a great twelve-string guitar and already has a couple of successful albums out on Folkways. (Also in the group is sax/flutist Willie Wait, who had played sax on Gene Vincent's "Be-Bop-A-Lula.") We had a string of gigs around San Francisco at venues like the Matrix, Hungry I, Berkeley's Jabberwocky, and once shared a flatbed truck with Carlos Santana for a charity concert. Bonnie designs and sews my clothes for the band: psychedelic shirts, turquoise bell-bottoms, and even a velvet jumpsuit. Jade Muse's career culminates in our appearing at The Big Sur Folk Festival. It's held at Esalen, the human potential center of California, right atop huge cliffs with the ocean hundreds of feet below. About 3,000 people show up. Esalen is known for its hot springs. A highpoint of the festival is cavorting in the hot springs bath with Joan Baez, Joan Baez's mom, Mimi Farina, Paul Simon, Art Garfunkle, Al Kooper, and the entire Chambers Brothers band. When we are ready to be paid, we are told, "Sorry, the box office has been robbed."

Deflated, we go back to San Francisco more broke than ever. But all is not lost. Mark has arranged a demo recording session paid for by Warner Bros. Records. If they like what they hear, we may get an album deal. Dave Hassinger, who recorded most of the Stones' albums in the Sixties, is the engineer. (He later worked with such groups as Jefferson Airplane, The Monkees, Love, Crosby Stills Nash & Young, the Grateful Dead, and The Jackson 5.) We are ready for him to make us the next great thing. As he mics my drums he asked whether I play "crash" or "tinkle." I tell him, "With this band, tinkle." Word comes back. Warner's passes because our soft rock sound is out of fashion. Sure, five years earlier we would have been fine, but not now when Jimi Hendrix and psychedelic rock have completely altered the sonic landscape. Discouraged, Mark pulls the plug on his electric group, goes on to become a preacher, releases a few more solo albums, and has a ton of kids.

A few weeks later, after rehearsing with another band, I am too tired to drag my drums up the flight of stairs. I leave them in the station wagon on the street. Big mistake. I return in the morning to an empty car. No drums. Is a life of music really what I want? I'll put it on hold for now. I take the $500 insurance money I get from the drums being stolen and invest it in what later becomes my graduate thesis film, *Messages Messages*.

UNDERGROUND MOVIES

When one door closes, another opens. In film class at the Art Institute, a new guy appears who I haven't seen before. At least I think he is a guy. Steven Arnold moves like he's underwater, a human sea-horse. He has big hair, an aquiline face, and with the flourish of a magician asks if I can see his resemblance to Jean Cocteau. He claims he is a reincarnation of Jean Cocteau. (Cocteau died in 1963, so Steven would have been about 19 years old already, but I don't challenge him on this.) He wears rings on every finger and dresses in 1920s European clothes. He said he spent a few years studying painting at the École des Beaux-Arts in Paris. I have never talked to anyone this exotic.

Stephen had just shot his second short 16mm black and white film — *The Various Incarnations of a Tibetan Seamstress* — and says he needs my help finishing it. "Dahling, come to my studio and I'll prepare a fine dinner." His apartment is ornate, but on closer inspection everything is thrift shop, albeit beautifully displayed. "Dinner" is a heated up can of Chef Boyardee spaghetti but served as if it were *filet mignon*. Steven has a way of embellishing reality, and time and time again I'd fall for it. But maybe he really does see the world differently.

His film is magical. It looks as if it had been shot in another era in another dimension. Perhaps it's his old wind-up 16mm camera with its dysfunctional shutter that gives it that streaked, jumpy early-cinema look. The film is filled with the same elaborate sets, props, and costumes that hang everywhere in his cluttered apartment. He is an extraordinary visionary even if he is entirely innocent in how to set a proper camera exposure or edit two pieces of film together. His influences, as I would learn, were Jean Cocteau's *The Blood of a Poet* and Georges Méliès' *A Trip to the Moon*.

Even though he is four years older, we become fast friends and filmmaking partners because we each have something to offer the other. Having studied at R.I.T., I am more technically competent than any of the other students. I have even made some films before. Steven, on the other hand, has enough visionary panache to launch his own Bauhaus.

Bonnie moves back East, so Steven and I rent a warehouse on Fillmore street, a few blocks from the Clay Art Theater. Steven works part-time at India Imports in Haight-Ashbury, so our studio is furnished with the cheap Indian spreads he "borrows" from the shop. On a loft overlooking the vast studio space, we each have an Indian bedspread tent which serves as our bedrooms. They are backlit with indirect lighting and filled with cushions. The look is kind of *Satyajit Ray* meets *Nights of Arabia*.

In the studio we build several huge sets out of butcher paper. Everything is a set. Pat Eddy, a high school friend of Steven's, lives there with us. As well as helping out in the studio, she appears in our films and models for our paintings. There is no heat and some nights we have to put our hands around one of those infra-lights that cafeterias use to keep turkeys warm just to keep ourselves from freezing.

Bonnie returns for a visit. I am ready to impress her with our wondrous studio, my new lifestyle, and my artistry. I am sure she'll want to move in with me again. "Isn't it incredible?" "Pompous," she says. A woman of few words.

Steven is busy drawing storyboards for the first film we will make together. His drawings and paintings are cast with Fellini-esque circus people, angels and Hindu gods. His work is powerful because of its provocative range: it's both homoerotic decadent and highly spiritual. Steven's genius is his ability to embrace and integrate extremes and in itself is perhaps a definition of art.

My job is to take the storyboards and figure out how to shoot and light them. His stories are all visual and don't depend on language. Our first film project is for our class at the Art Institute. It's called *The Elements*, in which actors personify earth, air, fire, and water. These are, of course, cast from Steven's collection of unusual looking friends: the more bizarre the merrier. The opening shot is of a dried lake-bed. The earth cracks open. A naked man is born from the earth to the sound of horses neighing. The film has its first showing at the Haight-Ashbury theatre, where it plays before The Beatles' *Magical Mystery Tour*.

San Francisco's hippy scene is exploding. The streets are filled with young people who've come from all corners of the country to explore and experiment with new lifestyles. Drug experimentation, revolutions in politics, music, sexuality, and spirituality are erupting. Everything is up for grabs. Old structures are crumbling. Steven is gay and proud of the countless lovers that he can attract. Sex for gays, and straights, is free and easy.

The upside of being the only straight guy working in our studio in a gay environment is that there is no competition for the women. One day, Cherel Winette comes over with her friend, Kaisik Wong, an extraordinary young fashion designer who is sewing the costumes for our next film, *Messages Messages*. When I first see Cherel she is the spitting image of Penelope Tree: skinny, big eyes with black eyeliner, and a very well put together thrift shop look. She is lots of fun besides being a very committed and fearless photographer. She also studies at the Art Institute and her portfolio of portraits of plantation blacks and Native Americans is very powerful. From that moment on she would be a major part of our films, and my life.

MESSAGES MESSAGES

Messages Messages takes Steven and me a year and a half to make. When finished it costs about $800 (most of the money coming from the insurance money from my stolen drums) and runs 28 minutes. It's peopled with freakish characters: goddesses with huge noses, slaves with shaved heads, and transvestite seductresses. The weirder the better. We are inspired by Dalí, Buñuel, Cocteau, and the German Expressionists. Jung inspires us to explore the "collective unconscious" through the imagery and archetypes in the film.

We dive in with great gusto. All our elaborate sets are made from a $50 roll of white butcher paper that I crumple up and staple to wooden frames. Afterwards the images are projected onto this uneven surface. We create a whole world with crumpled paper! I shoot it on black-and-white 16mm film with an Arriflex S which I borrow from the school. We add an experimental soundtrack that is performed entirely on a piano string-board using mallets and bows. The story — if it has to have one — is the journey of the psyche or soul into unconscious realms. Remarkably, the audiences fall into the dream world of the film and surrender to it, paper sets and all.

Steven and I enjoy cultivating a mysterious and enigmatic reputation at the Art Institute. We separate ourselves from our fellow students by refusing to show *Messages Messages* to our graduate class at school. We want a proper premiere at a real theatre. Trouble is, no theatre wants to show it.

I go to New York on a do-or-die plan. It's snowing heavily as I wait freezing outside the St. Regis Hotel. Finally I see the famous handlebar moustache appear through the snowy whiteness. Salvador Dalí appears as an apparition. I scurry up to him and tug on his cape. "Mr. Dalí, sir? You inspired us to make this film. Can I show it to you?" He agrees and over the next week I meet with him several times at his table in the Cole Porter Bar, where in a mix of four languages he tries to instruct me in alchemy and how art manifests something from nothing. He demonstrates what he means when a large man in a tight vest proposes a new Dalí exhibition. By the time he finishes, Dalí has secured $100,000 in license fees and won't have to lift a finger. Dalí smiles, "One day it will have to be officially admitted that what we have christened reality is an even greater illusion than the world of dreams." *Voilà*, alchemy!

Dalí likes the film and rents the hotel ballroom for an evening screening. The film isn't exactly finished — that is, the picture and soundtrack have not been married in a single film print. I borrow a Siemens double system projector that has a sound reel on one side, and a picture reel on the other, and hopefully they will roll together in perfect sync. The picture is a workprint chock-full of cement splices. I am not sure whether the splices will hold, so I am terribly nervous. Dalí's wife, Gala, sits next to me. When I turn on the projector she holds my hand. Dalí's guests include Andy Warhol and his actors from The Factory, Masters and Johnson (the famous human sexual response researchers), dancers from the New York City Ballet, a sprinkle of Hell's Angels, and other up-and-coming young artistic misfits. When the film ends, there is cheering and clapping, followed by surreal canapés supplied by Dalí.

I return triumphant to San Francisco. Steven arranges a press screening at socialite Katherine Cebrian's house. We invite the famous film critic, Stanley Eichelbaum, and others. Since Dalí endorses the film by giving his surrealistic stamp of approval, everyone wants to see it. Dalí knew exactly what he was doing and I shall be forever grateful.

We rent the Chinese Palace Theater in North Beach, a venue that caters to the Chinese opera and kung-fu set. The night of our premiere we hire a big klieg light that scans the sky over North Beach and announces to the world the emergence of two new young filmmakers. Inside, 2,000 patrons sit waiting to be the first to see a 28-minute, black and white, surrealistic short, blessed by the Great Dalí.

The Chinese owners are impressed by the sold-out box office, a rarity for the old theater. They pull me aside. "Could you find other films like this?" "Of course, piece of cake, all my friends are making them." They confer and then ask if we would like to book these films in their theatre. I say, "Sure, but when?" They say, "You can have it starting at midnight on Fridays and Saturdays." We grab at the opportunity, not really knowing if we can pull it off. We launch a very successful weekend of midnight movies called Nocturnal Dream Shows which run for several years. Other theaters throughout the country see how profitable we are and start their own midnight movies. Initially we show what I like, serious European art house films, but in order to appease a bigger and bigger late-night San Francisco gay audience, my two gay partners, Steven and Sebastian Myron, want to screen more campy features. Two votes to one, straight vote loses.

Messages Messages is invited to the San Francisco Film Festival and someone from Cannes sees it, so it's invited to the prestigious "Director's Fortnight." Unfortunately I can't afford to go to France. (For years Steven tells people that our film wins "Best Director" at Cannes. This is repeated in Steven's press clippings. For years I try to explain to him that it didn't win. Then I realize, on some level for him, it did.)

Noctural Dream Shows is thriving. Every weekend the 2,000-seat theatre is nearly filled. People come to be part of what has become a stoned, dressed up, see-and-be-seen scene. The movies are secondary.

The income allows Steven, Sebastian, and me to rent a 4,000-square-foot warehouse for an even larger studio in the Mission District. Steven, Skosh

(Steve's current lover), Cherel and I live there together. We start another film called *Pyramid*, which is to be about an ancient pharaoh who comes to life in an ancient tomb and travels into the future. Our friend Gerhard Samuels, composer and associate conductor of the L.A. Philharmonic, is to write the score. Beat poet ruth weiss and Joseph Zaccarelli (both appeared in *Messages*) are to be in the film, along with Cherel and Skosh. Funders from The American Film Institute come to visit and promise us that we will be given a $10,000 grant during the next cycle. On that basis, we foolishly start our film, but the grant is not forthcoming. (No Dad, I didn't get it in writing.) We only shoot the beginning few minutes of the pharaoh coming to life and traveling on a barge with his wife and slave before we run out of money. (The film is never finished, but a clip appears in my 1974 film *Silver Box*.)

NAKED AMBITION

Never mind, we'll find another way to get the money to finish our masterpiece. Friend and underground filmmaker Scott Bartlett (*Off-On*) introduces us to two guys who look like Laurel and Hardy dressed as gangsters. Carl, the tall skinny one in the acrylic leisure suit, thinks he's Frank Sinatra, and Bob, his walrus-shaped pal in the spaghetti-stained T-shirt, have built a film processing lab. They had paid Scott to make a film for them and they offer us the same deal. "We make nudies," Carl boasts.

Carl explains what he wants, or rather what he doesn't want. "You can't show the woman's... you know... her... well, down *there*, that *place*. You know what I'm talking about?" "No," I say to wind him up. "You know... *there*... down *there*... and you can't show the guy's... you know, his *thing*." "No, I don't know." For tough guys, they sure have a hard time trying to tell us what not to shoot in the middle of San Francisco's sexual revolution.

What they want is a movie with lots of naked people. Pretty innocent fare. Back in those days, people would go to "art films" for a flash of flesh and that's what these guys financed and distributed. Steven and I write a script about two ship-wrecked sailors who hallucinate about two women on a desert island. Steven draws a couple of storyboards. They like the idea and say they'll pay us $500 each to make it, plus all expenses. We advertise for actors in Haight-Ashbury's underground paper *The Oracle*. The weirdest porn stars, prostitutes, and junkies strip off in our studio auditions. These people really creep us out, so instead we cast our art school friends.

We all drive up to the Russian River where Steven's family has a cabin and shoot outside in forests and fields. Our last day in Sebastopol, we are shooting a naked couple dancing through a field when suddenly, from out of nowhere, we find ourselves surrounded by eight deputized men with rifles pointed at us. "What the... ?" They identify themselves and say we are trespassing and are indecently exposed. They say a Girl Scout troop often walks through this field. We are arrested and thrown into jail. The police confiscate our camera equipment, which belongs to Carl. Fortunately they don't open some of the film cans that are marked with a grease pencil, "Film — Do Not Open," or they would have found some of the country's best marijuana.

I am in court on July 12, 1968 — my 21st birthday. The judge warns me, "I never want to hear that you are making films again!" Standing before him with my fingers crossed, "Oh, no sir. Promise. I'll never make a film again." The charges are dropped.

A PARTY FOR FELLINI

The San Francisco Film Festival announces that our hero, Federico Fellini, will be attending the festival in October so we plan a huge party for him. We figure if we sell tickets to the party we can raise money to complete our Egyptian science-fiction film, *Pyramid*. Dozens of our friends help decorate and prop the entire warehouse. We already have the huge Egyptian barge we'd built for *Pyramid*. We have grottos and light projections everywhere. People dress in outrageous costumes. We have several swings with scantily clad trapeze artists who swing the length of the studio. Members of the Jefferson Airplane play in one part of the 4,000-square-foot studio and a string quartet plays in another. We have clowns and magicians, and people wearing nothing but body paint. Viva, of Andy Warhol fame, holds court in a tented throne. It's a photographers' paradise.

There is a commotion outside the studio. The sleazy part of 18th Street is lined with two dozen limos from the Festival's season ticket holders. People are shoving and pushing to get in to the hottest party in town. I am standing at the door when director John Schlesinger (*Midnight Cowboy*) "blags" his way in. A thousand people pay $15 for tickets, but after covering the event's expenses there is little left for our film. And in the end, Fellini did not come to the Festival, nor to his party.

The studio doesn't have heat and it's freezing. It's too cold and too drafty to work. Sebastian and Steven are showing campy films at the Midnight Movies. The serious European films I occasionally get to show have much smaller audiences. People don't come to the theatre to contemplate existential issues; they come to get stoned and get laid. It's a huge social phenomenon, completely out of control, and getting weirder all the time. More and more of Steven's gay friends have no place to stay and crash at the studio. Sometimes I find people in my bed and have to throw them out. I am miserable and want time alone. I want to be making films and the Midnight Movies aren't generating enough money to support us and all Steven's friends, let alone make a film.

Cherel is not happy either. We are not getting along, so she calls her uncle, the musician Herb Alpert, to come and pick her up. I become depressed. No girlfriend, no money, a freezing place to live, and a project that we can't get off the ground.

Steven has an idea for another film called *Luminous Procuress*. He says if we will just put in one real straight sex scene, then the owners of India Imports and their friends will invest $34,000. I am suspicious. This is a sure way to have our work completely compromised by investor's demands that wouldn't stop there. I have a bad feeling about this. I don't want to get steered off course again. Steven and I are moving apart. This is probably a good thing. His vision and sense of himself are so big, I am not sure what part of all of this is really me, if any.

Altamont. The Rolling Stones' concert comes to a fatal end when some Hell's Angels stab a guy to death. The sun has set on "The Summer of Love." The scene is turning dark.

Then the capper: I receive a notice to appear for a physical at the Oakland Induction Center. They are going to draft me and send me to Vietnam! I burn the edges of the notice and send it back to them. "Thank you for inviting me to your war — BUT I'M NOT GOING!" Not only do I believe it to be a corrupt and immoral war, I am not going to spend any part of my life killing. I am also not going to play the conscientious objector game either. There are many ways to get yourself rejected. I decide to do them all.

First I collect letters from doctors sympathetic to the anti-war movement describing my allergies and unfit psychological make up. When the day arrives for the physical, I put on a velvet jumpsuit and Kabuki eye shadow. That should make it clear that I am not going to fit in. I smoke a few joints on the bus ride over but I am so nervous they do nothing. Hopefully they'll alter my blood chemistry if they do a urine test.

I expect to see many others who also want to get out of the draft but I seem to be the only one. Instead, there are several hundred uneducated guys my age, raring to "go to 'Nam and kill some gooks." Several guys make wisecracks trying to start something with me. I expect that I will probably be beaten up, but just when things start to escalate they became obedient and follow the orders that a big Sergeant shouts out. His Popeye arms are the size of trashcans. A dozen of us are called in a room and asked to form a circle and then turn around. I've been told about this part and I know just what to do. The Sergeant shouts "DROP TROU!" and everyone pulls their pants down. I am not wearing any underwear. Ha!

Someone grabs me roughly by the shoulder and hustles me down a hallway to the shrink's office. Yes! Right on schedule. He runs through a list of questions which I refuse to answer. I tell him that I am a natural leader and that if I am drafted I will convince the others to protest the war. He stares at me, sighs, and then stamps my papers "4-F, Unfit to Serve." I am outta there in a jumpin' jack flash.

It becomes clear to me that I want no part of anything that seems to be on my horizon. Time to make a radical change.

I love the work of Ingmar Bergman, especially *Persona*. I manage to puff up my sense of self worth by recalling the success of *Messages Messages*. I write Bergman and send him a copy of *Messages Messages*. I say that I want to be his apprentice and that if I don't hear back from him in three weeks inviting me to Sweden, I will go to Japan and study with Kurosawa. Bergman, in his infinite wisdom, never writes me back. He must know my sensibilities are better suited to Japan. The film gods have spoken. I am off to Japan.

I sell my station wagon for $400, buy a $200 one-way ticket from L.A. to Tokyo, and hitchhike to L.A., where I meet Cherel for a goodbye dinner on Sunset Strip. Outside the restaurant a black Bentley is parked. Something about this car... I don't know what it is, but something....

Questing in the East

"You will be more disappointed by the things you didn't do than by the things you did. So throw off the bowlines. Sail away from the safe harbor. Catch the trade winds in your sails. Explore. Dream. Discover."

— Mark Twain

....

Michael in the Sudan

San Francisco was the Petri dish of my creativity. I had come from Illinois — a relatively ordinary world — and landed wide-eyed and flat-footed in a magical land of music and color. I loved it. I swam in the pool with passionate artists, psychonauts, political radicals, gays, psychedelic musicians, and underground filmmakers in the greatest free-for-all game of "52 Card Pickup" that America has ever seen. No rules. Have fun. Play hard. Nobody gets hurt. As it turned out, this was a short blip in time and the doors of perception slammed shut. I knew I had to leave. I didn't know why or even what I was looking for. After having no desire whatsoever to travel, I felt an enormous pull from the East, and I declared to my parents and friends, "I am going to Japan!" The pure energy of exploration welled up inside of me. I left everything and ventured East.

JAPAN

I arrive with the rising sun at Tokyo's Narita airport with $200 in my pocket and a single name scribbled on a scrap of paper. They stop me at immigration. They apparently haven't seen many hippy travelers like me in black leather pants, black shirt and black boots. But it's the Afghani shoulder bag that really gets their attention. They search it and find my film print of *Messages Messages*, which they take from me. I stand at the customs desk for about half an hour and then realize that the hall is empty. There are no guards on any of the desks and not a single passenger. What's going on? I walk around. I open a door and there are fifteen customs guys, some with their feet propped up on a desk, cheerfully watching my surrealistic movie.

I am taken into an interrogation room and without the benefit of a translator discover through pantomime that I am being hassled about the one miniscule nude scene in the whole movie. They won't give me back the film unless I agree to cut out the scene with the frames of ruth weiss' pubic hair. "It's not pubic hair, it's a shadow!" For hours they keep me there. I argue. It's the principle of the thing. "This is a great art movie that I will show in Japan." They put me in a holding room. When I am bored and exhausted they bring me out. Behind the power-hungry official who is harassing me is a nude pinup calendar. The irony is too great. I take a picture of it, which makes him mad. Ultimately I cave in and cut a few seconds out of the film. They put the clips in storage (with a daily storage charge). When I leave the country I can pick them up.

Eighteen hours later it's nearly midnight when the police car drives me from the airport and drops me off in Ginza, Tokyo's entertainment district. Bright blazing signs everywhere, all in Kanji or Katakana. All indecipherable. *Arigato*, guys!

I check out a few hotels but they are very expensive, five-star jobs. I have no map and don't know which way to go. I find the train that circles the city and get on it. There I meet a student who speaks a little English. He offers me his floor to sleep on. Done deal.

The next day I take out my scrap of paper and find my way to Takahiko Iimura's house. Taka is an experimental filmmaker who has collaborated with Yoko Ono and is my only contact in all of Japan. He takes me to a Japanese *ofuro* (public bath) and then we eat *yakitori*, which is a bonsai-sized version of fried chicken. He and his wife are extraordinarily generous and set up several film showings for me which enable me to earn some money. My films are a big deal because there are very few "underground" filmmakers in Japan, so I get a lot of national press even if they are clueless as to what my films are about.

I make my way on the bullet train to Kyoto and spend many months there living in an unheated paper-thin apartment. It's January and unbelievably cold. I wake up with my face frozen to the tatami mat. Except for sleeping, it's too cold to stay there during the day, so I spend my days in coffee shops, bars, noodle tents, and cheap public baths. I venture all over Kyoto and visit the beautiful temples again and again. It's good being alone. I can think on these long walks.

Near Kinkaku-ji Temple, I meet Ben Franklin (the great, great, great grandson of Benjamin Franklin) and his friends Joanna and Charlie, a big Scotsman. I often go over to Charlie's house and have tea with Joanna while Charlie finishes his morning meditation. Many of the Westerners I meet in Kyoto are studying Zen and teach English classes to survive. Most of my Japanese friends are musicians, artists, or performers.

Coffee houses come in all styles and shapes. They are mostly very small, seating only a dozen people, and are thematic. So you may have a London teahouse, a high-tech video coffee shop, a jazz coffee shop, or the kind that are coffee shops by day and transform into nightclubs in the evening. I even find one that is dedicated to American underground movies that has dozens of our Midnight Movie posters all over the walls! We are big in Japan!

It's in one of these coffee houses that I meet *So-en* magazine (Japan's *Vogue*) top model, Hiromi Oka. She knows little English and my Japanese is less than stellar, but through drawing and pantomime we are able to communicate. By coincidence, I meet her again the same night at a party for fashion designer Issey Miyake. Is some kind of fate at work here? A romance evolves and I find myself making frequent trips on the bullet train to Tokyo to see her. Eventually I move into her apartment. It's a challenge communicating, but I am proud that we were able to do so, even if it's on a very superficial level. Deep down I knew the relationship would be doomed because not only are there significant cultural differences, but we can only talk about things using the language of six-year-olds, so, through no one's fault, intellectual stimulation is missing.

Since there is no one to talk to, I read a lot. Someone sends me Stewart Brand's *Whole Earth Catalog.* Here are many books by Buckminster Fuller. I order them and read them all. Tokyo is a futuristic city designed to accommodate and service the needs of its teeming population, and therefore it seems like a good place to think about how best to make the world work for everyone. In a world convinced that scarcity is the norm, Bucky is the first person I've ever heard of who is certain the world holds abundance and that by employing design science we can raise the standard of living for everyone. He writes some amazing things that inspire me to no end: "I look for what needs to be done and then try to best work out how to do it. After all, that's how the universe designs itself." "We now have the resources, technology and know-how to make this world a 100% physical success." "Humanity is taking its final examination. We have come to an extraordinary moment when it doesn't have to be you or me. There is enough for all. We need not operate competitively any longer. If we succeed, it will be because of youth, truth, and love." Sitting in a temple in Kyoto, it occurs to me that Bucky may have taken the vow of the *bodhisattva.*

I have run out of money as work is hard to find, but in Tokyo there are many opportunities. I draw a surreal comic strip which a magazine publishes. I model ski pants. I meet Hiroshi Teshigahara, the director of a film based on Kobo Abe's novel *Woman in the Dunes* (one of my favorites). His father is the famous Sofu Teshigahara, founder and grand master of the Sogetsu School of Ikebana the emperor's flower arranging school. He arranges a film showing of *Messages Messages* for me at Sogestu, one of Japan's top museums.

The Fugetsu Coffee Shop in Shinjuku is the hang out for travelers and Japanese kids who want to brush up against Western culture. I get to know quite a few bands who imitate the Grateful Dead, Bob Dylan, or John Lennon.

I am invited to attend a big, all-day concert at Tokyo's Hibiya Park. *Messages* is projected without sound as a backdrop behind the bands. I am backstage with various Japanese pop stars, most of whom I have never heard of. There is a rehearsal room in the back of the amphitheatre where I jam with some of the other musicians. It doesn't sound bad. One of the organizers who jams with us is a former rock star who must miss the spotlight. He convinces us that we should surprise the audience and play a few tunes. I am game and so, as a lark, we go in front of 10,000 people, the biggest crowd I've ever played for. We start jamming and about two minutes into the driving tune I realize I am completely out of shape. I haven't played in ages and I have no chops. My arms are starting to cramp up just as the Japanese paparazzi start firing off shots of me — the only Westerner on stage. I am sinking fast. There is another drum kit on stage and I look over to see if anyone is on it. There is. I am able to draw back and basically fake it. I barely make it through the song. With newfound humility, I bow my way through the cameras and get off stage as quickly as possible. Yes, I am chicken. A chicken teriyaki.

With my good friend and television producer Hideki Kimura, we launch a five-day event in Tokyo called Global Dream Shows in Shinjuku's Art Theatre centered around my films. It's a direct throwback to the San Francisco Midnight Movies except this time we have dancers, singers, and bands as well as my movies. It's packed every night and generates enough money for me to live on for a few months.

I take the train to Osaka to Expo 70 to hear Lani Hall, who is a singer with Sérgio Mendes & Brasil '66 and is Cherel's best friend. (Lani is now married to Cherel's uncle, Herb Albert.) It's my way to check in and see how Cherel is doing. After a visit to Lani backstage, I go next door to the Indonesian pavilion and stare at Balinese shadow puppets for the first time. They are propped in a display case, but still their power is mesmerizing. They embody spirits and I feel them calling to me.

Back in San Francisco I had become excited about Balinese theatre when I read Antonin Artuad's book *The Theater and Its Double*. After seeing a single performance of Balinese Theater in the 1930s, he was inspired to write, "In a spectacle like that of Balinese theatre there is something that has nothing to do with entertainment... The Balinese productions take shape at the very heart of matter, life, reality... All of which seems to be an exorcism...."

Earlier, while living in Kyoto, I'd met some travelers who gave me their tape recording of Balinese gamelan. I listened to it until the batteries ran down. Gamelan is an orchestra of drummers and vibraphonists. Thirty musicians play interlocking patterns with metallophones, gongs, drums, and flutes. Staggering! An orchestra made up of percussionists — music for the gods — a drummer's dream if I ever did see one! It called to me more than any music I'd ever heard. Who plays this amazing music? Who animates these shadow puppets and performs ritual theatre? Whoever they are, they must have an extraordinary culture. I've got to find out.

I tell Hiromi that I have to go to Bali. I'd saved enough money so that if I traveled for many weeks by boat I could make it. I ask her to join me and she says she will, but I doubt it. She is desperately trying to hold onto her position as Japan's number two model and is afraid of slipping further. She is working hard, doing several photo shoots a day, many in foreign locations. During my last week in Japan, her former boyfriend, an older top fashion photographer, shows up more and more. They talk heatedly for hours and whatever they are talking about certainly doesn't include me. The writing is on the wall. I'll go it alone.

ROAD TO BALI

I had been writing friends from the Art Institute about my plans. Steven Arnold won't be joining me because he is starting to make *Luminous Procuress*. He has trouble already. I knew it. His investors are demanding explicit sex scenes, which are compromising his art.

Larry Reed, who I knew only a little, had helped on filming *Pyramid*. He writes that he'll join me on his way to South America. I tell him that Bali isn't exactly on the way, but that doesn't matter. He agrees to meet me in Okinawa. When I get to the shipyard I learn that his boat has already come in and he's nowhere in sight. I wander around for a day and only through sheer luck do I see him relaxing at an outdoor market and we begin our journey to Hong Kong. There we see and are enchanted by Chinese Opera. We go backstage and meet the actors.

One night we engage a skinny little guy in black pyjamas who whisks us through a maze of back alleys, restaurant kitchens, and upstairs to an opium den. It looks exactly like those dens in Charlie Chan movies. Old parchment-skinned men in bunk beds lay askew like rag dolls with their heads sunk into wooden headrests. The air is heavy with the sweet pungent scent. We watch how they heat a ball of opium and fill our pipes for us. We smoke for about an hour. At some point they must have figured we'd had enough (or were afraid they'd be busted for serving Westerners, which is illegal) and they hustle us down the stairs and push us into the streets. "Hey, what are you doing?" We are still very stoned. I can hardly stand and my eyes hurt from the bright lights. We find ourselves in a busy thoroughfare surrounded by honking cars and trucks! Somehow we crawl our way into a darkened sports stadium. We are sick and spend the night stretched out on wooden bleachers. A pattern is emerging. Larry and I find something we've never done before, then challenge each other to do it.

I want to travel on to Bali, but Larry wants to stay and join the Chinese Opera. We have a heart to heart talk and he agrees to continue the journey.

We arrive in Singapore, but the customs guy won't let me in. My hair is too long. The current regime is very nervous and does not want Western hippies to influence their young population, 70% of which is under the age of eighteen. I try every excuse in the book, but it's only when I tell the truth of how my sore tooth is killing me and I want to get someone to look at it does he let me through. Larry and I watch *Let It Be* in a Singapore cinema, a further reminder of the end of the hippy days. Even The Beatles are breaking up.

We have a great time hanging out in the carnival atmosphere of Bugis Street among the night vendors, transvestites, hookers, and fortune-tellers. We see puppet theatre in the street and again Larry is hooked and wants to stay. My heart is set on Bali.

We arrive in Jakarta, the capital of Indonesia, on National Independence Day. We have to wait around for the government offices to open the next day. We carry with us a letter of introduction from the San Francisco Art Institute that I have embellished with a gold seal (bought in a stationary store) and some red ribbon. It looks very official and we pull it out whenever we need to impress someone. This stunt gets us the very first press pass issued by the new Indonesian Press Office, which allows us to score a one-year visa.

We don't like Jakarta, so as quick as we can we take a train deep into Java, stopping for a few days at Borobudur, the spectacular Buddhist monument, where the life of Buddha is depicted in friezes. It's quiet and I meditate.

BALI

We are here! The island of gamelan music. Here fantasy, idealism, and dream blend into a single reality. We find ourselves on an empty Kuta Beach. You can see in both directions for miles along the white sand. There is only one *losman* (a four-room guest house) where we stay for fifty cents a day which includes breakfast. Across the sandy road is a *warung* that sells tea and stale cookies. There are only a handful of travelers passing through and spectacular sunsets every night. The beach is fine, great really, but I am eager to get into the interior, the heart of things.

Suddenly, I hear live gamelan for the first time! It's a walking gamelan. The gongs, drums, and genders are carried and accompanied by a lion-like character,

Barong, in a ritual ceremony right outside our *losman*! Barong battles with Rangda, the witch, as dancers fall into trance. Sarong-clad women of every age line the road with offerings towering on their heads which they carry past us to the beach. I've never seen anything like this before.

One day Madé Gina, a painting salesman, comes to our losman and unrolls his collection of fantastic images. I want to meet the artists who made these, so he draws a map and invites us to his village near Ubud. A few days later, after getting very lost in the rice fields, Larry and I find Pengosaken village. We are taken to the compound of the village head, Dewa Nyoman Batuan. He feeds us as hundreds of villagers gather around and watch. We must be the first Westerners to visit.

Fortunately Batuan, who had been a schoolteacher, knows a little English. We talk for hours and Batuan shows us many paintings from the Community of Painters that he founded just a few weeks ago — on July 12, my birthday. He invites us to stay in his compound and gives us each a sleeping platform in a room only slightly bigger than the bed.

Everything is new and exciting. Batuan and his family and the painters are kind and patient. It's really hard not knowing the language, eating strange food with our hands, bathing in the streams, and surviving the equatorial heat of mid-day.

For me, Bali is a perfect world. People live harmoniously with nature, animals, and each other. If they cut down a tree or kill an animal, they will use all of it. There is no waste. They appear selfless, putting the community first and sharing everything. They are highly artistic, musical, and spend half their lives engaged in spiritual practices. This is how I want to live; free of San Francisco, the studio politics, Cherel, Steven, and the draft. On my own, sink or swim.

My goal is to live as simply as I can. I hope to strip away my Western habits to see what is really important. In Bali, I am like a child again. I will be mindful of everything. I want to be impeccable in eating, sleeping, talking, walking, bathing, and even thinking itself.

Months pass, and during meals a dozen people will still gather around — amused — just to watch us eat. We are the only show in town. There is always someone watching me, sometimes through slats in my hut, no matter what I do. They are as fascinated by me as I am by them.

They share everything with us. Even when they are close to starving they give us food. We go into Denpasar every few weeks to buy coffee and sugar for them in the market.

One afternoon Batuan comes rushing in. He's got something special for us to eat. A delicacy. We sit on mats and are handed something wrapped in a palm leaf. Batuan watches our faces as we open it. It's pig with the bristles still in it! Urgh! I can't eat it, but I also don't want to be rude. So I pretend to eat it. I wait until Larry engages Batuan's attention and then I fling the pig over the compound wall. Batuan looks back at me and asks how I like it. I tell him, "*bagus*," it's good. Just then there is a horrible ruckus on the other side of the compound wall as a pack of dogs fight over the pig scrap. Everyone rushes to see what is going on. Busted. I've never been so embarrassed.

Laba is one of the better painters. He also plays lightning fast gamelan. He has made it his mission to teach me. Every day he comes around and we sit at two genders. He teaches me to strike a key with the mallet in my right hand and then, before striking another key, to dampen the ringing key with my left hand. This requires some coordination, but I get the hang of it.

There is no written music. You just have to hold it in your head. Laba teaches me patterns to play, which get longer and longer. Once I learn them, he plays a counterpart pattern, which results in an interlocking flurry of notes. Wow! After a month of this I know the basics of a single piece. It's time to have me join the gamelan in a temple ceremony.

Batuan's wife dresses me in a sarong, several waist sashes, and a headpiece. She tops it off by sticking a red flower behind my ear and a dagger in my sash. When I arrive, there are thirty musicians deeply immersed in a powerful piece. Hundreds of villagers watch as a beautiful Legong dancer shimmies past in a golden sarong. Only a single lantern illuminates the walls of the temple.

Geckos feast on the moths that get too close to their long tongues. They die a fluttery death.

When the piece finishes, one of the musicians slides from behind his instrument and motions to me to take his place. I barely get comfortable before the piece kicks off. With all eyes on me, and with all my concentration, I clip along at a fast pace. Not bad. Suddenly, they notch up the tempo. "Hey guys, what are you doing? We never rehearsed it this fast!" I am holding on for dear life. Suddenly a curtain bursts open and Celuluk, a she-witch, jumps forward. She circles the audience looking for a child to eat, but all the kids quickly duck for cover behind their laughing parents. She licks her long nails and turns her bulbous eyes to me! Slowly she comes in my direction as the pace of the drumming intensifies. I look down and continue to hammer away determined not to leave my post. Now she is standing over me, just a few inches away, flouting her gigantic droopy breasts and grinding her hips suggestively. She's so close I can smell her necklace of entrails. Then, imitating me, she pretends to play gamelan. Suddenly I no longer feel I am at a performance, but something else... another reality. I look up at her. The teasing is over. The monster prepares to pounce on me. I fumble in my sash for the dagger and try to play at the same time. Celuluk spins away, laughs, and wipes her brow, imitating my panic and then fades away in the darkness. The crowd erupts in laughter. Relieved, I find I am still playing as it comes to a close. Laba gives me a "thumbs up" as I leave my instrument dazed and confused, not quite sure what has happened here.

It's a moonless night. After the ceremony, Laba and Sena hold my hand and guide me down the muddy path through the dark jungle back to the compound. Laying on my sleeping platform I recall the night in my mind. I fall asleep with a smile on my face.

Ketut Liyer is the village shaman. I haven't been feeling well and Batuan takes me to his compound. Turns out we both speak a little Japanese. He learned his when the Japanese occupied Indonesia during WWII. We hit it off. I visit him frequently and watch as he heals a seemingly endless line of villagers. Some have physical illnesses while others want good fortune in courtship, marriage, childbirth, or business. Sometimes he does magic paintings on cloth, which he folds into amulets to be worn. Other times he will write sacred Sanskrit letters on his patient's forehead or tongue while chanting healing mantras. I sit for hours, fascinated by this Balinese medicine man.

Sadly, for Larry and me, it's time to leave Bali. Batuan gives me a huge roll of paintings. He asks me to sell them in my country and come back.

The experience of living in Bali profoundly affects my life. I will return more than twenty times, deepening my relationships with countless dear friends.[*]

On the way back to San Francisco, Larry and I stop for a layover in Tokyo. Hal Sloane, a concert promoter, picks us up at the airport in his black Bentley. (Hey! I've seen this car before on Sunset Strip the night before leaving for Japan!) In the backseat is a Buddha-faced Japanese guy with a goatee and a silver streaked ponytail. He holds a cane and wears a Tibetan necklace of carved bone skulls. He doesn't say a word, just smiles, or looks silently out the window. Two months later he is my best friend.

RETURN TO CORN COUNTRY

Back in Champaign I stay with my folks for a week or so, long enough to host an impromptu exhibition of the village paintings that Batuan has given me. I feel a lot of pressure. I want the exhibition to go well and to sell a lot of paintings because I know the village can use the money to build a schoolhouse. Good fortune! Half the paintings are sold to friends of my parents and to University of Illinois professors. They are some of the best paintings I would ever see come out of Bali. The rest I sell through exhibitions at the San Francisco Art Institute and the Bank of America.

My mother knows from my letters home that I've been reading everything I can get my hands on by Buckminster Fuller. Turns out he is speaking at my mother's Art Club. As the red Jell-O desert is being passed around, the din of silverware on china is hushed by a loud noise as Bucky bangs his shoe on the podium. "It's

---

[*]Note: I have written a novel *On the Edge of a Dream: Magic and Madness in Bali*, written a screenplay, *Bali Brothers*, published a book of Batuan's paintings, *Mandalas of Bali*, and made a documentary film, *Talking with Spirits*, about my experiences in Bali.

five minutes to midnight! This is humanity's final exam!" There is a shocked silence among the coifed and manicured ladies. Inwardly, I cheer, "Go Bucky Go"! Afterwards, I hurry up to meet the great man.

JAPAN — TAKE TWO

I can't wait to go back to Bali, but I am out of money so I head back to Japan.

Rock promoter Hal Sloane meets me at the airport in his black Bentley before taking me to his house where I will stay. Hal is working on a big Woodstock-style concert on the slopes of Mt. Fuji. I get involved in a very small way and again meet the mysterious guy that I saw in the back of Hal's Bentley on the way back from Bali.

Teiji Ito was born in Japan but was sent to the States when he was seven, a few days before Pearl Harbor. He is a composer and played drums for his mother, who performed Balinese dance and Gurjieff's Movements, which were based on cosmic mathematical principles and generated spiritual energies. Besides our both being drummers, we were also both involved with film. He had once been married to underground filmmaker Maya Deren, and composed the music for her underground classic, *Meshes in the Afternoon*.

Teiji and I are both fish-out-of-water in Japan except that he can speak Japanese and I can't. We help plan Fuji Odyssey with Hal Sloane and his Japanese partners Hideki Kimura and others. One night we convene in a hotel room with "Hurdy Gurdy Man" singer-songwriter Donovan, encouraging him to join our festival. About 9:30 p.m. Donovan's dad-manager sticks his head in and says, "Time for bed, Donny." End of meeting. Fuji Odyssey is never to be. Like Singapore, the conservative Japanese government was never going to grant the permits to allow this to happen. We were kidding ourselves.

Teiji has many jobs composing music. He looks out for me and gives me little jobs whenever he can. On one recording session for a saké commercial he hires me to play mbira (African thumb piano). He lives in a big room with tatami mats. On his altar is a samurai sword. We sit and talk while I watch him make protective ritual objects, which he learned when he lived in Haiti with Maya

Deren when she made her film on trance and voodoo. Teiji is always talking about his favorite Vodou spirit, Ghede, an intermediary between the living and the dead.

After a few months in Tokyo I've saved enough to continue my journey. I am planning to go back to Bali, but I figure that since Balinese Hinduism and its powerful art came from India, I should go there and check it out. I want to go to the source, perhaps where the spirit is stronger and more pure. At least that's the idea. I am pretty sure Teiji will join me.

A day before I leave Japan, Teiji does a ritual and gives me a dagger with a praying mantis on its handle and a shakuhachi flute. He also presents me with a cobra-skin passport holder. Inside he has woven a protective Tibetan dorge. Besides a miniature camera and a notebook, these are the only things I will take with me as I travel alone over the next year. As Lin Yutang says, "The wisdom of life consists in the elimination of nonessentials."

KATHMANDU AND MANALI

I fly into Kathmandu and arrive at night on Buddha's birthday. Tibetan horns can be heard from a temple near the hotel blasting throughout the city. I rent a tiny room. In the morning I discover I am in a scene from Hell. When I open the shutters I am at eye level with hungry vultures. They cling to a huge leafless tree anxiously waiting for any scraps that drop off the carcases. My balcony overlooks a slaughterhouse!

It's the rainy season and they have a most primitive sewage system. The streets and paths quickly flood, so anywhere I walk in my sandals I am ankle-deep in shit. It's little surprise that I am sick pretty much the whole time I am in Kathmandu.

Next I go to Varanasi (Banares) on the Ganges, one of the holiest cities in India. Thousands of people bathe, cook, and cremate their dead on the Ganges river. Nothing prepares me for India. It's sensory overload. Bali at least had a homogenous kind of Hinduism. It looks the same from village to village. But Benares is another story.

My first day there, I sit frozen in shock at a tea shop and watch retinues of devotees attend their gurus as they walk to the river to bathe and pray in the *ghats* or temples that are jammed along the muddy corpse-strewn riverbanks behind me. A monkey steals a *chapatti* from a food vendor who pulls out a small pistol and starts firing at it above in a great banyan tree. A procession of elephants stops traffic when a high priest riding in a tower gets tangled in electrical cables. A tiny policeman in khaki shorts tries in vain to redirect the flow of thousands of bicycles nearly getting run over himself. A naked dreadlocked *saddhu* covered in ash limps across the street, picks up some fresh steaming elephant dung and holds it high above his head and chants. There are as many ways to talk to god as there are gods in India.

A man in a bright yellow shirt gets in my face and won't go away. He wants to be my guru and have me pay him to teach me how to play Indian flute. "Don't worry, I am your guru, come with me." This is too much in this unbearable heat. I cool off by swimming in the Ganges because I am told it has healing properties, but after a partially cremated body part floats into me, I practically walk on water to escape and never swim there again.

I make my way by train to Delhi and then travel north by bus. It's a terrifying ride as we rise higher and higher in the mountains on roads not to be trusted. The bus driver has driven for two days and stays awake by popping blue pills and blasting his tape recorder that plays the same bloody Hindi pop songs over and over and over. Dead rusted cars, lorries, and busses can be seen hundreds of feet below; unlucky ones whose drivers fell asleep or got too close to the edge.

We finally arrive in Manali in Kulu Valley, a hillside settlement in the foothills of the Himalayas. I rent a mud hut for $5 a month. I have a blanket and the few things that Teiji gave me in my Afghani bag. I am keeping things simple. Every morning I walk down the mountain through pine tree forests to the village for *dahl* or yogurt. It looks like a Wild West town. Every day I see the same legless beggar with a skateboard. He zooms down the main street accosting rich Sikhs on holiday for a donation. I give him some money and talk with him. I see many tented communities of Tibetan refugees who'd escaped the Chinese by trekking over the snow-capped mountains. They are extremely poor and do the heavy roadwork that even the Indians do not want to do. They are always cheerful.

Manali is just starting to get a reputation for its large marijuana bushes that grow everywhere along the roads. All you have to do is rub your hands on the leaves during the day and roll the sticky resin into hash balls. Or not. Hash is readily available for free at the chai shops, like salt and pepper.

I go to the Poste Restante to see if I have received any mail from friends in San Francisco or Japan. I also send mail, but I make sure to watch the clerk cancel the stamps, because if I don't the postal workers will steam them off and resell them, keeping the money in what could amount to a day's wage.

One day I buy a cone of peanuts from the street vendor outside the post office. The peanuts come wrapped in paper. Paper is expensive, so the vendor uses whatever paper he can get his hands on. As I eat the peanuts, more and more of the paper is revealed. I look at the wrapping. The writing looks familiar... Hey! It's a letter I never received from my mother! Those rascals! I write back, "Dear Mom, thank you for the peanuts...."

New York musician and artist Henry Wolff has a big house in the forest. It's filled with gongs, singing bowls, sitars, tamburas, tablas, and all kinds of instruments that he has collected on his travels. I go up there, wiping my hands on the plants on the way, and jam for hours with whoever is there. A year later he records the world music meditation classic *Tibetan Bells*.

One morning as I am having my chai and yogurt in a smoky street side shop I see someone I think I know through the haze. No, it can't be. I think it's Kent Hodgetts, a fellow filmmaker and artist from the Art Institute. No, couldn't be. It takes days on death-defying buses to get up here and why would he be here anyway?

It's him! He says he's come to fly his hot-air balloon. And sure enough, as he fires up the flames, the balloon fills out and up it rises. He gives me a tethered ride. Henry and his pals organize some Tibetans with bleating horns to ritually celebrate the ascent. Going up is easy, but absolute madness coming down because there's only rocky terrain. If you land wrong you will crush your skull.

I travel to Bombay, stay briefly with some sitar students, then buy a $75 ticket on a freighter that is to stop in the Seychelles before going on to East Africa. I need some rest after the non-stop intensity of India.

If I would have paid attention to what happened before we pulled away from the dock, I would have wondered if boarding this freighter was such a good deal after all. As hundreds of people on the dock are saying goodbye to hundreds of people on the boat, a loading crane is dangerously swinging hooks over everyone's head. It catches on the railing of the boat, but instead of someone being calm about it and unhooking it, the operator yanks at the lever that jerks the hook, tearing off the railing, which then swings back and forth above the heads of the crowd. Fortunately no one gets hurt.

Off we sail into the Indian Ocean. I am in third-class accommodation, which is a half-notch above what it must be like to travel on a slave ship. I am crammed with hundreds of people in the airless hold of a freighter. The smells of people cooking, sweating, cleaning themselves, and eliminating is a constant source of nausea. First-class accommodations for a dozen people are on the top deck above us, but locked off. I climb up a railing to the top deck and spend an evening playing a game of hearts with a German guy and a Japanese traveler until they catch me and throw me out.

The captain is drunk most of the time, which accounts for us going off course and never finding the Seychelles. At least this is my theory, or maybe it's intentional. Late one night we come alongside another ship and there is much commotion with something being loaded on. Being lost has cost us an extra week at sea and we are nearly out of food and water. A very angry Indian man (who sleeps next to me on a sheet of swinging metal that serves as our beds) organizes a vigilante group to raid the kitchen for food. He tries to enlist me on my 24th birthday, as I lay sick as a dog on my bed. To him, it's the greatest of insults when I refuse. He threatens revenge. He takes several dozen men and breaks into the first-class food storage. When they've emptied that, they break into the little shop and take all the candies. I can hear their yelling and footsteps on the deck above me. When I learn he is looking for me, I go up to the outside deck and find an out of the way place under a tarp to rest, hoping he and his gang will forget about me.

When we get to Mombassa we are all taken to the top deck and made to stand in the sun for three or four hours while the Kenyan police scour the ship. What's going on? They find a dozen stowaways who are part of a slave trade scam. Indians pay agents large sums of money because they are told that they will have jobs and a better life in Africa, only to end up as slaves with no passports or papers. Besides that, our late-night rendezvous was some kind of arms deal. The police uncover and confiscate crates of rifles and bags of grenades. By now the police are furious and frustrated. When we are finally free to go, the police shove and hit most people with their batons. But they don't hit me, the few other foreigners, or the wealthy first-class-ticketed Sikhs.

EAST AFRICA

Exhausted, all I want to do is rest. I go to Lamu, which is an island off the coast of Kenya and north of Mombassa. It's the oldest town in Kenya and was a Swahili settlement. It's the home of pirates, slave traders, and merchants who export ivory, mangrove, turtle shells, and rhino horns. I stay near a mosque with its nearly constant blasting of prayers throughout the day, and later live in a hut in the nearby sand dunes for a few weeks.

I'd considered going south, but stories of apartheid in South Africa put me off. There is a big war in Uganda, so I don't want to go West. So North it would be, hitchhiking through Kenya, past Kilimanjaro, past vast expanses alive with lions, elephants, giraffes, and zebras, to Addis Ababa and the throne of Ethiopian Emperor Haile Selassie, to the high plateaus avoiding village, civil, and regional wars as much as I can. Little did I know at the time, there were thousands of refugees fleeing from wars in Chad, Eritrea, Ethiopia, and Uganda all around me. Crazy… dangerous, really, but I had no fear. I had the feeling I was protected, and I was.

Traveling through the desert in Sudan is mostly by hitchhiking rides in trucks loaded with animal skins. Whenever we arrive in a village or an oasis the local chief of police would always check me out to see if he could coerce me into buying him a drink. Once they determine I'm not a spy or a mercenary, they leave me alone. By now I am dressed in Indian linens and have shoulder-length hair and a beard — like Jesus in a student film. My bag — which sometimes is examined — is now filled with flutes that I have collected in India. When in trouble I show that I pose no threat. I play the Fool — the one on the Tarot deck.

Once walking alone in the bush I hear a lion growl. Another time a gang of guys are following me. Each time I take out the shakuhachi (thick bamboo) flute that Teiji gave me and turn the holes toward me so it will look like a weapon.

Whenever I enter a village, I am quickly surrounded by kids. At first this threw me, but now I know what to do. I take out my flute and entertain them. I always ask to see their instruments but in one village they didn't seem to have any. But they did have reeds with big shafts. So I got the kids to collect a bunch of reeds. I cut them, burned finger holes in the tubes and taught them how to get a sound. By the time I left it was one noisy oasis. I always wondered what an ethno-musicologist would think if he happened into this village.

On the way to Khartoum an educated man about my age climbs into the back of the lorry. We talk all the way to the next oasis. Mohammed is the first person that I have met in weeks who speaks English. The two of us go to a dusty food stall in the market and sit down. He asks me in a very serious way if I am Muslim. When I tell him no, he asks if I want to convert. I tell him while I have a lot of respect for Islam, no, I don't want to convert or join any religion. I tell him I believe that everyone has his own experience of God which happens outside the structure of religion. He then says that I am an infidel and that he is going to have to kill me. ("Dear Mom, I was almost killed again yesterday.")

I notice as I travel north you can almost track the history of weaponry. In Kenya the Masaai warriors only have sharpened sticks. In Ethiopia they have metal barbs at the end. In Sudan they have rusty Russian rifles. By the time I hit the Nile in Egypt they flaunt Uzi submachine guns.

Near Wadi Halfa, I board a riverboat heading north down the Nile. It's late afternoon and up ahead there is a black cloud a few feet above the water. I watch as we get closer. Maybe it's the heat, or a desert mirage? Everyone ducks for cover. I don't understand their panic until I am trapped in a cloud of insects buzzing in my ears and eyes, crawling up my nostrils and buzzing in my mouth.

LUXOR

In Egypt I rest in Luxor. I spend several days there. On the night of the full moon, I sneak into Karnak temple. Jerry Burchard, my Art Institute photography teacher, has sent me a few rolls of high-speed missile tracking film with 12,000 ASA. There is enough light to photograph the columns and rows of sphinxes with my half-frame Olympus Pen W camera. I spend the night there, never seeing a guard or anyone. It's very spooky.

After a long train ride through the hot and dusty desert, I finally arrive in Cairo. It's impossible to shut the windows on the train and so I am completely covered in dust. I try to check into a small hotel, but the manager won't let me in because I am too dirty. Kids heckle me and throw stones at me in the street.

Overall I feel safe and protected by the travel gods. I feel that as a world citizen, I am entitled to walk the world, my home. I trust I'll be fine, and I am. It's like I have spirits around me protecting me and keeping me from harm. Wherever I go, people are genuinely generous beyond their means. They invite me into their homes, however meager. It's a paradox; in the wealthiest countries people hoard, in the poorest countries people share.

SANTORINI

Crossing from India to Africa and then dragging myself through the desert has worn me out. In Greece I stop the incessant traveling. I look for a retreat.

I settle down in the small village of Ioa on the Northern tip of Santorini. I rent what amounts to a cave dug into the porous side of a giant volcanic rim. I look down into the crater that forms a crescent to the horizon. This is the volcano that blew in ancient times, creating the tidal wave that destroyed Knossos and the northern coast of Crete. I stay for six weeks in retreat in my little white-washed cave. I eat in the village tavern and drink ouzo with the locals. Some days I climb down the enormous cliffs and swim in the cold, clear Mediterranean.

Alone and quiet, I meditate. I write. I draw and I draw... long into the night. This activity takes me into an altered state. Drawing takes me to other places where something seems to guide my hand and gives me information that comes as marks on a page. Of course I'd seen the Balinese shadow masters channel the gods and ancestors through their puppets. I'd seen trance dancers inhabited by Hindu deities. I don't think much when I draw. I am empty. I don't remember much at all, but when I stop I am amazed at what I see. The communications take the form of film storyboards. Ha! Something I can understand — but they seem to be fragments of ancient teachings. I don't know where they come from. Maybe the walls of the cave? The subjects aren't of anything I'd thought much about. For years I have kept these drawings safe. I now see they are a prediction of events in my future, or perhaps in the future of the world.

But then, wouldn't you know? I receive a long letter from Steven Arnold. Two years have passed and he's finished his film *Luminous Procuress* — the film that was to be made quickly for investors. Of course he struggled to make the film he wanted and the process almost gave him a nervous breakdown. (I had nothing to do with that film, although I am frequently credited for it, but I was out of the country the whole time.) It's a four-page handwritten letter with Steven's careful drawings on the borders. He must have spent hours writing it. It's very seductive. He flatters me by writing that he "needs my marvelous eye" to shoot his next film. I feel the flattery but don't really want to climb back into that San Francisco craziness. I have discovered the source of my own power, my own vision, have traveled the world on my own, and learned a great deal. I want to put that experience to some worthwhile use and not get caught up trying to realize another Steven Arnold fantasy.

Steven wants me to return to make the film, *Monkey,* that we'd been talking about with fashion designer Kaisik Wong. It is the 12th century Chinese story of a monkey who protects a monk on a journey. The story is filled with magical transformations and encounters with demons. It's an allegorical tale about bringing Buddhism from India to China. In many ways I see my own journey and myself in this story of enlightenment and transformation. I put down Steven's letter but find myself picking it up again and reading it over and over. A story of bringing Buddhism to China. Hmmm. I am already getting ideas about how to shoot it. The more I think about it, the more I want to return and put what I've learned back into filmmaking. The hook goes in.

Returning
Home

1973 1974

*"A man travels the world in search of what he needs
and returns home to find it."*

— George Moore

....

Inter Ice Age Four — Steven Arnold

I smile at the Michael I see returning to the West, adding spiritual colors to his artistic palette as he grows. The story of his life, or any life, is all about expansion and consciousness. We start out not knowing, we experience something and gain a momentary knowing. There is no end to this. Our job is to open our senses, engage in the world, and learn from the universe. It's a job we cannot screw up. Whatever kind of life we lead, wherever we live, whatever we accomplish, in the big picture it's not counted. We simply have whatever experience we have, and for the universe, it's perfect. Fear not. Admittance to Heaven is guaranteed.

My Eastern journeys were, like a space probe sent to Mars, an exploration of different worlds, different ways of being. There are a number of ways to live, none more valid than the other and all to be appreciated. I lived simply and without many attachments so I would not be distracted. I wanted to let it all in. I wanted it to change me and I felt it had. What would I do when I returned home? Who had I become? Could I put to use what I had learned in the East?

SADDHU IN NEW YORK

After being away the better part of a year, I land in New York with no money. Teiji is there, so I stay with him. Bali is exotic, India weird, Africa intense. This is to be expected. But I am not at all prepared for America. I have reverse culture shock. People seem utterly mad, racing to their jobs, chasing money, and buying things they don't need. The insane race to acquire, to possess, to control. I'd dropped out of this life and now it does not attract me.

I sit down near 55th and 5th and eat an orange and try to center myself. It's crazier than Benares and what's worse, this is my home.

Cherel comes down to New York from Silver Springs to see me. It's great to see her. There is no romantic draw from me. She is disappointed and lonely. I've become someone else.

Life in America is surreal. I feel as if I keep waking from one dream to find that I am in another. My body is in America, but my spirit is somewhere in India or Africa or in-between. My dreams are all jumbled. It's hard to tell what is a dream, what is reality.

Teiji, his brother Genji, Mara Purl and some of their friends have a music group. They ask me to join them for a gig in a hotel club in Massachusetts. Why not? I will play my Egyptian *dumbac*, a tile-encrusted clay drum, which is the one treasure that I have carried back from Cairo. Mara calls ahead and books an additional room for me. When we all drive up to the restaurant there is a big marquee announcing, "Tonight. Michael Wiese and His Orchestra." Everyone looks at me as if I am trying to pull a coup. But I'm not. It's fun to play with a band again, but this is no longer my calling. What is?

After I leave New York, Teiji and Cheryl tell me they've gotten together. They marry a few years later. I am extremely happy for them both.

I hitchhike to Champaign. It's slow going. The beard and long hair put people off. When I arrive at our house no one is there. I let myself in with the key that's under the mat. I am finishing a shower when I hear Dad calling from the hall. Dressed in my Indian linens, I open the door. It's been a long time since we've seen each other. A lot has happened. In jest — although not completely — he takes one look, raises both arms, and bows low. The father bows to the son.

SAN FRANCISCO REDUX

I return to San Francisco and sleep on the couch in Steven's small apartment. Both the studio and Midnight Movie scene have run full course and have collapsed. Steven is at a bit of a loss about how to relate to me. I don't seem to be the same person I was when I left. I tell him about my adventures, but after a short while he looks away. He's really not interested. We are glad to see each other, but don't fully engage. I tell him I want to get settled a bit and will talk to him later about *Monkey*.

I rent a basement room in a house with Larry Reed and his partner Jane Levy on 7th Avenue near Irving in San Francisco's Sunset District.

I want to turn my travel experience into something. Share it. Express it. So I start work with Steven on the script and storyboards. We get a little money from a wealthy patron and are able to hire Joe Landon to work on the script. My idea is to shoot in colorful paper-constructed sets and experiment with highly saturated video electronic colors. We want it to look like something no one has ever seen before. We shoot video tests at KQED (the local PBS station) of Kaisik Wong dressed in fantastic costumes as *Monkey*.

Steven and I attend the San Francisco Film Festival. *The Godfather* has just been released and director Francis Ford Coppola attends a question and answer session after the film. A young filmmaker asks, "If I want to pitch you a project, how should I do it?" Francis thinks for a moment and then says, "Do something different, show me some slides, surprise me." Steven and I look at each other. Different? Slides? Come on, you want something different? We'll give you different.

By the end of the next week we had put together a synopsis of our *Monkey* film, storyboards, and a four-foot-high foam-core cutout of Kaisik in his *Monkey* costume. It's folded in such a way so that when you open the large envelope, out pops a large smiling monkey holding the script (and color 8" x 10"s) in one hand and an invitation card in the other with our phone number.

How to get it to Francis? Turns out we know a carpenter who is working on Francis' house in Pacific Heights. We give him the pop-up with explicit instructions. We knew exactly where he should put it for maximum effect.

We go back to Steven's apartment and raise our glasses in a toast. This can't fail. We wait. One day. Two days. We have pizza brought in. Nothing. No call? Impossible. He wants "different." We gave him "different." Why don't we hear from him?

Flash forward two years later; my bookkeeper Rohanna takes me to her house in Mill Valley. When I walk in, there on the wall are the 8" x 10" color glossies of *Monkey*! "Where did you get these!?" (She previously worked at Zoetrope as Francis' personal assistant.) She says, "One day Francis storms in and flings these photos on my desk, '*Some freaks broke into my house and put these in my bed! Get rid of them!*'"

More and more friends of Steven's show up. Getting more than a little ahead of himself, he is offering everyone a part in the film and we haven't raised a penny of financing. The script is not a script, but a loose collection of sequences. There is no through line. Steven expects financing based solely on an extravagant look. Maybe this works for student films, but not a feature-length film. Many disagreements and jealousies break out. There are power struggles over who will do what. The people in his entourage whom he has "hired" want to be paid and there is no money! This is a real mess and I extract myself from the process. I learn you can't go back.

Even after many months in San Francisco, I still feel out of it. Larry Reed does too. We tell our traveler's tales to friends, but after a short time you can see their eyes glaze over. I finally find myself not speaking much for over a year.

ASIAN REFUGE

Relief and shelter come when we discover ASEA (The American Society of Eastern Arts). I arrange a Balinese exhibition of paintings in their gallery in downtown San Francisco. At last I can share something from Bali in the West. I write descriptions on cards that are displayed next to the paintings. At the opening, we play gamelan music in the background, light incense, and serve saté.

ASEA is starting a summer program devoted to world music. Sam and Louise Scripps are its founders. Sam is an heir to the Scripps-Howard newspaper dynasty. He is a very shy and large man with a great vision. Working with his director and musicologist Bob Brown, they bring world-class musicians and performers from around the world to teach Western students. The line-up is not to be believed. India's legendary Bharatanatyam dancer Balasaraswati, master Javanese composer and gamelan leader K.R.T. Wasitodipuro (Pak Tjokro) and shadow puppeteers Oemartopo and I Nyoman Sumandhi from Java and Bali, and many others from Korea and Japan, all teach at the school. These aren't just run-of-the-mill teachers, these are some of the world's most accomplished performing artists and national treasures! And sixty white kids get to study with them. One-on-one.

The first World Music program is held at Mills College in Oakland during the summer. Larry and I sign up for both Balinese and Javanese shadow puppet classes and Balinese and Javanese gamelan. In Sumandhi's puppet class there are only four of us. Larry and I learn the movements, the voices of the characters, their songs, and how to signal the beginning and end of the musical pieces. Eventually we all have to perform short shadow plays for the other students and the public. For us, it is an extraordinary learning experience to tell stories with shadows. This is the original "movie." The puppeteer channels the ancestors, voices all of the characters, signals the musicians who sit behind him, and animates the shadows across the screen, enchanting his audience, who sits on the other side. He choreographs great battles between princes and monsters, evokes philosophical debates among the gods, and instigates comedic romps with clown servants of the kings. He is a shaman, a spirit channeler, a teacher, and a healer of the community, and for a brief moment we get to experience that role.

Maybe we can't get our old friends to understand how our lives have been transformed by our interests found in foreign lands, but now we have a small, safe community of like-minded new friends where music, dance, and performance all blend together and inspire us. Everyday we perform, play music, and laugh with each other, trying to understand the broken English of our esteemed gurus. It's a musical Mecca.

Larry, Jane, and I rent an apartment right off campus. Next door lives Judy, an elegant Japanese woman with very long black hair cascading down her back. She is also a student in the summer program. It's not uncommon among many of my Western friends who study Asian arts or religion to fall in love with partners from other cultures. These relationships are a way to delve deeper and make stronger connections with a culture that you also love and want to be a part of.

When I see Judy in a Javanese dance performance I am mesmerized. She is exquisitely graceful, almost dream-like, gliding ever so slowly on the regal tones of a Javanese gamelan. She becomes pure spirit when she dances and embodies the high essence of the warrior prince she portrays. We spend as much time as we can together between classes and share an appreciation for Asian arts. Some evenings we lose all sense of time in the slow Javanese shadow plays that Oemartopo performs, which start at dusk and finish at sunrise. After the summer program she goes back to her home in Hawaii. We write to each other frequently. She makes a couple of trips back to her folks in Torrance near Los Angeles every few months and visits me in San Francisco. It's a long-distance relationship that moves very slowly and is very hard on everyone.

AN AQUATIC FUTURE

America still feels like a foreign culture, but I am settling in. I am part of an artistic community studying Asian music. I have a Japanese girlfriend and live in a house in the Avenues.

When I am not studying shadow play or gamelan, I am adapting a screenplay of Kobo Abe's best-selling science fiction novel, *Inter Ice Age Four*, that I'd read in Japan. In a bar in San Francisco's airport I meet Creative Artist Agency's legendary agent Kay Brown, who represents Kobo Abe in the States. (Kay is also Arthur Miller's agent. Miller married Marilyn Monroe in a ceremony in Kay's house.) It's my enthusiasm that convinces her to give me a free option for a year on Abe's novel. To get a screenplay written, I have to work fast.

This is a project I really like. I can bring my experience of East and West together. A Japanese story for an American or even worldwide audience.

A year later when I have finished the script, I fly to Japan to meet Abe, who must approve the screenplay before I can take it any further. Kobo Abe is now the number one novelist in Japan (after the hara kiri of novelist Yukio Mishima and the suicide of Yasunari Kawabata). Abe's stature is so great that a Shibuya department store provides a small theatre where he stages his avant-garde plays. He is best known in the States as the writer of *Woman in the Dunes*, which was nominated for two Oscars and won the Jury Prize at Cannes. Teshigahara, who was so kind to me during my first trip to Japan, directed it.

Inter Ice Age Four starts as the next ice age approaches and the sea levels are rising. A scientist discovers a secret organization that keeps the fetuses from abortions alive, and clandestinely raises a race of aquatic humans who will survive the coming ice age.

Apropos to this theme, I meet the distinguished Kobo Abe and his producer at a restaurant in Tokyo's Akasaka district where the walls, floor, and ceilings are giant aquariums. It feels like we are underwater. I don't remember eating, but I do remember that our sake cups were never empty. Abe-san and I try to hold each other up as we stumble into trashcans in Akasaka's back alleys. At the time, this is uproariously funny. I'm not at all a drinker, but never mind, this is how males bond when doing business in Japan. You get rip-roaring drunk.

The next morning we meet. Anxiously I ask if he approves the screenplay. He says he's written so many novels and plays that that he doesn't remember much of the novel and that he is sure my screenplay is fine. In a celebratory mood, we go to his theatre where I play ping-pong with Tatsuya Nakadai, star of Kurosawa's *Yojimbo* and later of *Ran* and *Kagemusha*. I also chat with Kazuo Miyagawa, who was the cinematographer on *Yojimbo*. For a while I wanted Nakadai to play the lead scientist in *Inter Ice Age Four*, but no one in Hollywood knows who he is, so I try to cast David Carradine, who was then the lead in the *Kung Fu* television series.

I assemble my package. For the special effects and underwater cities, I meet with John Dykstra in his studio and see the great model spaceships he had built for Doug Trumball's sci-fi classic *Silent Running*. A few years later he did special effects and spaceships for *Star Wars*, and more recently *Batman*.

I manage to get appointments with all the Hollywood studios because times are changing and the old system is failing. It's a rare moment in history when the studios are looking to young talent with fresh storytelling skills. Many new directors were making their breakthrough films: William Friedkin, Steven Spielberg, George Lucas, Dennis Hopper, and Martin Scorsese, to name a few.

I have written a screenplay that is exactly like the novel because I am too intimidated to change much of Abe's original work. He's a great literary master and I'm 26 and I want to direct, which of course stops most discussions cold. And the story of aborted fetuses — in any context — even if they are kept alive and save humanity from extinction — is just not something that is going to wash in the mid 1970's era of Richard Nixon and Gerald Ford. Nevertheless, I persevere and even get Kay Brown to extend the option another year.

I get a commitment from Marshall Naify, the owner of the United Artists theatre chain, with some 2,000 theaters, one of the largest in the U.S., who says he'd book the film. But with a sci-fi special effects film, I am still too inexperienced. I didn't have a clue how to leverage all these assets to get financing.

Ultimately, after three years of trying, both *Monkey* and *Inter Ice Age Four* remain unmade. This is disappointing, but one must toughen up. It happens to all filmmakers. I can see these films in my head, but I don't have the personal power or financial support to make them. I begin to do what I always do. I look for an end run. I do not give up. I draw back inside. I inventory the resources around me and see what I have.

LIVING IN THE AVENUES

I move into another house with friends Howard Steinman, Jim Bray, and Joe Landon, on 8th Avenue near Irving. I have the attic. I paint it Zen white and put down tatami mats and sleep on a futon on the floor. I build a big shadow screen and make my own shadow puppets.

To pay the rent I use my one marketable skill — as a lightning fast typist — and take temp jobs in a railroad engineering office and as a legal clerk in flamboyant attorney Melvin Belli's office. I thought I might learn about universal law. Ha! Instead I learn about litigation. Belli is the country's most successful lawyer at winning lawsuits. The mere mention of his name brings large settlements to his clients who include Zsa Zsa Gabor, Errol Flynn, Chuck Berry, Muhammad Ali, Jim Bakker, the Rolling Stones, and Mae West. In his career he has won over $600 million. While he is busy suing people, I type depositions.

I also have a job as a secretary for acupuncturist Effie Chow, the founder of the East West Academy of Healing Arts. This is a great opportunity because I want to learn acupuncture.

One day as Effie is leaving the office to give an acupuncture demonstration I ask if I could go with her. "What for?" she asks. "To learn," I smile winningly. "You are not here '*to learn!*' Get back to typing those letters!"

SILVER BOX

Okay, I couldn't raise the money for *Inter Ice Age Four*. Fine. What can I do for no money? What resources do I have? I have just been around the world. How about I use the experiences of traveling to make a film? No, better still, I'll use my entire life.

I collect all the stills, drawings, writings and film clips that I have made up until now and examine my life over the past 27 years. Much like I am doing now in this book. Perhaps if I dig deep, I'll discover the "secret of life" or unravel a few mysteries. *Silver Box* will be an autobiographical study of my journey and of travels in Japan, Bali, Nepal, India, Kenya, Ethiopia, Sudan, Egypt, and Greece.

The combination of having returned from Asia, the difficulties of readjusting to American life, self-exploration and human potential practices led me to want to explore my life thus far. Who am I and what am I doing here? This is exactly what I do as I edit. *Silver Box* refers to that place where we store our most precious memories of friends, lovers, teachers, and experiences. It's what we hang onto and are attached to that we think defines us. But as Carl Jung says, "It's not what happened to me; I am what I choose to become." So, how did I choose what I have become?

For a year and a half I re-photograph my collected material with a 16mm optical step printer that cinematographer John Knoop kindly lets me use in his studio. It takes me all day to shoot twenty seconds of finished material, so I am a permanent fixture in his studio for many months. The whole film costs $3,000 and hundreds of hours of work. When I perform the sound mix I inform the recording engineer that I only have enough money to afford 90 minutes of time in which to mix the 60-minute film, so we pretty much mix it on the fly, only redoing a few bits. (Normally this process would take a day or two.) My old high school band buddy from Champaign, singer/songwriter Don Kennedy, provides all the songs for the film, and writes the melodies for my lyrics for the opening and closing titles. The look is very funky and visceral and has an editing style of what appears ten years later on MTV. The film covers my early childhood through all the traveling through Japan, Bali, India, and Africa. It culminates with a futuristic ending with dolphins, foreseeing a film that I will make four years later.

I meet Brenda when she stops for me in her Volkswagen as I hitchhike home. She's striking, has a great sense of humor, and is no-nonsense when it comes to work. She had been a fashion model and now manages a typing pool in San Francisco's financial district. She gives me many "temp" typing jobs. I tell her that I am the world's fastest typist. She says, "Sure you are" and then in a side-by-side type-off she wipes the floor with me by typing 120 words per minute without errors.

Thanks to the paying work that Brenda sends my way, I am able to finish the film. She then chauffeurs me in her little Volkswagen up and down the West Coast on a *Silver Box* tour. We screen the film in Vancouver, Seattle, Portland, and Mendocino. The showings are sold out, but when we hit Mendocino there is only one person in the audience. He is the local DJ who had read the promotional copy on the air and thought it sounded interesting. Ha! In Seattle, the film receives one bad review and is criticized because it's seen as an egocentric autobiography. Of course it is. Aren't all autobiographies egocentric? It's a film about me, the only material I had to work with. Painters and writers don't get hammered when they paint self-portraits or write autobiographies. Nevertheless, it was so upsetting that I don't show the film again for thirty-six years.

At the same Seattle screening, a film professor comes up and tells me he thinks *Silver Box* is an amazing film. He says that years later I will look back on it and see it as one of the best things I'd ever done. He is right. It's a kind of naïve template for the "personal sacred journey films" that I am making now. It has a very transcendent quality and is not really about me, *per se*, but a soul traveling through space and time," which is how Esalen founder Michael Murphy and author Sam Keen describe it when I show it to them. I also screen it for playwright Arthur Miller, through the kindness of agent Kay Brown. I didn't know it at the time, but I'd found my own voice.

Instead, I rejected my process and my truth. I went looking for validation outside. I no longer trusted myself.

Questing
in the West

1975 ◆ 1980

*"Look into yourself and if you do not find yourself beautiful as yet,
do as the sculptor of a statue does: cut away all that is excessive,
straighten all that is crooked, bring light to all that is shadowed. Do not
cease until there shines out of you the Splendour of Beauty."*

— Plotinus

....

John Knoop

I kick myself for being oversensitive in response to one bad review in Seattle. Had I carried on and experimented more with this "autobiographical form" I may have found my "groove" much earlier and produced a different body of work. Now I've matured and I don't put too much stock in how people respond. It is what it is. It's best to carry on with your own work, be it writing, filmmaking, or shadow puppets. Do what you are called to do while listening to your inner voice.

est

Living in Japan and Bali exposed me to new experiences. I intended to keep the quest going in the States. An opportunity arose.

Consciousness expansion, without drugs, is booming in San Francisco. All my friends are taking and enrolling others in the Erhard Seminar Trainings (est) which is the brainchild of Werner Erhard. It is a brilliant composite of spiritual practices perfectly suited to the Western sensibility. I recognized elements from Zen in the practice. In his biography, Werner said, "Of all the disciplines that I studied, practiced, learned, Zen was the essential one. It was not so much an influence on me, rather it created space. It allowed those things that were there to be there. It gave some form to my experience." Werner is a genius in constructing a space where people can experience themselves, their authentic selves, and realize they are responsible for creating their own lives. As they say in est, you can be at "cause" instead of "effect." I take the training which improves my communication with other people, strengthens my creativity, and uncovers a greater purpose to my life. It demonstrates that I can choose to be in charge of my own emotional and psychological states.

The est training ends with an experience of "getting it." There is a lot of discussion among est graduates about what "getting it" means, which is ridiculous because it's a non-verbal experience that cannot be described in language. For me, "getting it" is simply being aware moment by moment and experiencing yourself as co-creator of your own experience.

est is launched in many cities throughout the U.S. and the world, with hundreds of thousands of graduates. Like any large movement that is impossible to describe, it becomes very cultish and controversial. During the heydays of est,

I am hired to video many days of Werner training est's trainers, which gives me an inside look into his passion for his work.

EXTRAORDINARY POWERS

I start hanging around with Michael Murphy. He is very kind and open to me. He's got great energy, and his eyes twinkle with excitement when he talks about breakthroughs in human potential. He has twenty-seven not-to-be-believed acres on the cliffs of Big Sur with a natural hot springs and a magnificent view of the ocean. He co-founded Esalen in 1962 as an alternative center to explore what Aldous Huxley coined "the human potential," which attracts leading spiritual teachers from all over the world including Fritz Perls, Stanislov Grof, Joan Halifax, Will Schultz, George Leonard, Al Huang, Aldous Huxley, Henry Miller, Abraham Maslow, Eric Erickson, Ram Dass, Ida Rolf, Joseph Campbell, Andrew Weil, and Deepak Chopra.

Murphy had written his classic book *Golf in the Kingdom* a few years earlier, and was now especially excited about runners who display almost supernatural skills, or what might be called *siddhis*, which are extraordinary states exemplified by yogis. Murphy is researching and writing his classic *The Future of the Body* at this time. He sees athletes as modern-day yogis. In his book he writes, "We can identify four kinds of metanormal movement: the extraordinary agility attributed to certain athletes, dancers, shamans, and saints; partial or complete levitation; traveling clairvoyance (sometimes called bilocation); and entrance into other worlds."

Whenever I see Michael he enthusiastically tells me about his latest insight into Western-style siddhis. I show him *Silver Box* and he becomes my first investor on my new short film, *Extraordinary Powers*, which explores professional track athletes and how their beliefs influence their performance. Appearing in the short film are Esalen notables George Leonard and Will Schultz. This is exactly what I want to be making: films that explore consciousness and the human potential. This is a momentous occasion to have someone else actually support my filmmaking with a cash contribution. It changes everything. I feel what I am doing is supportable. I'll always be grateful to Michael.

I continue to explore the mind-body theme with my next short film, *I Move*. It's funded by a $10,000 grant from The American Film Institute and a $2,500 grant from est. *I Move* captures the big "I" (Creator/God) moving through the human body in sports, dance, and the martial arts. I can't say that I was able to capture the divine spirit in this film, but it did set a challenge for future work.

My self-esteem and personal power derived from est, spiritual disciplines like Tai Chi, and Michael Murphy's support, takes me to another level in my creative life. The more I am able to take in, the more teachings are available to me.

Talk about extraordinary powers! At San Francisco's UC Medical Center, just up the hill from my house, I take a series of classes with a being who exemplifies the extraordinary! Jack Schwartz is a modern-day yogi, educator, and one of the first to teach the integration of body, brain, mind, and spirit. Scientists from all over the world study him because of his ability to self-regulate many psycho-physiological processes of the body. He can voluntarily achieve specific brainwave states, control the pain of physical trauma, regulate blood flow, blood pressure, and heart rate; and heal his body within hours after being injured. Readings from an electroencephalograph confirm that the electrical output of his brain has a greater amplitude and voltage than other humans.

One day in class he demonstrates the power of his mind over his body with his favorite parlor trick. He pushes a long sailmaker's needle through his biceps, and there is not a drop of blood. Jack's sensitivity to light exceeds the norm and allows him to see the band of electromagnetic fields that surround every organic body. He can see auras and halos around all living things. Based upon years of observing these energy fields, Jack Schwarz can describe the physical, emotional, mental, and spiritual conditions of people, and he teaches others how to do the same.

Extraordinary as he is, he is always kind, light-hearted, and makes sure that we students understand his principles. I tell him about my film work and he is interested in doing a film together. One day, Jack introduces our class to his friend Joseph Campbell, the great mythologist who gives an outstanding lecture. I have read his books, but it's the first time I've heard Campbell speak. His talk inspires me. Every story connects to an ancient past, alive and loaded with meaning. Schwartz' physical demonstrations and Campbell's interpretation of myth make the world a more magical place.

SAN ANSELMO

I am meeting a lot of new friends involved with est, consciousness raising, or various spiritual practices. It's time to move out of my tatami attic in San Francisco's Avenues where I'd lived for five years. I move into a house in San Anselmo in Marin County, its occupants frequently coming and going. The core group of housemates include Bucky assistant/designer Roger Stoller, gemstone artist Lawrence Stoller, businessman Evan Blankman, workshop leader Brooke Medicine Eagle, therapist Shoshona Friedman, writer Mary Earle, graphic artist Dustin Kahn, and writer Neal Rogin. All of us come together around the shared interests: est, Bucky, spirituality, ecology, magic mushrooms, and trance channeling.

BEING WITH BUCKY

Werner Erhard can't attend my *Extraordinary Powers* premiere, so he sends Ron Landsman in his place. Ron and I become fast friends and start talking about producing a series of events called "Guardians of the Planet." We plan to hire speakers like Bucky Fuller, Jacques Cousteau, Frederick Leboyer and others to present day-long seminars at the Masonic Auditorium on Nob Hill.

Ends up that we don't get any further than Bucky. We meet Jamie Synder, Bucky's grandson, at est and through him a series of seminars is set up to be called "Being with Bucky."

I'd read Buckminster Fuller in Japan, first heard him speak in Champaign, and now would be facilitating his talks. I arrange my life so I can work on events and films with Bucky, anything to be in his presence.

I get a job editing a film on Bucky for the USIA and raise private money to shoot my own Bucky film. Inside, we shoot Bucky with his many synergetic models. Outside at Pajaro Dunes, Bucky walks along the beach and talks about how design science employs Nature's principles for maximum efficiency. Suddenly he stops, stoops down, and scoops up a handful of white foam from the surf. "Dear boy, you don't think Nature uses pi when she creates these magnificent bubbles?"

I have the good fortune of sharing a birthday — July 12 — with Bucky. We are able to celebrate it together a couple of times. Once, in 1977, we celebrate in Bali. It doesn't get better than this! Working in my favorite place in the world with my favorite teacher! He invites friends and colleagues to a mini-conference to share global and universal experiences. Attendees include Kenneth Clarke, Werner Erhard, Lim Chong Keat, Nina Rockefeller, Arie Smit, Shirley Sharkey, Steve Parker, Medard Gabel, and others. I am blessed to attend as a "junior varsity" member and tape record and film the event. At the birthday party, the Balinese surprise Bucky with a bamboo dome they have constructed. They also bring blessings, flowers, and offerings in his honor. Bucky loves the Balinese. He says they exemplify natural cooperation and, like the crew of a sailing ship, spontaneously know what to do.

It is inspiring to be hanging out with a small group of great Western minds. But being in Bali can be difficult. In the U.S. Werner is in complete control. Here he seems vulnerable and I want to help. We spend some time together outside of the conference. We go to a cockfight and I help him buy a lot of stone sculptures.

The conference is difficult for me too. I love being with Bucky and company, hearing their expansive ideas. But it's the first time in seven years that I've been back to Bali and I am eager to see my painter friends in the village and to dip back into the magic. I go to Pengosaken and find Batuan. He asks if I am coming back to live there. He takes me to the bamboo house that the village had built for me. The deal was that when I was not there they could use it. An American couple is living there. After a few hours, Batuan again asks when I am coming back. I tell him I won't see him again this time because I am busy with the conference. It's hard having a split agenda. I feel very divided.

When we return from Bali, my housemates host a celebration for Bucky. After dinner, Neal Rogin and I perform a shadow play we have written especially for him using a shadow puppet I made, that in silhouette looks like Bucky. The story takes place in heaven as a spiritual being is sent down to Earth by the gods on a mission to save the planet. Naturally, that being is Bucky. Bucky stretches out in a lawn chair, surrounded by young people, totally transfixed by the shadow play. Then Morgan Smith sings a song she has written for him called "Great Grandfather," which expresses for all of us our deep affection for Bucky. He doesn't say anything, but I can see tears well up behind his thick glasses.

Another time, on a beautiful October afternoon, as the leaves change to red and yellow, I visit Bucky in Maine. He has just returned from a stint in the hospital and is eager to get his beloved sailboat *Intuition* back into the water. We film him sailing around his house on Bear Island. We watch in wonder as dolphins ride the bow wave, weaving in and out below us. "Beautiful, just beautiful. Nature wouldn't have given the dolphin such a large brain unless she was doing something quite extraordinary with it."

As a mentor and teacher, Bucky is inexhaustible. During dinner together, he fills the tablecloth with drawings of tetrahedrons and tutors me in synergetic mathematics. Not more New Math! I tell Bucky that I just don't get it, but he persists, knowing that unless we all understand how to employ Nature's principles, humanity will be doomed with its antiquated agenda of exploiting the Earth's resources.

Many years later, at 86 years old, Bucky is still traveling around the world, speaking to an average of 2,500 people a day (he keeps track of these things). He is giving a public lecture at the Frank Lloyd Wright-designed Marin Civic Center just north of San Francisco. The event is sold out. Morgan Smith and I hadn't planned to go, but at the last minute we do. It has been arranged that someone will drive Bucky back to his hotel after the lecture, but the young woman who had agreed to do it drops the ball and doesn't show up because she heard that John Denver (Bucky's friend), whom she wants to meet, is not going to be there after all.

After the lecture, when I learn this, I go backstage to see if new plans have been made. Bucky isn't in his dressing room. I find him backstage: tired, lost, and confused, wandering among the theatre flats. Bucky has given his all. Morgan and I take him to a restaurant in Sausalito for his favorite: steak and potatoes. When his strength returns, he asks Morgan to sing "Great Grandfather" *a cappella*! After she agrees, he bangs a spoon on his glass and announces to the silenced diners that Morgan is going to sing now.

Once, when Bucky is in New York to give a lecture, I arrange to meet him. Afterwards we go to dinner. Bucky is very tired but still tries to teach me synergetics by drawing on the table cloth. I take him upstairs to the room in the hotel and he goes to bed.

A few days later, his wife, Ann, is ill and goes into a coma. She has told Bucky she is afraid of dying first, and so Bucky has promised her that he would go first and meet her on the other side. He sits with her, holds her hand, and then dies. She dies shortly thereafter.

In Boston, a double funeral ceremony is held in the country's oldest cemetery, where we learn of Bucky's great love for Ann. He had built the great Montreal dome — his Taj Mahal — for her. Later, when I tell friends about it, I keep having a kind of Freudian slip: I say, "I was in Boston for a wedding," because that's how it felt to me when they were buried side by side.

ENTER KASKAFAYET

One day we meet a young Edward O'Hara, who tells us that a strange thing has happened: he finds that spirits come through his body to teach. Master Kaskafayet (whom Brooke Medicine Eagle writes about in her books *Buffalo Woman Comes Singing* and *The Last Ghost Dance*) is a Persian master from centuries ago and is the primary spirit channeled by Edward.

Initially, Edward is freaked out and disoriented by the visitation of Kaskafayet. We encourage him to channel with us present and gradually he learns how to allow the spirits to talk through him. He says he doesn't remember what happens in these trance sessions, but is chosen by his spirit to use him like a radio. This is not too different from what I had seen in village rituals in Bali, but I'd never met a spirit channeler in the West.

After sitting down and centering himself, Edward's eyes roll back and his voice changes pitch and carries a foreign accent. At first it's just a few of us from the house who gather to hear Master Kaskafayet. The spirit's intent seems compassionate, but he has a fierce and penetrating side that sees right through you and aggressively challenges you. Many people have emotional breakthroughs in these sessions. Once Kaskafayet tells the core group of us, "You will each make a major contribution to the world." Pretty heady stuff. Who wouldn't want to sit around to hear this about themselves?

Very quickly word spreads and now hundreds of people pay hundreds of dollars each for group sessions and private readings with Kaskafayet. Edward has a harem of women waiting on him, and two of them live and sleep with him. The Master advises Edward and others to buy a Mercedes. The idea being that if you buy one, you are acknowledging your own potential success, thus real success will follow. A kind of New Age "build it and they will come" philosophy. Many people do buy a Mercedes only to have it repossessed a few months later.

I am in at the beginning as this fascinating story unfolds and think it will make a great film. I meet with the executive producer at the local PBS station KQED and pitch him the idea. He wants me to find out the details of Kaskafayet's life and then take a film crew to the Middle East to confirm the facts of his previous existence. We'd either uncover a fraud or a true master of the spirit world. Either way it would be a great television program. Kaskafayet gets angry and refuses to go along with this line of inquiry, so KQED pulls out.

Not to be thwarted, I ask Kaskafayet if I can film the channeling sessions and he agrees. I raise a little money from my housemates to pay for film and processing. We shoot a couple of sessions.

As Edward's audience grows, he sometimes lectures as Edward and does not channel Kaskafayet. Those attending want Kaskafayet and not Edward. (Is Edward tired of playing second fiddle, or being the mouthpiece for Kaskafayet?) Debates and arguments rage among us. Is this phenomenon really a spirit, or is Edward acting, or is this Edward's higher self, or does he have a split personality? Does it matter? The information is powerful and that is all that matters. Right?

Hard as it is, I feel myself pulling away and one day I do. The whole scene is becoming a cult and critical thinking has gone out the window. I call into question the whole thing. If the spirit is an authentic teacher, then should I be confused? I lay low in my office and work on my films. Edward comes by and says that Kaskafayet has asked him to retrieve the footage from me and that I am no longer worthy of doing the film. I honor Kaskafayet's wishes and return the film to Edward, even though I am not really sure who is doing the asking. It's never seen again.

Not long afterwards, the whole scene implodes. Edward quits channeling. Just because a channeler claims to have insights from another dimension does not mean that he is enlightened. After all, in one sense, we are all channelers for higher and lower selves. I prefer to seek a path of self-realization, where the teacher is your own experience.

AN EXPERIENCE OF LIGHT

Knowing this, Michael Murphy tells me about a woman who has had an "experience of light" that changed her life. She is writing a book about it. I meet Dorothy Fadiman at her house in Menlo Park, California. Within minutes, the living room table is filled with piles of religious and mystic art that she has collected for her book. With eyes sparkling, she takes me on a journey of her own experience of light and muses that perhaps the light that surrounds holy men is real, and that all of us are light energy bodies. I like it already.

Using two projectors and a dissolve unit we first create a slide show titled *Do Saints Really Glow?* Dorothy's soothing voice narrates the journey and transports the viewer deep into a mystical trance. In every showing, many people go into altered states, some weeping in gratitude. This is powerful stuff. If the presentation takes you somewhere you've never been, then it's a success.

We are invited to show the slide show at The Psychic Explosion, which is attended by 500 people in San Francisco's Masonic Auditorium on Nob Hill. The other presenters are a "Who's Who" of the consciousness leaders of the day, including Timothy Leary, Uri Geller, Edgar Mitchell, Jack Schwarz, and Olga Worrall.

The slide show allows us to work out the flow of images, which brings us to the next step: reshoot the dissolving slides on 16mm film. The 22-minute film asks the question, "Is the halo around mystics like Jesus, Mohammed, and Buddha a metaphor for higher consciousness, or do these beings really emit light?" The film is retitled *Radiance: The Experience of Light* and takes the audience on an experiential journey revealing humans as energy bodies filled with light. The film wins a number of festival awards and becomes a new-age classic. (Dorothy catches the filmmaking bug and her skills blossom. She goes on to create over a dozen documentaries, one of which receives an Oscar nomination.)

HARDWARE WARS

My film explorations are not only on human potential themes or spiritual quests. Sometimes I just like to have fun. I begin to work on another short film in which I shall forever be associated. It's the brainchild of satirist Ernie Fosselius, who is the funniest man I've ever known. Ernie is a neighbor of mine and attends our almost weekly parties at the house in the Avenues where we would entertain Japanese, Balinese, and American friends with shadow plays. I had made a bunch of puppets of whales and dolphins and one night Ernie and I perform an improvised shadow play parody of *Jaws*. Ernie is in top form and it's a big hit.

The next day, over egg rolls in a crowded restaurant, Ernie acts out a film idea that he'd like me to shoot and produce. He wants us to make *Hardware Wars*, a "coming attractions" trailer for a sci-fi film that doesn't exist that will parody big-budget, special effects-laden science-fiction films. He waves chopsticks and soy sauce bottles in the air to demonstrate how household objects (like steam irons and toasters) can double as space ships. I can't stop howling even though our Chinese waiter is scowling.

The film we will parody would be *Star Wars*, which had recently been released.

We raise $5,000 from an old friend of Ernie's, who also makes the costumes. Ernie writes, directs, and also acts in the film as "Darph Nader." John Fante and I shoot in an empty warehouse for about five days and shoot another three days on locations.

Scott Mathews dons a lopsided blond wig for the starring role of "Fluke Starbucker." (Later he becomes a platinum-selling record producer who has worked with everyone from Barbra Streisand to John Lee Hooker.) Paul Frees, who voiced the original *Star Wars* trailer, performs a hilarious narration. At the end of the film the narrator tells us, *"You'll laugh, you'll cry, you'll kiss three bucks goodbye."* We go over budget, spending $8,000, which includes paying ourselves $300 each.

We test the first cut of the film in a friend's restaurant to see how the laughs are stacking up. If something doesn't get a laugh, we cut it out. If the laughs are too close together and drown out the dialog, we space them out a bit more. We edit it down to thirteen minutes.

Our dream is to show it to George Lucas, who (in the pre-Skywalker Ranch days) has his Sprocket Systems office only a few blocks away from my tiny office in San Anselmo. Ernie's first idea is to attach the film to a parachute and throw it over the fence in the front of George's house with a note, "From outer space."

Instead, we discover we have a friend who is working as a carpenter at George Lucas' house who has been invited to Thanksgiving dinner at George's. (Secret fact of life: You can get to anyone if you know his carpenter.) The friend reports back that as George was finishing his pumpkin pie he calls our film a "cute film." Not quite substantive enough to use for a blurb on our poster.

I call George's office to try to get a longer quote. Instead, and maybe even better, through Lucas' assistant, a meeting is arranged for me with Alan Ladd Jr., who is the head of 20th Century Fox studio, the distributor of *Star Wars*. They probably want to see what we are up to and then sue us.

I fly down to Hollywood with the 16mm print of the film clutched under my arm. I am very nervous. An executive assistant ushers me into an executive screening room with a row of huge, super-plush velvet chairs. Mr. Ladd — "Laddie" to his friends — is seated next to me, and behind us are three lawyers in expensive suits. Accustomed to getting huge laughs, this is absolutely the worst screening I've ever endured. Dead silence. No one makes a sound during the movie. Someone coughs once and I reassure myself, "That's a laugh."

When the lights are turned on, Laddie turns to me, "Well, kid, so what can we do for you?" I say, "How 'bout you show it with *Star Wars*? You know, make fun of your own movie!" He says he'd get back to me on that, and I'm sure he still will.

A few months later someone offers to finance a full-length low-budget feature of *Hardware Wars*, but we pass. We know that what we have is basically a one-joke movie and the joke won't sustain feature length. Of course that doesn't stop Mel Brooks from "quoting" us — or as some might say, ripping us off — with *Spaceballs*. Janet Maslin, film critic for *The New York Times*, writes a scathing review of *Spaceballs*, but in her opening paragraph praises its source: *Hardware Wars*. I write her a letter of thanks.

I find distribution for the short almost instantly through Pyramid Films in Santa Monica. They lock the doors and won't let me out of the building until I sign a deal. It's a great thrill to have a film that everyone wants.

We enter it in every festival we can and win fifteen first-place awards. Pyramid sells and rents 16mm film prints mostly to schools, libraries, and institutions. We receive 25% of all sales and rentals, and then 30% when the gross surpasses $100,000. The film is also licensed to HBO, Showtime, and every other pay cable station imaginable; it's blown up to 35mm film and is shown in fifty theaters with *The Adventures of the Wilderness Family* in Australia! (Go figure.) We even have showings as the short before *The Empire Strikes Back*. We license MCA the videodisk rights and Warner Bros. the video rights. It shows on PBS, on ABC's *The Dick Clark Show*, and we receive a broadcast contract from NBC's *Saturday Night Live*.

The film earns about $500,000 for its distributors in the first few years, making it the highest-grossing short film of its time. After distributor's fees and the recoupment of expenses we (Ernie, our investor, our sound designer, and myself) split nearly $150,000; not bad for an $8,000 investment.

Every time George announces a new *Star Wars* film we do something to ride its promotional coattails. When George Lucas announces "The Force Is Back" and adds new special digital effects to *Star Wars*, I announce that "The Farce Is Back," after Fred Tepper, a *Hardware Wars* fan and special effects creator from Digital Domain, adds some twenty new digital video effects. *Hardware Wars — The Special Edition*'s video packaging parodies 20th Century Fox's campaign. The main thing this little film taught me is that if you have a strong pre-promoted element that your audience recognizes and you make a good film, you can have great success by selling it across many platforms.

By now our cheesy $8,000 production has grossed its various distributors more than $1 million. George Lucas finally goes on public record on *The Big Breakfast*, a London TV talk show, and says it's his "favorite *Star Wars* parody." After waiting twenty years for this, I immediately post his comment on the Internet. Later, Lucasfilm gives our film the "Pioneer Award." You couldn't wish for greater exposure than this.[*]

KETAMINE

One day housemate Brooke Medicine Eagle brings her anthropologist friend Eva to our San Anselmo house.

We talk for a long time. Passionately, she shares her extensive knowledge of myth, world cultures, psychedelics, death and dying, and shamanism. I tell her of my interest in transcendent states of consciousness. She lets me read some of her writing for an article she is writing on shamanism. "A common thread among shamans seems to be an awakening to other realms of reality and the experience of ecstasy." I show her *Radiance*, which I like to think of as a filmic shamanic initiation of light. We also view a rough cut of a new film I have just started. She encourages me by the depth of her interest in my work. This is important to me and makes me feel that what I am doing is on the right track.

She lives in New York and at the time I am doing some photo research for one of Werner Erhard's Hunger Project presentations, so I stay with her whenever I am on the East Coast. She tells me she had recently introduced Paddy Chayefsky

---

[*] An entire chapter in Clive Young's *Homemade Hollywood: Fans Behind the Camera* is devoted to the story of *Hardware Wars*. (For those wishing to learn every little detail about this film, read Clive's excellent chapter on our website: *http://shop.mwp.com/products/hardware-wars-star-wars-spoof*. Even I learned a lot.)

to ketamine while he was writing *Altered States*. Eva is not only a scholar and a psychic-explorer, but a spiritual muse to other creative masters.

I am honored when she offers to guide me on a ketamine journey. Ketamine is a general anaesthetic that's used before operations on humans and animals. I am a bit apprehensive, because unlike other psychedelics which are taken orally or smoked, ketamine must be taken intravenously. We prepare a sacred space in her loft, then take the drug. Its effect on my body is that it turns off all motor functions — I become pure mind.

I cannot move. I no longer identify with my body. I am pure consciousness. I enter vast universes of light at an atomic or quantum level. I travel in the cosmos. I am everything and everything is me. I find that the ketamine space is kind of like a cosmic party line: I can enter or share the mind of anyone. Werner, Bucky, Campbell, Eva: everyone is here, a vast interconnected web, of which I am both part of and the whole thing. It's all energy, exhilarating, expansive. Is this a preview of where the soul goes after it leaves the body and before its next incarnation?

We journey again a couple of times over the next few months. I feel myself wanting to stay in the experience and not wanting to return to the harsh and loud New York streets. I also begin withdrawing somewhat from friends who can't possibly understand this experience. A year later Dr. John Lilly warns me, "Ketamine will kill you." I understand what he means. We can visit these realms, but not live there. Not yet.

SPY-HOPPING JOE

One day I am invited to a lunch with Joseph Campbell, which is a real treat. Although I never worked with him, Joseph Campbell keeps showing up in my life as if he is peeking around the corner, occasionally checking up on me.

Campbell's latest book is being published by Alfred Van Der Marck and edited by Robert Walter, who together created some of the most inspiring high-end books ever published. I become great friends with Robert (who now heads up the Joseph Campbell Foundation). Years later I am hired to find video distribution for Campbell's *Hero's Journey* video series, and later I publish *The Writer's Journey*, a best-selling screenwriting book based on Campbell's "Hero's Journey" mythic paradigm.) On reflection, it appears as if some magical cosmic board game is being played out. People show up in my life, be they teachers or colleagues, to work together, serve one another, and interact in different creative ways. Trusting, awakening, and enjoying these synchronicities appear to speed up the process and bring about more connections.

DOLPHIN BLISS

Like me, Hardy Jones is a student of Buckminster Fuller. Hardy and I quickly become friends and he invites me to test his new isolation tank, a sensory deprivation environment designed by dolphin researcher Dr. John Lilly. In the soundproofed tank, the Dead Sea-like saline solution allows you to float in complete silence. The water temperature is exactly the same as the body, so all body sensation goes away (not dissimilar from ketamine or deep meditation). Hardy shuts me in this thing for a couple of hours where I do "nothing very carefully." Floating without sensation or feeling, I observe my mind. It occurs to me that the dolphin may be a pure mind in an ocean of consciousness.

I tell Hardy about an experience I had years ago that has haunted me. In the late '60s, a few months before moving into the Mission Street studio with Steven Arnold, I lived alone on 47th Avenue a few blocks from the ocean. An extraordinary, unexplainable thing happened.

It is foggy and cold near the ocean. I am walking on the beach. I see a group of people gathered around something at the water's edge. When I get closer, I see a stranded dolphin. People of all ages gather around trying to push or pull it back into the water. I squeeze in to help. As we free the dolphin it looks directly at me. I hear, or maybe feel, a high frequency sound inside my head. Was it saying "thank you"? The dolphin swims off slowly, its dorsal fin disappearing under the first breaker.

What happened? I felt a deep intelligence behind those eyes. Afterwards, I read everything I can find on dolphin research, especially the work of John Lilly.

Hardy too has studied Lilly and is equally curious as to whether this creature with a large brain might be more than what we assume. (Asking this question implies that we humans are also more than we assume.) Dolphins have lived on earth for fifty million years through many ice ages and have, we presume, a highly organized language. What, if we could speak with them, would they tells us?

Hardy had been a CBS field reporter and writer. We plan a film together. He will write, I will produce, and we will co-direct. Steve Gagne, who has worked as a concert tour mixer for Bob Dylan, the Grateful Dead, The Band, and Crosby Stills Nash & Young agrees to do the sound recording, but more importantly he pitches us that he wants to design and build an "underwater piano." It sounds like complete madness until we read Aristotle who wrote, "Dolphins care for man and enjoy his music." Can we engage dolphins through music? Is Steve onto something? Can we do so, not with captive dolphins, but with dolphins in the wild? Steve modifies a Hohner Melodica (a big harmonica), encases it in a waterproof box, powers it with the scuba air exhaust, and amplifies the sound through a Navy speaker. Brilliant. It's actually a primitive communication device like you might find in *Close Encounters of the Third Kind*.

A filmmaker is always on the lookout for money. I am no different. I have to find someone who will fund my film projects. I meet Gene, a real estate developer, who encourages us to go to Hawaii where we are to stage our first dolphin shoot. He says when we return he will have raised all the money. No sweat. So we go to Hawaii, rent helicopters, underwater camera crews and dive boats. We try playing the piano for the spinner dolphins we encounter, but they are aloof, wary. When we return I have major bills to pay. I meet with Gene. He has raised no money. We'll have to raise it ourselves.

Mary Earle, who lives in our San Anselmo house, works with us to set up some investor presentations. We invite some forty people. We show twenty minutes of the best footage from Hawaii, display flip charts of projected revenues, answer questions, and follow up with wine and cheese. About midway through my pitch to the investors, I catch the bright green eyes of a gorgeous woman in a buckskin jacket. She sits attentively in the front row. I don't look back at her because I don't want to get distracted from my pitch, but I make a mental note to find out who she is when I get off-stage. When that time comes, she's not to be found anywhere and no one has a clue who I am talking about.

The evening's cash commitments amount to $60,000. There are still a few names on the list that say they will get back to us. A few days later, we are making the rounds to the uncommitted investors when Mary takes us to a flat in Pacific Heights. I expect to meet a white-haired patron of the arts. Imagine my surprise when the door opens and it's the green-eyed mystery woman!

Morgan Smith is the co-manager of jazz diva Pilar du Rem and her band, who are rising in popularity in San Francisco and Los Angeles clubs. I do everything I can to generate some animal magnetism, but Morgan will have none of it. She's all business and makes clear her intentions. She wants to know if any women are going on the expedition. She feels if this is truly an interspecies communication experiment, it would be a great error not to include women on the team. After all, "there are female dolphins out there too." Hard to argue that. Hardy says "No, it's too dangerous out at sea, and there are confined quarters, and women will distract the crew." Mary sees her chance and chimes in, "Yeah, guys, I agree, women should be part of this expedition too." Morgan says that she will invest if she can go on the trip and that she has a lot more to offer the project than just money. Hardy and I discuss it later. I have no objection because I am smitten and I also see her point.

With three-quarters of the $165,000 budget raised, we set out for the Florida Keys, stopping first at the Dolphin Research Institute where we film semi-captive dolphins in an interspecies communications experiment. Then we head off to the Bahamas on a 75-foot gaff-rigged schooner (used by Crosby Stills Nash & Young on an album cover and once owned by Burl Ives). It's a gorgeous vessel, but hard to work from. We have to be careful when we drag heavy diving gear and cameras across its beautiful wooden deck.

We get a tip from a treasure diver where we might find wild dolphins, but after a week of looking, encountering storms at sea and treacherously shallow water, we don't see any. I never do get my sea legs. I am sick as a dog for most of the journey and at one point beg to be left off on a small atoll. It's getting serious. We've spent all this money and no dolphins. Looks like we will have to go back to our investors empty-handed.

Finally, late in the afternoon on one glorious day, just I as say, "How beautiful, if only we had dolphins," they appear. We lower Steve and his piano into the water and instantly seventy spotted dolphins are cavorting around him like Busby Berkeley dancers in a most exquisite underwater ballet. The water is filled with their squeaks and whistles. Steve swims with his piano for hours until he's exhausted. The dolphins are fascinated by the piano's sounds and sweep past in ever-tightening circles for a closer look. The music works! We swim with the dolphins for three days, for three hours a day, until we are physically exhausted. I find that the dolphins are just as interested in studying us as we are in studying them. In the water they are the faster learners and if you don't start another behavior quickly, like taking off your flipper and dropping it ("Yikes! He just took off his leg!"), they will get bored and swim away.

We are thrilled that Steve's genius pays off. Oceanographer Jacques Cousteau tried unsuccessfully to swim with wild dolphins, but then he didn't have an underwater piano. His approach was to put out a net around a school of dolphins. Our approach is to let the dolphins choose to be with us or not. It is the first time to our knowledge that anyone has recorded a human/dolphin encounter in modern times.

Being with these magnificent creatures brings out the best in everyone. Maybe it's the incredible light on the water or the feeling in your brain from floating in the ocean, or the harmony of being with the dolphins, or succeeding in our mission, but whatever the reason, the experience opened our hearts and created a love for one another that sustains to this day. Maybe the dolphins were showing us our own potential for love and compassion as human beings. It is an incredible life-changing event and the film conveys that experience.

We rent the Palace of Fine Arts theatre and three other theatres around the San Francisco Bay area and launch our own theatrical release. We pack the 2,000-seat theatre for the premiere. We come in number three in San Francisco movie grosses for the week. The film also plays the film festival circuit, winning a Golden Eagle at CINE and the Cup of the Prime Minister of Italy in the Milan Film Festival. The film is distributed to television internationally and is seen in thirty-five countries including the UK on the BBC. In the U.S., Atlantic Richfield sponsors a nationwide release on PBS and later it is aired on The Disney Channel. Films Inc. distributes it to the educational non-theatrical market and Vestron releases the video. Today it is being streamed on iTunes.

It is shown by Greenpeace, Save the Dolphins, and at an international gathering of the International Whaling Commission. The film has some influence on changing the tuna fishing practices that accounts for countless dolphin deaths. The film launches Hardy Jones as our generation's Jacques Cousteau. He goes on to spend a lifetime making some forty television programs on marine mammals.

PEOPLE WHO LIVE IN GLASS HOUSES

We return to the Bay Area, sky-high from our experience with the dolphins. This exuberance lasts for many months as the romance with Morgan blossoms. We rent a glasshouse in the Sausalito hills with a magnificent view of the bay. She works launching Pilar's band and I work distributing *Hardware Wars*, *Radiance*, and *Dolphin*. My income from producing and distributing my films is about $1,000 per month. Even with Morgan's additional income, we find we are financially way over our heads with a monthly rent of $800. And we hardly have any furniture.

Luckily, compared to my fellow filmmakers, I am making films and getting them out there. I know how to pitch, get them financed and distributed, and I'm actually making money, albeit not much. I am supporting an editor, a secretary, a bookkeeper, and a small office, but most of all I am making the kinds of films I want to make.

Because my filmmaker friends are always calling me for advice, I decide to put on a filmmaking seminar. I rent a room, folding chairs, and put up some posters. No one was giving filmmaking seminars in those days. Seventy people show up and pay $35 each for the all-day event. I tell them everything I've learned in the hopes this will help them realize their own dreams. Over the next three decades I will present countless seminars all over the world for The American Film Institute, Kodak, and many others; this is the humble beginning. With just about everything, one day you have an intention, take action, plant a seed, and many years later when you turn around your fields will be filled with trees. Every thought, every action, has a result — so plant your seeds well.

FIRST BOOK

I buy an Apple II+, Apple's first computer. It had about 64K of memory. I learn the word processing program and VisiCalc, which is the precursor to Excel, on which I can prepare budgets.

By now, Morgan and I come to our senses and give up the glasshouse high on the hill and move into a modest one-bedroom apartment in Sausalito. Here I write my first book, *The Independent Film and Videomaker's Guide*, that has evolved from the handouts I create for the seminars.

There is only one other "how-to" film book out at the time. I send my manuscript out to a dozen or more publishers. They all reject me. Certainly there is a market for this hard-to-obtain information. Once again, I have to figure out how to do it myself. I borrow $3,000 from my mother, print out the text on a printer, and have the book assembled by a local printer. I get a few good reviews and it starts selling through direct mail. Every day I go down to my post office box in Sausalito to see if there are any orders. Money is really tight. If I get a check for $13 (the price of the book), I immediately rush to the bank to cash it so we can buy food.*

I spent a lot of time writing my new film book and various spec proposals for other films. This is development hell. It is definitely not bringing in the lean green. I owe my Mom money, and Morgan and I are talking about getting married. Going to need some money to support us. To the outside world I look successful because my films are widely seen in San Francisco and I am getting a

---

*As I am writing this book I receive a Facebook message from a filmmaker I don't know. He invites me to the premiere of his new film which is showing in Hollywood. He says he read my first book when he was ten. Now he is thirty-six years old and has two sons. He said he just wanted to thank me. Sometimes we have no idea of the impact that our work may have in the lives of other people.

lot of press, but in reality, my attention is focused on whether there will be a $13 check in the mail or not. I feel a lot of pressure to come up with something. I may have to put my own projects on the shelf and go to work for someone else, as painful as that feels. I stood at the crossroads and sometimes I wonder if I took the wrong road. I had success following my instincts, and hard as it was, my films did come together. Perhaps I should have kept going, but then there were "real world" concerns that led me down another path.

In 1980, Morgan and I get married at the Swedenborgian church in San Francisco. We have a big turnout, with hundreds of friends. Due to health problems, her parents are not able to come. Months earlier I'd gone to Chevy Chase, Maryland, a suburb of Washington, D.C., to ask her father for her hand. Hugh likes me, and despite his busy schedule he is proud to attend the American Film Institute screening of *Dolphin* at The Kennedy Center. But little does he know I can't sustain a living on one wildlife documentary, a few short films, and the occasional seminar. Now that I am married, the eyes of both her parents (and mine) are upon me. I have to get serious. It's time to make a real living and not scrape by as an independent filmmaker making save-the-world films. I need a real job.

Working in Entertainment

1981 ◆ *1985*

"Let's go to work!"

— On the Waterfront

....

Nancy Weyman

I give gratitude to the water spirits that brought the dolphins to our cameras and opened that world to us. Our film was a success and gave me confidence. I wanted to keep that high going, and getting married was a way to fix that momentous high in amber. If I could settle down, refine my filmmaking, make a living by reaching a wider audience, then all would be well. Wouldn't it?

"ROBOT WARS"

I hear of a job opening for a segment producer on a talk-variety-entertainment show at the local NBC station — KRON — in San Francisco. It's Friday morning when I call and the secretary tells me they think they have already found someone but the producer hasn't decided yet. I go for it. "I'm your guy, don't hire anyone until you've at least seen me! Really. You won't be sorry." I beg, I grovel, I plead. Finally she caves. "Okay, okay, come in this afternoon." I take a bus into the city and meet with the host/producer, Steve Jamison. I am desperate, but act cool, exude success and confidence. He asks if I have seen the show and what do I think of it? Yikes. I haven't seen the show. Think fast. I tell him that I have lots of ideas for segments for the show. He asks what they are. I say, "You know, I'd rather not present them in a haphazard manner. Tell you what, I'll write down fifty ideas and give them to you on Monday. If you like them, you can hire me. If you don't, fine, you can use the ideas just the same." He agrees.

I rush to the bus and get home just in time to turn on the TV. I watch the show and spend the weekend writing down fifty ideas. I get the job.

SFO is a five-nights-a-week talk-entertainment-variety-show rip-off of *The Tonight Show*. The host even pulls his ear lobe and adopts other mannerisms he's copped from Johnny Carson. The show has three guest segments a night and is shot before a live studio audience in a single take and aired the next night at 7 p.m.

They want me to come up with ideas for segments, book local characters, and write the questions for Steve, which go on cue cards. (I don't know why I prepare the cue cards, because Steve always ignores them.)

My job is also to warm up the audience, ask them where they're from, and tell a few jokes. Five minutes before we go on air, the audience is primed with coffee and glazed donuts so that the caffeine/sugar rush hits them, causing unwarranted enthusiasm and applause just as Steve appears on stage. The producers want to appeal to a young, hip audience. Instead we get an elderly crowd who are bussed in for an afternoon outing.

I am pleased to have my first media job and a steady paycheck. I run into some friends from my filmmaking class at the Art Institute. They snub me and turn their backs when they discover I've gone "commercial." I think it's a step forward, but their reaction gives me a sliver of doubt that perhaps I've taken the wrong road. But then Bucky once told me that it's okay to take a regular job to support yourself as long as you still "do your own thinking."

After a few weeks I am up and running. I am booking one or two segments each night (that's five to ten segments per week if you are counting). Morgan is interviewed and gets hired as a production assistant.

I book all sorts of weird people on the show, from cooks who make dinners of insects, to sexual surrogates, martial artists, dancers, singers, street performers, you name it. I go through my list of fifty ideas pretty quickly, so that whenever I am out on the street and see an interesting person I think, "Maybe he would be good."

Steve explains to me, "Our goal is to get good ratings, which brings in greater advertising revenues. That will make the station owner happy. It's not about saving the world. Got it?"

But the show is not getting good ratings, so everyone is skating on thin ice. Steve hires a marketing expert to do a survey which asks a focus group every question under the sun — do they like the segments, the guests, the live studio band, the name of the show, ad infinitum. The only question he should ask — but doesn't — is, "Do you like the host?" But then why should he? He may find out something he doesn't want to know.

There are two other segment producers, both of whom book Hollywood celebrities. I supplement this with unusual characters who will appeal to younger audiences.

I am proud when I discover edgy artist Mark Pauline, who has been getting a lot of buzz in the art world press. He builds huge animated sculptures by welding together junkyard pieces of scrap metal. His metallic inventions look like the love children of *Mad Max*. Together Mark and I design a show called "Robot Wars" which is staged in the parking lot next to the studio. The lot belongs to a Cadillac dealership. We get them to move their new Caddies and Mark unloads two huge post-apocalyptic metal monsters.

The elderly audience circles the perimeter of the lot while cameramen manipulate huge studio cameras with cables running back inside the building to the control rooms where the feeds are edited live. Another 100 spectators show up unexpectedly. There are skinheads, bare-chested punks, and tattooed freaks, friends of Mark's who cheer, jeer, and act out for the cameras.

A deafening, growling electronic soundtrack fills the air while two monster robots shoot flaming metal arrows at each other. Suddenly one gives birth to a flaming *papier-mâché* calf embryo. Mark is hyped up, adrenaline pumping, ready to make his anti-war statement to the world as the metal robots scrape along the concrete in fierce combat. Another remote-controlled robot shoots a flaming arrow that "accidentally" misses its target and plunges into a huge billboard of the latest Cadillac above the parking lot. Post-modern symbolism, baby!

Poor host Steve Jamison is out of his comfort zone. Courageously he scrambles with microphone in hand to interview Mark, who is pushing buttons and pulling levers to control the out-of-control robots. Every time there is an explosion, Steve dives to the ground. It's definitely edgy — just like the boss ordered.

This is fabulous television. Far more engaging than sit-down host-guest chitchat. Maybe there will be a television Emmy in my future?

After the show, as the cables are being rolled up and stored, I proudly walk through the building having just made television history. I am walking on air.

But whenever I see another segment producer they turn away and disappear. What's going on?

One of the segments we are supposed to have tonight is Bob Hope, but he cancels. Someone forgets to tell the owner of the television station, who has brought several carloads of friends to meet Hope. Instead, he gets an anti-war overture of burning calf embryos, warring robots, and flaming arrows shot into Cadillac billboards.

Steve's boss, the executive producer who has until now never spoken to me, makes it crystal clear that 1) no, I would never get an Emmy, and 2) he never wants to see me work in television again; in fact he guarantees it. "You're fired!"

Stunned and crestfallen, I go to my car. When I put the key in the ignition, it bends by itself like a Yuri Geller spoon. Whoa! Then the car, without being started, puts itself into reverse and smashes into the car behind it. Am I psycho-kinetic?! I am totally freaked out. Is my energy causing this or is it carry-over energy from the show?

The changes made after the marketing survey, like building a new set, do not improve ratings. The show goes off the air a few months later. Years later, another show called *Robot Wars* is a huge hit in television markets around the world, making millions for its owners.

POLITICS IN NEW YORK

Morgan's father is ill and she wants to move back to the East Coast to be near him. My future is with Morgan, so we leave the Bay Area. I interview for a job on *The Charlie Rose Show*, but before they answer I am offered a job at D.C.'s PBS station WETA to executive produce a children's science series. We are busy packing when I get the call, "Sorry, we can't hire you, our legal office says we've got an equal opportunity rule we have to follow, so we are hiring a black woman."

So we send the moving van to Westport Connecticut and I commute to a job with DHS Films. It's my first job in New York. I wear a suit to work every day. Dutifully, I take a 45-minute crowded train ride from Westport to Grand

Central Station each weekday and walk the 15 minutes to our offices at 5th and 55th. (I pass the spot where that long-haired, bearded guy dressed in Indian linens and sandals ate that orange in another life.)

The agency is headed by David H. Sawyer. (In the film *Power*, Richard Gere plays David.) David's office is entirely black. Black walls, black glass table, no windows, pin lighting. It takes my eyes time to adjust to find David leaning back behind his desk. A circular cloud of cigar smoke erupts from the silhouetted head of the kingmaker: "We have only one goal: Win elections for our candidate clients. Got it?"

I am responsible for arranging the crews and the post-production of hundreds of radio and television spots for various political campaigns. It's 1982 and we have nineteen gubernatorial and senatorial campaigns going simultaneously, mostly liberal Democrats, plus the national campaign for the National Democratic Committee. It's a great job. I believe I can contribute to the political dialog by creating communication pieces that reflect the values of some of the country's smartest politicians. Enthusiastically (and perhaps naively), I bravely enter the political waters.

As head of production, I produce all the spots. Mandy Grunwald is "head of political." She deals directly with the candidates and campaign staffs in writing and approving the scripts. (Years later, Mandy becomes the key media advisor for both Bill Clinton's and Hillary Clinton's presidential campaigns.) Mandy is a billy goat gruff, determined and strong-willed. She keeps her cards well hidden and downs a constant stream of Diet Pepsi, which fuels an uncompromising need to win every argument.

They work me to death. Or rather I let them work me to death. Not having worked in New York before, I want to make a good impression. I get to work early and rarely do I get home before 10 p.m. This is a common fault of every young person in his or her first job because you can easily be exploited. Eventually I work 'round the clock in late-night editing sessions, finishing up spots and then shuttling them to the airports so they can be broadcast throughout the country the following day. I sleep in the editing room or in a cheap hotel room for a few hours before going back to the office. I don't see much of Morgan during the week. She is busy working for a telephone astrology service hosted by astrologer-to-the-stars Jean Dixon.

Everything at DHS is an emergency. The candidates constantly change their posture and reposition themselves as public opinion changes. Stakes are high. Our candidates want to win office and all nineteen candidates do except one. David has structured my job in a manner that pits me against Mandy, so there is often tension between "political" and "production." My greatest beef is that I don't get to see the TV or radio script that I am to shoot or record until I am in a taxi rushing to a studio. I only have minutes to prepare. And often when I get to the studio or location and am halfway through recording a spot, Mandy calls, changes everything, and gives me new lines to record. And... I am the one who is responsible for watching the budget. Even today, all I need to do is think of Mandy when I need to summon up the strength to open the stubborn lid on a pickle jar.

Most campaign strategies work like this. If a candidate is an unknown, he has to be mythologized to the voters of his state. It he is an incumbent, he will be shown to have the same position on issues as the voters. Polls are conducted to see how people feel about the hot issues; social security, crime, the economy, etc. If the public wants tougher law enforcement and more cops on the beat, that's how the candidate will be positioned. Never mind what he or she may really feel about it. What's important is to get the votes and get our man in office. Integrity? Integrity does not figure into the equation. I am told, "Do your job and mind your own business."

One morning we are filming a very wealthy candidate who is running for the Senate. We go to a baseball field in the black ghetto. He steps out of his stretch limo, takes off his jacket, loosens his tie, rolls up his sleeves. The makeup girl pats some powder on his sweaty forehead and he dashes towards home plate. We film the candidate surrounded by black women holding up their babies for a kiss or handshake from the wanna-be Senator. We finish and get back in his limo. He's disgusted, "Urggg..." commenting on what he just endured. I say, "Hey,

Fred, this is your constituency, these are the people you will be representing." He looks at me, like, "You gotta be kidding."

This is the beginning of the end for me. I am so put off by his attitude that I start to question the role I am playing trying to get him elected. I am creating a positive image for men who want to gain political power. Don't get me wrong, many of the candidates like Moynihan (NY), McCarthy (CA), and Babbitt (AZ), have a lot of integrity. But the rest of the bunch? I am not so sure. I resign after the last ballot is cast.

Mandy says, "But you can't quit. Didn't you hear? We're running the presidential campaign for astronaut John Glenn. Wasn't he your hero? It'll be great!"

MY FIRST REAL BOOK

Morgan and I can only afford to buy the smallest house in Westport. We fix up a two-story house not far from the river and train station. It has a tiny attic where I set up an office. The center of the room is the only place where there is enough ceiling height for me to stand up. Never mind, I can work anywhere. For a year, during any free moment, I rewrite my book, *The Independent Film and Videomaker's Guide*. I meet two lady typesetters who claim they have mastered a new publishing technique called "desktop publishing." In those days you type several symbols, like #B# or #I#, in front of words you want to turn bold or italicize and again at the end of words to turn off the instruction. You type other code numbers to format indentations or new paragraphs. It's really tedious and you really have to keep your wits about you or you will find when the text is printed out on glossy layout paper that you forgot to turn the bold off at the end of one bold word and so the whole paragraph prints out in bold. Drat! After several attempts, I get the layout how I like it and it goes to the printer. A couple of weeks later I get a call from *Publishers Weekly*, who want to interview me for an article they are writing. Along with a few other people, I am one of the first publishers to actually do "desktop publishing," although I didn't know it at the time.

Besides selling the book myself through mail order, I sign a distribution contract with Publishers Group West near Berkeley to get placement into retail bookstores. The second edition is professional looking and sells very well. In various editions over the years it sells more than 50,000 copies.

THE MOVIE CHANNEL

After a year or so of making several hundred political commercials, I have contacts with a huge voice-over talent base in New York. I know where to hire the best recording studios, camera gear, sound stages, and post-production facilities. I may not have made my own film for two years, but having spent millions of dollars making political commercials I know where and how to get the best deals.

This makes me attractive to Warner Amex, owner of The Movie Channel, a start-up pay cable channel. They are smaller and do not have as many subscribers as their competition, HBO. In 1982, Anne Foley Plunkett and Bob Pittman (who founded MTV a year earlier) hire me as Director of On-Air Promotion to oversee the production of all interstitial programs, such as star profiles (interviews with Morgan Fairchild, Jack Lemmon, etc.), network IDs, contests, and movie trailers — everything but the movies themselves. Anne tells me, "The goal is to keep people once they subscribe to The Movie Channel, make them feel they are getting real value, and not let them even think about cancelling. Got it?" This is tough, as HBO has more money and has licensed better movies.

I oversee a young staff and manage the production of 1,200 pieces ranging in length from about twenty seconds to ten minutes. Monday mornings are fun. We gather in the conference room and my team of young writers and producers go over the status of their assignments. All week long segments come into my office for approval before going on air. We are one of the first to use the Quantel paintbox (hardware and software technology) for broadcast television. The paintbox is an early precursor to Photoshop. It changes the look of broadcast television forever. *Saturday Night Live* had just started to use a soft, pastel look on their animated photo opening, so we hire the same people to do network IDs for us. While HBO is going for an expensive high-tech 3D look, we brand ourselves with a stylish hip/retro hand-painted look. We've got to push our graphic look and establish ourselves in the public's mind.

Although I get a lot of flack, I bring my Apple II+ computer to work and track production budgets as our segments are being made. This is what I'd done at DHS, and in both instances I am able to streamline the process, saving the companies hundreds of thousands of dollars. It's not rocket science. A budget template simply allows me to analyze a lot of information very quickly.

No one but me has his own computer at work. This is frowned on by the IT department because, as they tell me, "we are the ones who make and put out the financial reports." They tell me to keep my office door closed so no one can see what I am doing. The IT department can't deliver information as fast as I can. Since I approve the invoices, I have the information first. My boss, Anne, loves that she can see budgets in real time (any time she wants), whereas it takes the IT department a month to deliver their budgets. By then it is far too late to steer the ship.

The Movie Channel is bought by Viacom, the owner of Showtime. The staffs and resources are merged. Now the interstitial programming for both channels will be produced by one department. The Showtime staff has more clout in the transition, so many Movie Channel people are let go. I am among them. Eventually, with every job, you will either quit or be fired. It amounts to the same thing: change. Better get use to it.

I may be out of a job but, I am not troubled. Experientially, I had already learned everything I could in that position. I had managed a larger staff and overseen 1,200 on-air segments. I pushed my producers to try a lot of things that few people ever get to do in television. We'd used all kinds of new post-production video technology. I am sure I can use these skills down the road.

THE BUDGET BOOK

I have a few weeks before my next job will begin, so I work like crazy to finish my second book, *Film & Video Budgets*. Having created hundreds of budgets for commercials and pay TV segments and my own documentaries and shorts, I write a book about the budgeting process. Now I will have two books in release and a trickle of income from the sales each month. It also leads to some opportunities on the East Coast to present seminars now that I am an "expert

Bonnie, at Rochester Institute of Technology. I have to prove myself to her as an artist, a photographer, a musician, an awake human being, anything.

Steven Arnold and Michael at the San Francisco Art Institute in 1968. We refused to show our film at school. We wanted a real theater and a premiere!

Young Surrealists Film the Psychic

SAN FRANCISCO CHRONICLE MARCH 1969

By **Stanley Eichelbaum**

Steven Arnold and Michael K. Wiese are young film-makers who want to be recognized and seem to know what they're doing.

They have an interesting new film, which they call "Messages, Messages." It runs 30 minutes. But it took a year to make, with a cast of 50, in a store-front studio on Fillmore Street.

I was invited to a special showing of the work and found it quite d i f f e r e n t from the m o v i e s other young people are making today. There's no protest, no commitment, no psychedelic trickiness.

It's an a r r e s t i n g and beautiful study in surrealist imagery and it's done with remarkable c o n t r o l and discipline.

The filmmakers — Arnold is 24 and Wiese is 21 — have used a very reflective t h e m e of a young man's subconscious experience and a good deal of film is concentrated in facial expressions. But like Cocteau's old surrealist classics, t h e performers appear in bizarre makeup and costumes and move like dream c r e a t u r e s through some highly theatrical fantasy settings. There is no dialog, only the wailing of electronic music. This, explains Ar-

AUDREY
One of the dream creatures

nold, is because "the people d e p i c t e d speak with their faces."

Arnold and Wiese are both graduate students in film-making at t h e San Francisco A r t Institute. T h e y ' v e collaborated before, on s h o r t e r works. Their new film was personally financed and they expect Canyon Cinema to distribute it nationally.

Wiese calls the film "a vast tapestry exploring the phenomenon of p s y c h i c life."

It does have a spiritual quality (and is perhaps a

bit too private, except possibly for those trained in psychiatry).

But it did impress Salvador Dali, whom W i e s e called upon in New York last month and persuaded to have a look at it at a private screening arranged for Dali and a party of his friends.

In New York as well, the film was acquired for the M u s e u m of Modern Art Film Library.

But more prints of the movie are needed for potential distribution. The filmmakers have therefore scheduled a benefit for the movie. It will be shown at the Palace Theater (Columbus at Powell) on Thursday night, Feb. 27, at 8:30 i n an all-surrealist program that will also include works by Frederic Melies and Man Ray.

Since Salvador Dalí endorses the film by giving his surrealistic stamp of approval, everyone wants to see it. Dalí knew exactly what he was doing and I shall be forever grateful.

Steven Arnold

Michael and Cherel during a break from shooting a short film. When I first see Cherel she is the spitting image of Penelope Tree: skinny, big eyes with black eyeliner, and a very well put together thrift shop look.

MESSAGES MESSAGES

A FILM BY STEVEN ARNOLD AND MICHAEL K WIESE

MESSAGES MESSAGES   A VAST TAPESTRY EXPLORING THE PHENONENON OF PSYCHIC LIFE ENTERS THE MIRRORED CORRIDORS OF A WORLD RESPLENDENT WITH WINGED CLOUD CREATURES   INSECT WOMEN   UNDERWATER CITIES   GARDENS OF LUNAR LABYRINTHS   GROTTOS OF TRANSPARENT LEVITATING BODIES   MESSAGES MESSAGES IS AN OFFERING

MESSAGES MESSAGES   ONE YEAR IN THE MAKING STARS THE JOSEPH   LIAM O GALLAGHER   RUTH WEISS AND A CAST OF FIFTY WITH ELABORATE COSTUMES AND SPECIALLY DESIGNED MAKEUP   LIGHTING AND SETS

Our surrealistic student film is invited to Cannes Film Festival's "Director's Fortnight" after its blessing by Dalí.

133

Dennis Hearne

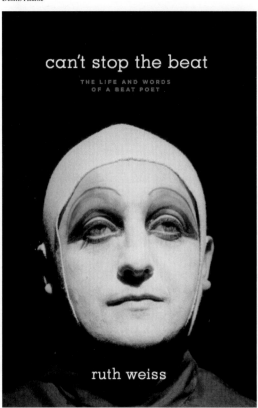

can't stop the beat

THE LIFE AND WORDS
OF A BEAT POET

ruth weiss

Dennis Hearne/Ingeborg Gerdes

*Suddenly, from out of nowhere,
we find ourselves surrounded by
eight deputized men with rifles
pointed as us. "What the...?"*

*This strking shot of Beat poet ruth
weiss was used 45 years later for
the cover of her book – can't stop
the beat – which we published
on our Divine Arts imprint.
Left and next page are images from
the unfinished Pyramid film.
Right: L-R Steven Arnold,
Sonia, Michael with camera.*

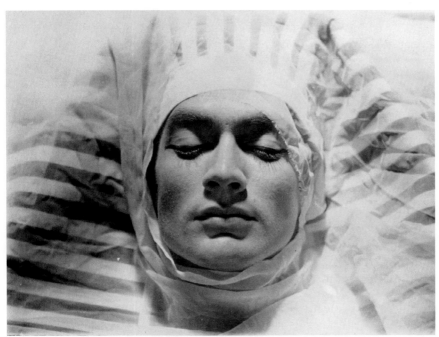

Michael Wiese

Gene Kenny

In my producing mode at our 18th St./Mission Street studio in San Francisco.

Michael Wiese

Exterior of the studio. An Egyptian eye marks the spot. Inside, we have built a giant barge and are filming Pyramid.

We went to Maine to film Bucky Fuller for our Dolphin *film. L-R Michael, Bucky, Hardy Jones, Jaime Snyder (Bucky's grandson), and John Knoop.*

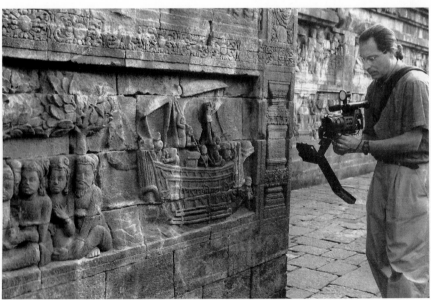

Geraldine Overton

Filming the friezes at Borobodur in Java in 1990.

By the time I left that village in Sudan all the kids were playing the flutes I taught them to make. It was one noisy oasis!

Cherel Ito

Teiji Ito, my best friend, during my Tokyo days. On one recording session for a saké commercial he hires me to play mbira (African thumb piano).

前から脱しなくっちゃ

マイケル・ウィーセ氏

I arrive with the rising sun at Tokyo's Narita airport with $200 in my pocket and a single name scribbled on a scrap of paper. They stop me at immigration. The photo is from my passport.

Michael Wiese

The sand dunes on Lamu, off the north-eastern coast of Kenya. It's the home of pirates, slave traders and merchants who export ivory, mangrove, turtle shells and rhino horns.

Michael Wiese

He takes me to the bamboo house that the village had built for me.
The deal was that when I was not there they could use it.

Michael Wiese

On July 12th, Bucky and I share a birthday. In 1977 we celebrated at a conference in Bali.
Someone gave him the crystal as a gift which prompted a spontaneous lecture.

One of the heavenly creatures shadow puppets that I made for our shadow play performances.

The shadow puppeteer choreographs great battles between princes and monsters, evokes philosophical debates among the gods, and instigates comedic romps with clown servants of the kings. He is a shaman, a spirit channeler, a teacher, and a healer of the community and for a brief moment we get to experience that role.

MAGICK

PAINTINGS BY THE ARTISTS
OF PENGOSAKEN VILLAGE

Batuan shows us many paintings from the Community of Painters that he founded, just a few weeks ago - on July 12th, my birthday. He invites us to stay in his compound. From a Bali painting exhibition in Champaign in 1971.

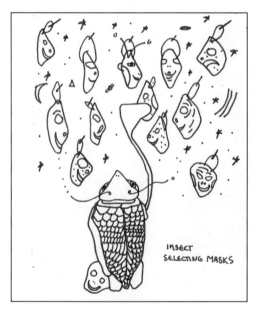

I draw...long into the night. This activity takes me into an altered state. Drawing takes me to other places where something seems to guide my hand. Made in my "cave" in Ioa, Santorini.

Steven Arnold/Michael Wiese

Kaisik Wong as Monkey. *"One day Francis storms in and flings these photos on my desk,
'Some freaks broke into my house and put these in my bed! Get rid of them!'"*

John V. Fante

It was a thrill to see lines around the block for the premiere of Hardware Wars *in
1977. "You'll laugh, you'll cry, you'll kiss three bucks good-bye."*

Jack McKinney

Maybe it's the incredible light on the water or the feeling in your brain from floating in the ocean, or the harmony of being with the dolphins, but whatever the reason, the experience opened our hearts and created a love for one another that sustains to this day.

I love being with Bucky and Werner hearing their expansive ideas. But it's the first time in seven years that I've been back to Bali and I am eager to see my painter friends in the village and to dip back into the magic.

In jest - but not completely - Dad takes one look, raises both arms, and bows low. The father bows to the son.

Jack McKinney/James Hudnall

*We lower Steve and his piano into the water and instantly 70 spotted dolphins are cavorting
around him like Busby Berkeley dancers in a most exquisite underwater ballet.*

The Great Ken Lee, Vice President of MWP. I told him I am not hiring anyone.

Right: With Shirley MacLaine and congresswoman Bella Abzug on the set of Inner Workout. *I am grateful to Shirley because our chakra work helped lead me back to inner work and reflection.*

Below: In Las Vegas with the funniest men on the planet: discoverer of The Titanic, Dr. Bob Ballard, Billy Crystal and Robin Williams. All appeared in home video programs for Vestron.

author." (Today, the book is still popular, in its fifth edition and now written by Deke Simon.)

When I learn new things through my work experience and want to share this experience, I first create a seminar, test out the material's usefulness, and then write a book. A process is emerging that brings me income between jobs but also allows me to do my own thing. Quietly I persevere... slowly, slowly.

VESTRON VIDEO

Ruth Vitale and C. J. Kettler are two of my colleagues at The Movie Channel who also find themselves out in the street after the Showtime merger. However, since I am busy working on my book, they land new jobs before I do, and want me to join them. Ruth calls and says she wants to meet Austin Furst, who has just launched a new start-up: Vestron Video. He is a pioneer in the home video business and has licensed some movies from his former employer, Time-Life. Vestron has just had its first big hit with Michael Jackson's *Thriller* video. They are eager to do more of the same and want me to find home video product for them. Austin says, "Our goal? Fill every video store in America with Vestron videos."

I meet Vestron president Jon Peisinger and he hires me as a Vice President to head up the "original programming" division. I ask, "What's that?" He says, "I don't know, go figure it out." So I think about all the different genres that could possibly be on home video, like exercise, music, sports, documentary, comedy, and children's videos. Another Vestron division focuses on acquiring the video rights to theatrical movies. My domain is "everything else." I just need to figure out what that is.

I study the book trade, which is a similar business, where everything is shelved by genre. I identify the key genres in home video and start by acquiring video titles and later producing them. These are the very early days of home video. The studios, with their star-laden "A" titles, are still sitting on the sidelines waiting for the Supreme Court to rule on the "first sale doctrine," which would allow videos to be sold to stores for rental purposes. While the legalities are being debated, Vestron rushes in to fill the barren shelves of 10,000 mom-and-pop video stores that have sprung up overnight all across America.

Vestron is an exciting place. I have a young and energetic staff. The pay is good and we are very successful. We are given enormous responsibility to "Just go do it." I can "green-light" most acquisitions, but just to cover my backside I pitch what I want to buy or produce to the sales and marketing department to make sure they can sell it. The question that always needs to be answered is "How many?" How many will a proposed title sell? If we know that, we can determine what we can spend on acquiring or producing that video. Nothing is done unless a profit can be made. But this is relatively easy, because there is so much pent-up demand for videos that the marketplace is very forgiving, and so 98% of what we release turns a profit.

Whenever someone has good news to share they stop work, go to the conference room, pick up a mallet, and strike a huge Chinese gong. This is heard throughout the building. Everybody stops work and gathers to hear the announcement. I am constantly ringing that gong.

Our department has the most fun. I've discovered that if people have fun they will come to work early and stay late and really do a good job. This proves to be true. The Vestron summer picnic is coming up, so I form a band with anyone who could play anything. We have two guitars, bass, me on drums, sax, and three female singers. (Morgan joins the band as an honorary member.) We call ourselves the "D Titles" because we don't want to raise anyone's expectations. I'd say "D" is generous, and so is our appreciative audience.

My mandate from the company's financial planners, with my small staff, is to acquire or produce 110 titles a year. This is a ton of output. Every two weeks I release six titles! I don't always like what we release, but that can't be a concern. We move forward like a hungry shark, finding projects in unlikely places.

One Friday I am pitched a video on pro wrestling and I pass. But just because I don't like it doesn't mean it won't sell, so on Monday I write a check for a wrestling video that I title *Lords of the Rings*. We release titles in every genre, but the areas in which we dominate are comedy, documentary, and children's videos.

We score big in the comedy genre. I manage to sign more big names than our competitors: Richard Pryor, George Carlin, Stephen Wright, Robin Williams,

Billy Crystal, and Whoopi Goldberg. When I meet Whoopi after the taping of her show, I give her a box of Vestron horror videos as I was told she was a big horror fan. She thanks me and then as I am leaving I hear her say to the crew standing around, "Who's the Suit?" Ouch! I discover I am no longer perceived as a "Creative." Only then does it dawn on me that I had become an entertainment executive.

I pitch Vestron's marketing department on the idea of creating a line of videos for National Geographic. They pass. They think people will just record these specials off the air. I ask, "Have you ever thrown away a *National Geographic* magazine? And even if you tried, didn't it eventually end up in your attic or garage? It's because of that yellow packaging; it's in our DNA to collect it! People will collect National Geographic videos in the same way." This argument falls on deaf ears, with the exception of Jon Peisinger, who supports me if I can make the deal "for a price."

In Washington, D.C., I meet with Tim Kelly, Head of Television at National Geographic, and offer to bring them into the home video business. They are reluctant. Congress has granted them their non-profit status and they are afraid to jeopardize it by appearing too commercial or profitable. Nevertheless, I am very persuasive, but so is CBS Fox, a much bigger, better-known New York-based video company with a name that means something to National Geographic. "Who are you guys and where are you from again?" "Vestron, in the backwoods of Stamford, Connecticut."

I tell Morgan that I can feel the deal slipping away. I can feel the power of CBS. She asks if I have done everything I possibly can. I think so, but maybe not. I look deeper. When I go back to the office I ask Jon if he would fly down to Washington with me for a final push. I want him to tell National Geographic that as the president of the company he will make their video line a personal priority. I want him to give them special attention. We make the trip and he does just that. A few days later I close the deal.

A month later I ask Tim Kelly of National Geographic why they went with us and not CBS. He said that they had already decided to go with CBS, but then

CBS didn't bring their company president to Washington! The deal brings in about $40 million in wholesale sales revenues to Vestron. I get the glory, but no gold trickles down to me.

After the success of National Geographic, I license series from Smithsonian, NOVA, and Audubon. I try several times to create a label with PBS, but there are many complex licensing and rights issues that can't be resolved. Acquiring lines is a more expedient way to fill 110 release slots a year than one at a time.

After the success of the wrestling video, I try to create a boxing series. I invite boxing impresario Don King out to our Connecticut offices. The man with big hair bursts out of his stretch limo, kicking aside half-empty buckets of Kentucky Fried Chicken.

To sell him on the project, I have the art department prepare a videocassette box mock-up with a big picture of Don on the cover. Ali and Foreman's pictures are also on the box, just smaller. I have an assistant secretly count how many times Don glances at the video box *Don King's Greatest Hits* during the meeting. It's a lot.

Don invites me and Jon Peisinger to come to Las Vegas as his guests at the Mike Tyson–Trevor Berbick fight. My philosophy is, "If someone invites you some-where you've never been — go!" I'd photographed many Golden Gloves fights when I was in high school, but a front row seat at a title fight for the Heavyweight Championship of the World is a whole other thing. It's nightmarish. Any one punch would kill an ordinary mortal and these guys are hammering each other. The crowd goes berserk and wants blood. I've never been in this kind of energy before. Blood and sweat splatter the front rows with every swing. It's sickening. The crowd is chanting. I am pinned in between hysterical people standing on their feet. I am looking for the nearest exit. I am glad when Tyson knocks out his opponent in an early round and the torture ends. Tyson wins his first WBC Heavyweight title.

Afterwards, we go to a party at the Hilton Hotel's rooftop penthouse. Spread out across the back wall is a huge buffet. There are a lot of celebrities and prize fighters balancing plates stacked high with ribs, cornbread, corn on the cob, black-eyed peas, and orange slush. Don King sees us and rushes up. I am impressed that he remembers our names and introduces us all around. We meet Muhammad Ali and a very shy Mike Tyson, whom we congratulate. I know Don has great footage from all his fights, but does he have photo clearances? Don pulls me aside and assures me that he can get clearances from all the fighters. I have my doubts. I've heard enough stories about semi-literate boxers signing blank pieces of paper to be skeptical. In the end, the deal never happens. I am relieved. One look into the world of professional boxing is enough.

One great thing about the job is that my position gives me access to anyone. I can think up a video project and call any agent, manager, star, musician, comic, or documentary filmmaker, and they will take my call. I am under no illusion. This isn't because of my glowing personality, but because I have a checkbook and Vestron is the fastest rising video company on the planet.

I am learning a lot about marketing, sales, and distribution. Every project is unique and has its own set of challenges. I like that. Creatively I get to experiment with the packaging and distribution of hundreds of videos. I am feeding a voracious beast. I just wish the product had more calories and something to say.

THE BEACH BOYS

Even as a teenager growing up in Illinois and playing surf music in The Torquettes, I fantasized about California when listening to The Beach Boys' music. So what a complete joy, in 1985, to be given the responsibility for the Vestron's first feature — a $2.2 million rockumentary, *The Beach Boys: An American Band*, on the life and times of The Beach Boys. Malcolm Leo (*This is Elvis*) is to direct and assemble footage from the Beach Boys' long career, from their early days at Hawthorne High to a recent Washington, D.C. beach party with an audience of hundreds of thousands. The film has 43 of their best songs and is a celebration of the Beach Boys' career.

A half a dozen filming sessions are set up, with each Beach Boy to tell his story, but the bulk of the film is from the Beach Boys' own archives as well as from fans around the world. Super 8, 16mm, 35mm, videotape in all formats are mastered together on one-inch tape and then transferred to 35mm film for theatrical release. This in itself is experimental. Video-to-film transfer was far from an established process and ever since *Monkey* I have wanted to try it. We were taking a big chance showing this "film" to the world.

The premiere is at the Director's Guild Theater in Hollywood, which has, hands down, the best projection system in the world. The theater is buzzing with music stars, music industry execs, and every film critic in town. When the curtain pulls back I am terrified that we'd be killed by the reviews. "That's not a film, that's video!" But once the movie starts, everyone goes along with the mix of media and no one utters a peep. The movie is captivating from the first frame and garners terrific reviews. Everybody loves The Beach Boys.

Vestron has its own press department, and every week I am quoted or make some product announcement in *Variety* or *The Hollywood Reporter* or *Video Business*. We are deliberately very high-profile in the press because this enables us to attract the top talent and their product as well as keep our name before the financial community. I send press clippings to my folks, who are delighted with my professional success. Morgan's parents are pleased as well. I am a corporate vice-president at the fastest-growing video company in the U.S. Now even bigger things can happen.

In 1985, Vestron's Chairman Austin Furst announces that we will take the company public on the New York Stock Exchange with an IPO (initial private offering) of $440 million. The timing could not have been better. There are more people wanting to buy the stock than is available and the stock price immediately rises. We have five hundred employees in seventeen different countries, selling videos in thirty countries, with gross wholesale revenues of $500 million. Vestron controls about 10% of the video market.

My division releases everything from comedy (Robin Williams, Whoopi Goldberg, Billy Crystal), to music (The Cars, The Rolling Stones, Bette Midler), kids (Care Bears, My Little Pony, Rainbow Bright, The Smurfs), sports (Arnold Palmer, NFL Football), exercise (Armed Forces, Low-Impact Aerobics), to entire documentary lines (National Geographic, Smithsonian, Audubon, and NOVA). Anything I thought we could sell we buy or produce.

But there are dark clouds on the horizon. As Malcolm Cowley says, "Hollywood money isn't money. It's congealed snow; it melts in your hand, and there you are."

By 1986 the major Hollywood studios are no longer sitting on the sidelines. The Supreme Court has ruled that videos can be sold and rented. The studios move into the video business in a big way with their star-laden blockbusters. These "A" titles take up more and more shelf space in the video stores. Initially, video stores stocked by breadth — lots of different titles. But with big-name studio titles, they are now stocking in depth. So where they once shelved twenty different titles, now they stock twenty of the same studio blockbuster. Vestron's less desirable B and C titles are being squeezed off the shelves.

Jon announces at the company staff meeting that we are restructuring to save on expenses and assures us that no one will be let go. Then I am promoted and inherit the staff of both the Vestron Music Video and Children's Video Library labels. I am now president of three Vestron divisions, including our production company, High Ridge Productions. The next day Jon calls me into his office and tells me "I know what I said, but times are tough, you are going to have to fire one of your directors." He adds, "It's your choice."

This is excruciatingly hard to do. I've never had to fire someone who is doing a great job. I call Nancy into my office. I tell her that her position has been eliminated and she no longer has a job. She laughs and laughs. I am usually a cheerful funny guy and so she must think this is just my bizarre sense of humor, especially after Jon had told everyone that no one would lose his or her job. I tell her, "No, really." She breaks down and cries. I tell her that I'll give her a letter of recommendation and help her find another job. This whole thing isn't right.

There are new realities that must be faced. With the video market maturing and shelf space more scarce, we can't release as many titles. Because I had a mandate to release over 110 titles a year, I focused on "lines" of videos, such as National Geographic, Smithsonian, NOVA, Audubon, and others. I'd built up an inventory of hundreds of titles ready for release. Now they are no longer needed.

One Friday morning during my usual breakfast with Jon at the greasy spoon diner, he says softly "Today is going to be a very black day." I ask why. He whispers,

"Because we're going to have to let some really good people go." I say, leaning forward, "Really? Who?" I don't see the punch line coming. "You," he says.

That afternoon I am packing up boxes in my office, as are three other vice presidents. Still in shock, I have forgotten to cancel an appointment with a producer who has come from New York to pitch me on a project. I say, "Sorry you have had to come all this way. I just lost my job. I no longer write the checks." He says, "Can I pitch you anyway?"

Later that day, National Geographic calls Vestron. They are very angry. They want to know why Vestron fired their main liaison and who was now going to take care of their line?

The next day I am in still in a daze. It all happened so fast. In an act of great compassion, Joseph Campbell's publisher, Robert Walter, takes the day off and comes up to Connecticut to console me. We have lunch and he cheers me up. Life goes on.

A week later National Geographic asks me to come work for them as a consultant on their video deals, both domestic and foreign. I tell Morgan that I can't go work on the other side of my own deal. I still feel loyal to Vestron! Morgan shouts, "Michael, Vestron just fired you!" I take the National Geographic job.

Vestron has a last gasp comeback with an unexpected hit from a $6 million movie called *Dirty Dancing* that brings in $170 million at the box office. The feature division is making low- and mid-budget movies. They have fifty in production, pre-production, or development.

Shortly thereafter, Security Pacific Bank pulls the plug on Vestron's $50 million line of credit. An independent distributor trying to make movies without A-list stars cannot compete with the major studios. With fifty films in various stages of production, everything comes crashing down. Live Entertainment buys Vestron and their library in January 1991 for a paltry $27.3 million. End of an era. Everything changes.

LIFE AFTER VESTRON

After Vestron, the home video bubble bursts and the field is littered with many independent home video companies that went belly-up. Never for a moment did I think my firing from Vestron was personal. It wasn't. Things expand. Things contract. For four or five years I was on the ground floor with one of the most successful start-ups of the decade that became internationally successful in a very short time. By the time I'd left, I'd executive produced or acquired, packaged, and marketed more non-theatrical titles than anyone in the video industry. Many bestsellers, earning Vestron $100 million in revenues. My experience taught me about business, financing, sales, marketing, distribution, and publicity aspects of the video publishing business. It was like getting a Ph.D. in the entertainment business. Our efforts had made Austin and a few others very rich, but not the rest of us. What we got was enormous experience that I planned to apply elsewhere. I had a huge Rolodex and many friends on both coasts. Next time though, I promise myself, I will have ownership in what I create.

Also, a lot of what we distributed was entertainment fodder with little redeeming value. It was very different from the save-the-world and human potential films that I made ten years earlier. Of course I was proud of National Geographic and a few other titles, but most of what we acquired was meant to feed the consumption machine. I'd started my filmmaking career wanting to make meaningful, important, and worthy films. Now I find myself in the deep end of commercial entertainment. The break from the frantic environment of Vestron was actually a good opportunity to re-examine where I was and where I wanted to be. I knew I did not want to go back inside. I knew I wanted to return to making uplifting films, videos, and books, at whatever level. I wanted to return to meaningful content.

I receive some job offers from large television and film companies, and while most of the other vice presidents at Vestron accept executive positions with the studios, I decide I want to do two things: return to making media that makes a difference, and build my own company. The next time out, I would succeed or fail on my own terms. But first I had to exorcize entertainment's demons.

GOIN' HOLLYWOOD

What happened to me at Vestron is typical in the entertainment industry. This happens to everyone sooner or later. Trends come and go. Everything changes. Contemplating the absolute madness of the movie business inspired me and my buddy Greg Johnson (sax player in the D-Titles and Vestron's VP of Business Development) to create a satirical board game called *Goin' Hollywood: The Movie-Making Game*. In the game, players make a movie however they can. It's a parody of the movie business, where you try to make the most money, not the best film. The game is a cross between Monopoly and *Saturday Night Live*. It's a cynical look at how the movie business does business. Ernie Fosselius (*Hardware Wars*) wrote some of the funniest game cards. The tagline for the game is *"Wheel and Deal, Schmooze and Steal, Do Lunch, Take a Meeting, Cheat Your Friends."* Clearly I had experienced some pain and disappointment after Vestron, and making this game was a way to exorcize it through humor.

Charlotte and Joel Parker, the publicity team who represent Arnold Schwarzenegger, get us a lot of coverage, including an opening feature spot on CBS Networks' *Entertainment Tonight*. We do well and initially sell 5,000 copies, mostly in New York and Los Angeles, which we manufacture and distribute ourselves.

A few years later I join some Studio City neighbors for a yard sale. All of our unwanted junk is spread across the front lawn. On a neighbor's card table is a brand-new *Goin' Hollywood* game, in its original shrink-wrap. He only wants $1 for it! (It's now a collector's item worth at least $150 on eBay!) I don't know whether to be crushed because our brilliant work of art is in a junk sale, or elated because I got a great deal.

Recently, I hear the game has a huge cult following in Finland. It helps them get through those long dark winters, I guess.

END OF A LIFE CYCLE

To earn a living while starting my own production/publishing business, I continue to consult with National Geographic and the Smithsonian on building their video businesses. The Smithsonian asks me if I want to executive produce the video ideas we've developed, however I am quickly tiring of the turbulent small plane rides that I take every week commuting between Westport and Washington, D.C., so I pass.

I finish writing a third book, *Home Video: Producing for the Home Market*. Even though I am out of a "steady job" I have plenty to do. Between consulting and book sales I can just cover the mortgage.

Change comes for Morgan and me as well. We are both working very hard in our respective careers. We've been drifting in different directions for some time. I take a diving vacation alone to Virgin Gorda and another trip to Bali to rekindle some of the magic of the past. But don't get me wrong, we are extremely compatible and enjoy each other's company immensely.

We both come to the realization that it is over. No blame. No shame. There is no big drama. No one has had an affair. No dishes are thrown. We talk lovingly with each other and acknowledge the truth about our relationship. Graduate school is over and we both pass with honors. It has run its remarkable course and feels complete. There is nothing else we need to do other than go on our individual quests and support each other in doing so.

Upon reflection, what really happened is that I'd lost my way. I'd quit following my own inspiration, my own bliss, for too many years, with the decision to leave San Francisco. I'd not trusted my own experience, my own unfolding. I hadn't made a personal film in years. Instead, I took jobs to support us and to make our families secure and happy. I'd given up my own dreams (something that I later learned my own father had done as well). The marriage died because I'd died. It took me decades to realize that you have to nourish your calling and everything else will take care of itself.

I met Morgan at an extraordinary time. We swam with dolphins! We made a glorious film about it. It does not get much more romantic than that. This was a once-in-a-lifetime experience, and the intoxicated feelings of love and connectedness that sprang from this interspecies encounter were rich and magnificent. We got married on this high, and rather than getting higher as we expected, everything went downhill because I quit following what truly inspired me. I quit doing inner work and got caught up completely in the "go-go" media worlds of commercial television, politics, cable TV, and home video. I learned a lot about the entertainment business, but I'd sold my soul at the crossroads of 5th and 55th. I'd lost what the Balinese call "taksu." I'd lost the divine connection. It would take me a while to find my way back onto the path.

I had been carrying around "lost jobs" and "a failed marriage" as a disappointment when in reality I'd been tremendously successful at everything, including jobs and marriage. Joy in life comes from how you hold something in your mind. I had not yet fully learned this.

Morgan and I split up our assets on a yellow pad and visit a lawyer to draw up the divorce papers. He says he can't represent both of us, only one of us. I said, "Fine, then represent Morgan, I won't have representation." He tried to make things unnecessarily complicated, but we said, "Look, we know what we want to do and how we want to do it, so please, just write it up." We set the world record for the cheapest divorce.

I didn't want to stay on the East Coast. I didn't want to go back to San Francisco. I'd spent a lot of time in Los Angeles on Vestron business, and while I never really liked it very much, I decide I would head out there.

I'd packed all my things and was "Goin' Hollywood." Morgan surprised me by hiring a limo to chauffer me to the airport and into my new life. As the limo pulled away, I shook my head and laughed. It was typical of Morgan to create a special moment. I'll miss that.

To this day, we still stay in touch and I see her whenever I am in New York. A few years ago she arrives with her partner at a film showing. Afterwards a bunch of us go out for dinner. One of our authors, who hadn't met Morgan before, asks, "So, how do you guys know each other?" I say, "We were married." Shocked, she stutters, "But... but... you're still friends." Morgan smiles, "Yes, we are."

Sowing
the Spirit

1986  *1987*

"Behold, a sower went forth to sow...and some fell among thorns...
But others fell into good ground, and brought forth fruit, some
an hundredfold, some sixtyfold, some thirtyfold."

— Matthew 13:4-8

....

Michael Wiese

SHIRLEY

A few months after I leave Vestron, I hear that Shirley MacLaine is searching for someone to produce and direct her new video. I'd been pitched videos starring Shirley MacLaine a number of times at Vestron, but every time I probed deeper none of the producers actually had Shirley under contract. I meet Shirley and we hit it off. I tell her about the human potential films I have made and show her *Radiance*. Before hiring me, she wants me to meet former Congresswoman Bella Abzug, who is her close friend and will act as executive producer.

I arrive at Bella's apartment in Manhattan. Bella is best known for serving in Congress for six years, representing New York State, and for her unsuccessful run for New York City mayor, which she has recently lost. She is a large powerhouse, known for wearing outrageous hats, and is affectionately nicknamed "Battling Bella" for passionately pioneering women's rights and helping to end the Vietnam war.

She peers over a formidable desk heaped with legal briefs. We chat for half an hour as she growls and tries to eliminate every line on the budget. "Too high! No, that's not right! You don't need this!" She clearly is bluffing and doesn't really know what she is talking about. She tries to steamroll me. I hold my ground.

The phone rings and she takes it in another room and leaves me alone. While I am waiting, the corner of a book shoved under the pile of papers catches my eye. I pull it out. It's my book, *Film & Video Budgets*! She has taken a yellow highlighter and marked points that interest her. "Challenge every price" is highlighted. She is using my own advice against me!

On Shirley's behalf I shop the project around the major home video companies. Vestron comes up with the best deal, plus I know how to eliminate the contract "magic" that can severely reduce a producer's royalties. Jeff Peisch, whom I hired and who was my protégé at Vestron, oversees the project. He has my old job and office, and now does an excellent job handling me just like I taught him.

I visit Shirley at her house in Malibu and we start working on the script for a meditation video based on the ancient Hindu chakra system which, simply put, are energy centers in the body. Meditation on these centers can help with healing and balancing the energy. The seven primary centers are located at the base of the spine, the groin, the solar plexus, the heart, the throat, the third eye and at the crown of the head. Shirley explains this using a manikin we had built with colored lights representing the chakras. There is an open-eye meditation with mandalas created by old friend and video artist Ken Jenkins, who had provided imagery for *Radiance*.

Shirley dictates the meditation sequences into a tape recorder, taking me on a guided visualization. ("You see yourself walking through a grassy green field, you hear a babbling stream, in the distance is a large tree, you walk slowly toward it....") while Bella bangs around trying to make tea, impatient with our long creative process.

I drive Bella back to her hotel. As I walk her to the lobby, there's a scraggly black guy with Coke-bottle glasses dressed in a shiny suit coming out of the elevator. In his hand, a strangely shaped guitar case. This could only be one guy! I introduce him to Bella. "Bella this is Bo. Bo this is Bella." I love it. My hero, Bo Diddley, tells me he is in Hollywood to record the soundtrack for a *Blacula* film. Bella never does get who he is.

Once Shirley and I finish the script, I book a crew and a studio in Hollywood. I already had a sensitive designer come up with drawings of the sets that will be built. It utilizes large shapes representing the chakras. Shirley loves the concept. I hire Bill Klages who has the best reputation in Hollywood for lighting leading ladies. With Shirley's vast stage and screen experience, she is acutely aware of how the light falls on her face. With actors, you want to make them feel as secure as possible, so having the best lighting man in the business is good insurance that things will go smoothly.

We build the set and light it. The morning of the shoot about a hundred people show up. This is the "rainbow coalition" that Shirley wants for her audience. Blacks, whites, Hispanics, Asians, green aliens (only kidding), etc. I desperately try to persuade her that we should shoot her looking <u>directly</u> into the camera with no studio audience. I feel this would be more intimate, as the viewers would experience Shirley talking directly to them, and not as if they were eavesdropping on a meditation workshop. Shirley says, "I need the energy of an audience to bounce off of." The audience stays.

So the set is ready, the audience is ready, I am ready. In comes Shirley. Excited, I take her to our magnificent set. "Don't you love it!?" She hates it. "It's all wrong," she says. "People in Watts won't relate to it" and storms off. (Never mind that people in Watts will never buy this video.) I am floored. She'd already approved the set. Now I have an expensive crew standing around, a 100-strong rainbow coalition, and no star.

Shirley disappears into her dressing room. I follow. "Shirley, what do you see?" She says, "I see green, I see earth, I see rainbows," and on that she slams the door. Right. Got it. Got what?

I go back to the crew, who stand around eagerly expecting praise. With a severe migraine coming on I use my best director voice, "Okay guys, tear the set down, we're going to do something else." The art director starts to cry. The others ask, "Okay, what do you want?" I say, "I want green, I want earth, and I want rainbows."

It is Sunday and all the prop shops are closed, so we raid the executive offices at the studio and put ferns on the stage and light them with many colored lights.

Bella is in the control room squinting at the monitors and bellowing, "This looks like shit. My kids could do better than this!" I tell her it's a shame that her kids aren't here and anyway we're not done, but she's right. It looks like a Don Ho Christmas Special. I go on stage and have them take down some of the "rainbow" to get a clean, Japanese *ikebana* look. Shirley comes out, thinks it's genius, and we shoot the first day.

Since it's a multi-camera shoot with a live mix, I am able to send Shirley home with a video cassette rough edit of the day's work. She calls me around 11 p.m. She says, "I don't like Her. I can't relate to Her." I saw this coming. I jump in, "That's because you are looking at Her, you are not <u>being with</u> Her. We should shoot her looking into the camera lens, and the viewers will feel She is looking at them." She agrees. The next morning, I thank the assembled rainbow coalition and send them home.

The editing of the footage is not going smoothly. I work for four hours each day before Shirley comes in after lunch. Whatever I show her she doesn't like, and she wants everything changed. After about three days of this, I discern a pattern. First thing she does is find things she doesn't like, then she makes some phone calls, signs a few autographs, finds something she does like, tells me I'm a genius, then drives back to Malibu.

I change tactics. The minute she comes in I show her sections that I plan to change anyway. Things go better.

I work for a long time to license a beautiful piece of music that's perfect for one section. She hates it. I know it's the right piece of music. So before she sees it again, I slip the music ten seconds later so it hits against different images, but it still creates the effect I want. She sees it, loves it, and asks where I found the new music.

Eventually, once trust is established and the video starts looking good, we learn to work with each other quite well. Making this gentle meditation tape is one of the most stressful projects of my life.

Shirley and I have made a new age meditation video. There really is no video genre for this tape. Where would a video store shelve it? It doesn't fit anywhere. Vestron titles the tape *Shirley MacLaine's Inner Workout*. She appears on the video box cover in peach-colored sweat clothes. Brilliant. It goes on the exercise shelf and yet people can quickly discern what it is. The video wins The American Film Institute's "Best New Age" video award and sells more than 250,000 units in a few months.

I am grateful to Shirley because our chakra work was responsible for leading me back to inner work and reflection. For the last seven or eight years my focus was on outer work: making a living, getting politicians votes, getting television ratings, holding onto subscribers, selling videos, and making a name for myself in the media world. Now I would slowly return to where I'd started: exploring consciousness. But not all at once.

PACIFIC ARTS

I arrive in Los Angeles in September and by October I have bought and moved into a house in Studio City. Vestron had been such an exciting place and I'd learned a great deal, so my knowledge was valuable to other video companies and clients like Mystic Fire, Republic Pictures, Hanna-Barbera, King World Television, The Apollo Theater, Deepak Chopra, and others.

I meet Michael Nesmith (formerly of The Monkees), who founded Pacific Arts Video, a very hip and forward-thinking home video label that echoes his eclectic and wide-ranging artistic tastes. He asks me to help him make a home video deal with PBS and start the PBS Home Video label. I'd been trying to do this at Vestron for a couple of years and knew the issues and difficulties. Along with Al Cattabiani, who is hired the same day, we are able to get things rolling and, after a few months, we conclude a deal with PBS for their programming by paying PBS a licensing fee for their name and another licensing fee to the rights holders. I stay on to help acquire and market programming such as *This Old House*, *Masterpiece Theater*, *The Astronomers*, *I Claudius*, and other programs. Michael has a great team of people working with him and I enjoy the job very much. After a year, the PBS start-up has earned about $14 million.

Nesmith honors me by asking if I would like to be president of PBS Home Video and run the label. I didn't see this coming, but I should have. Smiling, he says he wants me in the job "heart and soul." I tell him he could have one or the other and that there are many other things I want to do. He is upset with me when I don't accept the job. Any video company job seems like a step backward, so at this crossroads I keep my independence. The ultimate success is being able to do your own work in your own way.

THE GREAT KEN LEE

One day an enthusiastic producer friend calls and says, "You have to meet this guy, Ken Lee. He's great." I say, "Fine, but I want you to know, and him to know, that I am not hiring anyone. I'm still working out of my house and not earning enough to start a company." So Ken and I meet for lunch. I spot him right away as he perfectly fits the description he has given me: "very tall, Chinese, and handsome." I repeat the mantra of the day, "I'm not hiring anyone." He asks me about what I am doing now and what I want to be doing in five years. Basically he runs a kind of career consulting rap on me that he probably learned in a management seminar somewhere. But he is smart, and funny, and enthusiastic, and aggressive... so I say, "Okay, three days a week on a trial basis." That was twenty-two years ago! Now he's Vice President of the company and runs everything. Should I tell him he passed the test, or not, just to keep him on his toes?

I bring Ken into everything I am doing to get him up to speed. He comes to sessions with my consulting clients, helps with film and video productions, and markets our burgeoning line of film books. It's 1990 and I have published six books, including Steve Katz' *Film Directing Shot by Shot* (which turns out to be a bestseller with more than 200,000 copies sold and translations into twelve languages). We officially incorporate Desktop Broadcasting Inc, d/b/a Michael Wiese Productions (MWP).

One of the secrets to our long and great working relationship is that Ken and I complement each other perfectly. If we both excelled at the same things, then there would be a duplication of effort. Ninety-eight percent of the time he knows what I am thinking before I tell him. We are that locked in on our mission for the company and I can't imagine anyone who could support my vision better. I like to do the broad strokes and Ken handles the details. I guide the direction of the company and Ken brings it into reality. Whatever the dynamics, it's the best business relationship I've had and stands the test of time. And so does another important life-long relationship that is about to appear out of nowhere.

SHE SHOWS UP

I am working out of my house and have just finished writing my fourth book, *Film & Video Financing*. I need a photo of myself for the back cover so I ask Suzanne, my secretary, if she knows any photographers. She says she knows a great one and puts me in touch with Geraldine Overton, who is a top photographer at CBS Network and is well known for making celebrities look beautiful.

Sounds perfect! I call her and she quotes me a price. Darn, she's expensive! I try to get her down but she refuses to budge. I like that.

Suzanne is having a birthday party and invites me. She says Geraldine will be there and so I can meet her and discuss the photos I need. Reluctantly I agree to go because I don't really like parties. They are always too loud, with music blasting, and you have to shout to be heard. But I go anyway.

Sure enough, it is loud and crowded and you have to shout to be heard. Suzanne introduces me to Geraldine and it happens. Exactly what, I don't know. She shakes my hand and although she only lets me look into her eyes for a second, there is a powerful sense of recognition. Not only am I instantly aware that I have seen her before, but that we have been together, had many adventures, and knew each other very well a long time ago. I can't believe it. I smile and stammer to myself, "Fantastic! It's you again!" Basically, I am a goner. I spend the rest of the night trying to get close to her, which is a challenge, because there are half a dozen other alpha-male admirers all vying for attention. The pack backs off somewhat, but continues to circle as we sit outside and find a quiet space to talk. She's even got a picture of Blind Lemon Jefferson on her refrigerator! I'm captivated.

I ask her about the photos. She says to call her in a week and we'll set something up. I can't wait that long. I call her the next day. We talk on the phone for hours. A lot of energy is exchanged, causing things to crash around in my kitchen as if poltergeists are having a party. Bang, clank, crash! What's going on? It's nearly dawn. We should hang up. I tell her she can hang up if she wants, but I'm going to stay on the line forever. We still haven't hung up.

THE TEST

We both know from the start this would be a life-long partnership, but nevertheless we test each other. I take her to Bali. She has to love Bali as much as I do. We rent a little bamboo house near Pengosaken. We stop by shaman Ketut Liyer's compound. He does a reading and tells us we'll have a daughter. We visit remote villages and attend gamelan competitions. One pitch-black night walking through a village we are surrounded by a pack of wild dogs nipping at our heels. Geraldine courageously keeps them at bay by flashing her camera in their faces. When the pictures come back they are of the scrawniest, most pathetic looking creatures you've ever seen. Their bark was way bigger than their bite, poor things. We call the series "The Dogs of Bali."

Starting out at the crater's lake at 3 a.m. in the dark, we climb the massive Batur volcano. Just after sunrise, we reach the top. The sun is behind us throwing our shadow, holding hands, onto the clouds below us. Circling our shadow is a brilliant rainbow. It's surely a sign from the gods. She's the one. She passes the test with rainbow colors.

Her test for me is Cornwall. She'd been going there since 1980, drawn by the literary geniuses that she had read extensively. D.H. Lawrence spent a year and a half in Zennor and had written *Women in Love* there. Virginia Woolf wrote *To the Lighthouse* about her childhood in St. Ives. Dylan Thomas had his honeymoon in Mousehole at the Lobster Pot Hotel where, of course, we had to stay. This all went well and I totally loved everything about Cornwall and Geraldine. But I also missed my cue.

Those who know Geraldine know she's very stylish and puts together her own fashion-busting looks before they become trends. So picture this: on the Cornish cliffs she's perfectly composed, back-lit from the sunlight sparkling off white-capped seas below, wearing a Saville Row tweed jacket with a cashmere scarf, flat cap and jodhpurs. Imagine the hero of a romance novel and you'll get the idea. This posing *in situ* occurs daily and of course I take some wonderful photographs of her, but I miss the set up. Dummy! You are supposed to seize the moment, fall to your knees, and pop the question. When I finally do pop the question, we are in our living room in Studio City. We both have the flu and are wearing grey sweat clothes. Very lucky for me she is patient.

Here I am, in my forties, getting a second chance at marriage. I really hadn't expected this to happen. The love gods have been generous.

Our wedding takes place at the Bel Air Hotel, in a beautiful garden in the middle of Beverly Hills. Mom, Dad, and Jeff have flown in from Champaign. Geraldine's mom and aunt are thrilled with everything and have a great time.

We invite about 100 friends. Jane and Larry Reed come down from San Francisco. Larry hangs out with me, more nervous than I am, and Jane helps Geraldine into her Edwardian wedding dress. My Dad walks Geraldine down the garden path to a white gazebo to give her away. A string quartet plays as a dozen hummingbirds magically zigzag around us during the ceremony. The reception is an English tea.

The next morning, finally alone, Geraldine and I enjoy a late breakfast in the terrace restaurant. Ringo Starr sits at the next table by himself.

DIET FOR A NEW AMERICA

The business heads at Los Angeles PBS station KCET have been following my success at Vestron. When they learn I am consulting, they hire me to executive produce a *Lifeguides* series. The series explores social issues and offers positive solutions on adoption, aging, sexual abuse, alcoholism, and the environment. I jump at the opportunity. At last, something meaningful!

Walking the exhibition halls of the American Booksellers Association's (ABA) annual convention, I talk to Stillpoint, the publisher, who had launched the best-selling book *Diet for a New America*, a shocking and sobering account of the great American food machine and the inefficiencies (and health hazards) associated with raising and consuming animals. The power of the book comes in the connections it makes between diet and health and the environment, as well as the moral and ethical values of our diet. Its author, John Robbins, is the heir-apparent to Baskin-Robbins' ice cream dynasty, but he turned his back on the family business because of the health issues raised by consuming too much dairy and animal fat in ice cream. While I never have eaten a great deal of meat, I immediately become a vegan after reading his book. Stillpoint told me that the rights were already sold to cinematographer and socially conscious filmmaker Haskell Wexler. Too late, but that's fine, because Haskell is one of the greatest filmmakers in the country and there's no doubt he'll do the book justice.

A few months later Stillpoint calls and asks if I am still interested. Apparently Haskell had tried to launch it through his contacts at Turner Broadcasting but was rejected because it was too controversial and Turner couldn't find advertisers for the show.

With the approval of my bosses at KCET, I obtain the rights and we go into production. The resulting film reveals the commercial politics behind the so-called four food groups, the raising of cattle and poultry, and health issues that today are common knowledge and widely reported, but in 1991 was information that was still controversial and breaking news.

Right before the show is to be broadcast the station's management team gets a visit from an executive from The Cattlemen's Association, their lawyer, and a "cattleman" (who looks right out of central casting for a Marlboro ad). I am summoned to a meeting with the KCET executives. The Cattlemen say they'd been tracking our progress and although they haven't seen the show they are sure it's biased against them and would hurt their industry. They submit a huge research document that one of their paid consultants has put together refuting everything in the show. They are proud to tell us that it has cost them $50,000 to have it written. We too have done our research and every statement that we make in the film is substantiated by no less than three credible sources. When the Cattlemen's Association's executives see their pleas falling on deaf ears, the gloves come off and they threaten to have thousands of their members call PBS stations during pledge week and block the lines so that much-needed pledges cannot be made.

KCET starts to cave and looks around for a scapegoat. They are angry with me that an "advocacy" show has been produced. "How did this happen?" they ask. It happened because they had approved the project from the get go, they had read copies of the book, they had outlines, scripts, approved budgets, and saw dailies and various rough cuts. Suddenly it was a runaway production that no one knew anything about.

KCET backs down. Usually press kits and screeners are sent to hundreds of TV reviewers before a show goes on national air. This time, KCET doesn't send out any press kits or take out any ads in *TV Guide*. It's damage control. They are going to bury the show, and maybe not air it at all.

Regrettably, PBS can be bullied by corporate interests. Why? Because they are dependent on pledge dollars and corporate contributions. In our case, the health information in our show could have a negative impact on the meat and dairy industries. It's not in the financial interests of these groups to have this information in the public domain, which may cause people to consume less meat and dairy products. And the Cattlemen are flexing their muscles to thwart the word getting out.

This drama continues to escalate for several weeks. I don't know what to do — I am getting a lot of heat from KCET. John Robbins, in the meantime, is fearlessly contacting members of his EarthSave Foundation, which educates people about the powerful effects our food choices have on the environment and our health. They conduct a word-of-mouth campaign about the upcoming broadcast.

I call cinematographer Haskell Wexler and tell him what's happening. He is furious. He says if I want to, we can get his publicist working on it and we could take these threats from the Cattlemen to *The New York Times* and blow the whole thing wide open. He sees a feature article about how powerful lobbies control what we see on PBS, which is suppose to be a publicly owned non-commercial network.

I am conflicted. On one hand we had worked hard on the show, we diligently checked our facts and the truth could potentially affect the health of millions of viewers. I am committed to seeing it broadcast.

But I also have other shows to finish for KCET. If *The New York Times* runs a story, I am afraid of starting a forest fire that can't be put out. There is no telling how far the Cattlemen will go to keep the show from airing. They have deep pockets and aren't going to stop until they get their way. But I too have no intention of backing down.

At the last moment, KCET comes up with a compromise plan. They will broadcast the program but immediately afterwards will provide a half hour interview where experts from the Cattlemen's Association and the National Dairy Board could refute the points made in the show.

The broadcast date arrives. KCET does no promotion for *Diet for a New America*, but it has high ratings in Los Angeles because of the EarthSave campaign. Of the 270 PBS stations that are originally scheduled to show it, only 60 do, and only a few are in the larger markets. The Cattlemen's threat directed to PBS stations nationwide is great enough to scare off 210 stations.

Without the support of KCET, John Robbins launches a massive grass roots campaign and more than 50,000 videos are sold. Two years later the very same points we make in our documentary are echoed in a *TIME* magazine cover story about our food choices and its impact on our health and the environment. Our shocking truth is now common knowledge. Our program did its part in getting these ideas about our diet out into the public forum.

Ironically, *Diet for a New America* receives the Genesis Award for "Best PBS Documentary." There's always something to smile about.

VIGIL

Geraldine and I take a short honeymoon to Ventana and are treated to the most incredible massage at Esalen. Twenty seconds after laying down on the cliffs of Big Sur, we leave our bodies.

When we return home, there is a message from Ken Lee pinned to the front door to "Call home immediately." My mother is very ill. She has cancer. She knew about it before our wedding but had not told us. I fly to Champaign. The cancer has taken the best of her. She is thin, miserable, and anxious. There is a huge portrait of me on a nearby table facing her bed. I sit with her while she slips in and out of dreams. Sometimes she starts a sentence and finishes it twenty minutes later. She tells me about an experience of light. I ask her questions about it and she smiles, "I knew you'd be interested in that!" In the middle of the night she calls out for me. I go into her room. She asks me and Dad to hold her hand, and then tries very hard to die. As I hold her hand I say, "Mom, you have too much life energy, you're not dying."

My mother is the dramatic one in the family. She and Dad met in high school and both went to the University of Illinois. They'd both been engaged to other people when they decided to break it off and get married to each other. Dad studied law and received a degree but never practiced. He played trumpet in big bands. Mom studied drama and was in some college productions. She was the rebellious one in the Kuhn family and was always challenging the Victorian principles her mother had tried so hard to instill. A few months earlier, while I was filming an oral history with her, she showed me newspaper clippings about a fraternity house ruckus in which she featured prominently. Women were not allowed in the fraternity house, but someone saw my mother go inside and called the police. When the police arrived they found thirty fraternity brothers having a massive snowball fight on the front lawn and in the confusion my mother, dressed in men's clothing, jumped out of the window and slipped away. What a rascal. She was quite proud telling this story.

A few days later, we check Mom into a hospital. I have to return to California to meet a production deadline. Before I say goodbye she says be sure to come back for Dad's 75th birthday. I say I will. I really didn't expect that she would die a few days later. Geraldine and I return to Champaign for the funeral. The Wiese family is down to Dad, Jeff, and me. As the last person leaves the house after the funeral reception, Dad sits Geraldine and me down in the family room and tells us he also has cancer. This is a tremendous blow.

We immediately invite Dad to join us on our upcoming trip to Cologne where I have been invited by the Cologne Film Festival to lead a three-day film marketing symposium. Geraldine and I fly to Frankfurt and meet him in Kitzbuhel. Together we take a train to Cologne. I bring a dozen experts from the U.S. and Europe for the conference. A huge Nuremberg-style vertical banner hangs behind the raised stage where we are to sit. Five hundred people are expected to attend. Dad tags along. At the reception dinner the night before the event, Dad says, "I'm concerned about your translator." I ask him why and he says, "When I asked her how many people are expected to attend she says, 'Oh, about five million.'" Dad, are you winding me up, again?

After the event is over I am looking around the huge ballroom for Dad. I spot him behind the stage instructing a stagehand how to roll up the huge twelve-foot-high banner that reads "FILM MARKETING WITH MICHAEL

WIESE." I say "Dad, you're not going to drag that thing home are you?" He says, "Damn right I am." And he did, like a medieval pageant through the streets of Cologne. He was very proud of me.

A LITTLE THING

Geraldine and I are having the most wonderful life. We are perfectly suited for each other and share many interests. We love traveling, reading, and listening to music. We make our home an oasis of beauty.

Geraldine is a voracious reader and can easily read a book every couple of days, sometimes several at once. I am much slower as my time is spent with the book business, reading submissions, and working on my films. Three quarters of the books on our shelves represent Geraldine's interests, ranging from ancient history, sacred texts, mythology, early Christianity, English literature (especially D.H. Lawrence and Virginia Woolf) and much, much more. Some categories in my section are Bali, Japan, Tibet, shamanism, Buddhism, Zen, Hinduism, consciousness, Bucky Fuller, painting and drawing, writing, film. But regardless of whose shelf a book is on, we each introduce the other to new interests.

The backyard garden is filled with sweet-smelling fruit trees and flowers: orange, lemon, apricot, plum, honeysuckle, and wisteria. It's a paradise in the middle of L.A.

One day Geraldine and I ask each other if there could possibly be anything more, since our hearts and lives are so full. We say, well, maybe there is one tiny corner to be filled. But that corner was not so tiny after all.

In October 1992, our daughter Julia Bronwyn Wiese is born. Of course I film the birth. The room fills with an extraordinary holy light. A sparkling energy is tangible. It envelops us all. From that moment on, everything changes. The world appears as a sacred place filled with miracles.

I imagine that all parents go through a huge transformation when their children are born. We are attentive to Julia's every need. We are conscious of her all the time. I work at home, so I can be nearby. If we are going to raise a child I am not going to miss a second of it. I am 45. A bit old to start a family? Will I have the energy? Let's see, I'll be 65 when she's 20. I'll probably just make it.

One night as I hold Julia, I am overcome with the huge responsibility bestowed on me to raise a human being. I feel completely overwhelmed and incapable. But I would have to rise to the occasion and draw on every resource within me. This baby does not come with an instruction manual. How does anyone really know what is the best thing to do? I pray and trust that in every moment I will be conscious enough to protect and care for baby Julia.

WHAT OUR CHILDREN EAT

I become more passionate about finding out how to best raise Julia. My focus is still on food. I feel that what we eat is one of the most important choices we make in our lives and most people are blind to the healing (or destructive) power of food. I have other shows about this that I want to make.

One, in particular, has an attention-grabbing title: *What Your Children Are Eating Is Killing Them and What You Can Do About It*. I try but get nowhere with KCET, so through pediatrician and vegetarian diet advocate Dr. Jay Gordon I get a meeting with Jeff Sagansky, who is head of CBS programming. (Jay is his family's pediatrician. Fun fact #2: If you want to get to someone and don't know their carpenter, there's always their pediatrician.)

I take friend and producer Deke Simon to the meeting. We rehearse our pitch. I am to do the overview and Deke will do the details. I start the pitch. Jeff interrupts, "Love it. We'll do it. Important show. How much?" I am shocked and stammer, "Oh about $350 thousand..." "...to $500 thousand," Deke pipes in. We are accustomed to PBS and not commercial network TV budgets. These three words are the only thing Deke says the whole meeting. We can't believe it as we ride down in the elevator. CBS said "Yes"!

In a follow-up meeting with Sagansky's lieutenant, whose nickname is "Dr. No," we are told we can't produce it since we haven't produced anything before for CBS. We will have to get an executive producer that CBS approves. After a few weeks of meeting with other producers (thus raising the budget to $1.1 million) we go back to CBS. The project is then sent to the CBS sales group, who takes it to their commercial sponsors to see if they can pre-sell ads. Would cereal, candy, and fast food manufacturers want to sponsor this show? I don't think so, as these are the very products that are turning our kids into Michelin tire men. The word comes back that the show — as worthy as it is — is unsellable.

Never give up. As is my way, I look for an end run. Edison never failed, he successfully found 10,000 ways that did not work. Let's see... The networks won't show it, PBS won't run it. I know, I'll buy the TV time! Fortuitously, and as a result of *Diet for a New America*, Rick Cesari, who runs a successful info-mercial company in Seattle, contacts me. They have just earned $70 million with "The Juiceman" and are looking for other worthy health products to market via infomercials. We come up with the idea to take a "body of knowledge" — in this case vegetarian lifestyle — and slice it up in media products (instructional videos, audios, and books).

The first infomercial I produce is based on the work of Dr. John MacDougall, who gets amazing restorative results using healthy diets to treat very ill people. He is great to work with and his patients are remarkable. The infomercial is a hit, earning $5 million in revenues. I am suddenly an infomercial producer. Now while I hate infomercials, I see that I could at last produce the kind of content I want and use broadcast media to disburse valuable and affordable health information. Deke Simon and I produce several other programs that center on vegetarian lifestyles, such as *Good Food Today, Great Kids Tomorrow* with L.A. pediatrician Dr. Jay Gordon.

The lesson here, which I frequently have to remind myself, is not to get stuck in the form. If I can't do a film, why not a PBS show? If not that, an infomercial or a video or a book? All forms are delivery systems. They all require program development, production, distribution, and marketing. By now I have had experience in many media formats and platforms. Why not slice and dice your body of knowledge into many forms, each with its own revenue stream?

KNOXVILLE

For many years The American Film Institute has been sending me around the country to give seminars on the business of independent filmmaking. One weekend I travel to Knoxville, Tennessee. Dad drives down from Champaign. He agrees to meet my plane at the airport. My small commuter plane hits turbulence, so I get off the plane very green. My only desire is to hurry to the washroom, maybe throw up and wash my face. Dad has made other plans.

When I walk into the terminal there are five Dolly Parton look-alikes in fringed cowgirl outfits singing an out-of-tune "Welcome Michael" song. (Turns out Dolly has a dinner theatre nearby in Dollywood, and these are die-hard fans). I just want to get by them, but there are ten gigantic breasts blocking my path. I have to wait it out until they end their jubilant song. Behind them I can see Dad grinning ear to ear, really enjoying himself. It's obvious who has put them up to this. I point to him and mouth the words, "I'll get you for this."

Right before the lunch break at the seminar I tell the hundred or so filmmakers in the room, "You know, there are people all around you who are interested in financing independent films. In fact, there is a banker here who you should talk to at the break," pointing out the white-haired gentleman trying to slip out the door. A few minutes later I see Dad surrounded by a half dozen filmmakers who've cornered him in the parking lot. Gotcha!

ONE-MONTH BIRTHDAY

I stand in our backyard and light the torches. There's a full moon barely visible through the lemon trees; their scent permeates the air. Tonight is special.

It's Julia's one-month birthday. She wears a tiny white dress. In Bali they'd have a shadow play to celebrate her one-month birthday, and so that is exactly what we are doing. One hundred friends soon fill the backyard.

As synchronicity would have it, Wayan Wija, Bali's most popular *dalang*, or shadow puppet master, is passing through Los Angeles. Last night he performed at UCLA and tomorrow he goes to Hawaii for another performance before going back to Bali. When I learned that he'd be in Los Angeles, I asked Wija if he'd perform for Julia's birthday. He tells the best stories, makes the best jokes and fight scenes. A small gamelan group accompanies him. My Bali traveling buddy, Larry Reed, assists him with the puppets. A large oil lamp is suspended above Wija's head. He will move the puppets to create flickering shadows on the screen. Right now he is arranging the puppets; some good and noble, others greedy and demonic.

Geraldine brings Julia into the backyard and is quickly surrounded by admiring friends. I am very nervous. Some of the most fascinating people I know fill the backyard. Children monopolize the front row nearest the shadow side of the screen; their young faces illuminated by the blazing oil lamp on the other side. The dalang has already said his mantras evoking the spirits, and he has entered a light trance.

It's a magical performance and has something primal about it that my Hollywood filmmaking friends have never seen before and have never forgotten — an original movie — a shadow play. They still talk about it.

For me, it's an extraordinary evening. For just one moment my worlds have come together: Geraldine, Julia, and my best friends, all sharing something special from Bali.

Geraldine and I often marvel at the good fortune we have in our lives. We try to understand why we have this. We put it down to our appreciating it and being grateful for what we have.

Our life together is like a weave of many colors. Our stories merge and come together in powerful moments — each of us on our own life's journey. Geraldine and Julia also have as many extraordinary stories to tell of their lives — some include me and some do not. Life is like that for everyone. We can appreciate the crossings of our moments, and those of family are the strongest.

YOU HAVE TO TELL THE SPIRITS

Julia joins us on the first of her many trips to Bali. We rent a compound in Sanur near the beach. I make day trips to see my friends in Ubud, but we are careful to keep Julia in areas which we know are malaria-free. We visit a *balian*, a

Balinese healer, who tells us that Julia is sleeping poorly because we haven't told the spirits of the house who we are, what we are doing there, or how long we will be staying. A few days later we arrange a ceremony, make offerings, and tell the spirits. Julia goes into the temple and even at the age of twenty-two months seems to have innate knowledge as she repeats the prayers and lights the incense like someone well beyond her years.

THE MERRY MAIDENS

With Mom gone and my promise to look after Dad, we spend more time with him. In 1993, Dad joins us for a week in Cornwall. We rent a cottage near Gurnard's Head in Zennor from the Landmark Trust, where Julia celebrates her one-year birthday. Horses in the field outside peer through the window as she sucks spaghetti for the first time. We walk the coastal paths and Geraldine and I take turns carrying Julia in a backpack.

We visit the ancient sacred sites near Lamorna, such as the Merry Maidens. This is a circle of nineteen standing stones. Their use has been forgotten, but modern day Druids use the site for solstice ceremonies. For good luck, Granddad carries Julia around the circle, holding an intention in his mind as he touches every stone. Years later we set up our home just minutes away from the Merry Maidens. We like to think that Granddad had something to do with our good fortune; that he was guiding us somehow, maybe wishing us to this place as he walked around the circle. Cornwall is a mystical place.

One evening at dusk, Geraldine and I are pushing Julia in her stroller along the single-lane country road that winds from our cottage to the Gurnard's Head Hotel. To our left is a low stone wall. There is a single standing stone in the middle of the field. Suddenly, a huge black stallion appears out of nowhere and gallops along next to us, tearing along, just on the other side of the wall, nostrils flaring, its mane and tail flying. It gallops beside us for some time. When we get to Gurnard's Head we realize this cannot have happened. The horse was in full gallop and we were walking slowly, pushing a baby in a stroller.

STUDIO CITY

Back in Los Angeles, it's a magical time with Julia. Small simple things fill me with joy. She's up every day bright and early with that, "What we gonna do today?" look on her face, ready for whatever the day has to offer. She crawls through the grassy backyard into her castle under the plum trees. Sometimes she comes into my office and tells me it's time for tea. She takes her first pony ride at the Renaissance Faire. It's all we can do to get her to come home.

We live in Studio City in the San Fernando Valley, and although I have several offers of "free" office space with various production companies around the Los Angeles area, I know that "free" really means "Come on down and when we need to pick your brain for something you'll be available." Plus, I just don't see the point of driving 45 minutes through heavy traffic twice a day. I'll have an extra two hours a day if I just stay home. Anyway, I want to be a full-time dad for Julia. What's the sense of having kids if you are away from dawn to dusk? I design my work life around my family life.

I hire John Carpenter (great name for a carpenter) who builds an office above and around the existing garage. Ken Lee and Michele Chong have the top floor office and I am on the bottom. French doors open out into the small garden and in waft fragrances from orange, plum, lemon, grapefruit, and apricot trees. Some days Julia fills her wading pool with a hose draped through the tree like a jungle snake, providing a mini-waterfall. Some days she swings or plays in her castle. Or we walk to a near-by park, or lunch at one of the restaurants on Ventura Blvd. In the afternoon I ride my bike to the gym or up Laurel Canyon to Mulholland Drive and back. Life is sweet.

One day at the gym I am plugging away on the exercise cycle when Ron Deutsch, a screenwriter next to me, tells me about a memo that is making the rounds at Disney. As I learn later, it was deliberately left in a Xerox machine so that people would "discover" it. It was a memo written by Chris Vogler regarding his method of applying Joseph Campbell's "Hero's Journey" story paradigm to screenplays. I was immediately struck by the validity of the idea, met with Vogler and suggested he write a book. The result was *The Writer's Journey*, which has been one of our best sellers over the last 20 years and continues to sell well today.

This came about from an intuitive impulse. It was an intoxicating rush. I was starting to get a sense and deep knowing about what I was put here to do.

This reorganization of my priorities, lifestyle first, business second, did not come about overnight. In Connecticut, New York, and earlier in San Francisco, I put work first. Now I am seeking balance and will not allow myself to be dominated by the business. While most of my colleagues and fellow executives at Vestron go back into high-powered corporate and studio jobs, and still work sixty hours a week, I am very happy with a low-overhead office above a garage in our back-yard, a small staff, and a few projects. Remember, with a low overhead you don't have to do things just for the money.

The same is true for Geraldine. She leaves her CBS job after seventeen years as a celebrated photographer to be a full-time mom. This is a huge decision for a fiercely independent woman who is at the top of her game. Being with Julia full-time is clearly more important to us. We have been blessed to do it this way. This is how our life as a family began.

SHAKE RATTLE AND ROLL

One night I pack my suitcase and put it by the front door. I have an early morning flight to London. My book, *Film & Video Financing*, and Christopher Vogler's *The Writer's Journey* are short-listed for the prestigious Kraszna-Krausz book awards that are to be held in London in a few days. Lucky thing about that suitcase, because that night — January 17, 1994, at 4:30 a.m. — there is a 6.7 Richter scale earthquake in Northridge, a few miles from our house.

I wake up screaming and running down the hall. It sounds like a train is thundering through the house. The walls wobble and actually twist. Julia, fifteen months old, is standing up in her crib not sure what the fuss is about. Geraldine picks her up and we make our way in the dark over a mountain of fallen books, flowers, flower vases, lamps, everything. (It could have been much worse, but a week earlier we had earthquake-proofed our huge bookcases). I grab the suitcase and get dressed in the street.

Car alarms are going off, fires have broken out, and people are running about in their nightclothes. Some houses and apartment buildings in the neighborhood are reduced to rubble. Needless to say, I didn't make it to London for the book awards. When dawn comes, we go back into the house. It's in shambles. All the contents of the kitchen are in other rooms — a mixture of broken glass, honey, rice, and cooking utensils. A kitchen knife is stuck in the wall behind the refrigerator! The house has been jolted off its foundation. We sustain thousands of dollars in damage. I say then and there, "We're outta here."

But getting out of Los Angeles is not so easy. We have several things keeping us here. My Dad and brother are in Illinois and Geraldine's mom lives an hour or so away, near Long Beach. I have a fledgling business in L.A. And where would we move for a better quality of life? We knew we didn't like the L.A air, the traffic congestion, the noise, the sheer ugliness of a city with its mishmash of billboards anywhere and everywhere, the drug dealers that use our street and the proximity of a nearby freeway ramp (for a quick getaway), drive-by shootings, a holdup at a nearby bank, and race riots. Shall I go on? This isn't where we want to raise our daughter. Sure, we have a small but very beautiful backyard and garden, but eventually you have to go to the grocery store. I am not really into the Hollywood scene, regardless of how it may appear. I am "in it" but not "of it." I don't go to parties (except that one where I met Geraldine), and I am not interested in most Hollywood movies. Then what are we doing here, really?

For several summers after my mother died, Geraldine, Julia, and I go to Champaign. For me, now living in L.A., going back to Illinois is like going back in a time machine. We stay in the house with Dad. We join him for lunch to sip tomato soup in the family room. Jeff comes by after his construction job. He plays catch with Julia and helps her tie her shoes. He loves her and dotes on her. We pick and roast Illinois "super sweet" corn straight from a farmer's field. Julia decorates her bike with red, white, and blue crepe paper and then rides it, with trainer wheels and all, in a Fourth of July parade. She attends Big Chief Al's Indian Day Camp (just like I did), and jumps off the high dive at the Country Club, which she calls the "crunchy club." Geraldine takes ancient Greek at the University of Illinois. We go to every small country fair we can find so that Julia can go on the kiddie rides. She is especially fond of the small dragon roller coaster. Jeff has a birthday. We hang a piñata which Julia, not Jeff, manages to bash open for a shower of candies. Family life is great.

One morning, Geraldine and I take a walk with Dad. When we get about three blocks from our house, Dad finds a dime stuck in the tar in the road. Try as he might, he can't get it out. He walks back to the house, gets his pen knife and returns to retrieve his treasure.

As a lark, I organize a low-budget digital feature with U. of I. drama teacher Rick Barrows and his graduate students. We shoot in Champaign and Urbana and the cornfields. Julia, now five, joins in the filming. We put her in charge of the fake blood. She puts more on herself than the actors. Jeff helps out by driving his truck. Life is simple, fun, and what little family I have is still in Champaign. Geraldine and I go so far as to look at houses to buy, thinking Champaign would be a great town in which to raise Julia. The Midwest town seems safe and comforting, but I suppose the truth is there really is no going back home.

With Mom's passing, Dad's personality changes, or perhaps sides of him that I'd never seen start to emerge. He no longer has to be the person that he was around my mother. Like many men of his WWII generation, he is duty driven, very loyal, with a strong sense of personal integrity. All that is still present in his character, as is his great sense of humor, but now he does only what he wants without regard for social norms. "Michael, it's a free country," he declares, "I'm gonna do what I goddamn feel like doing." This new lease on life must be very freeing for him. He confides to me that he had worked in a job that he hated for thirty years. He loved my grandfather and so accepted his request to work for him "temporarily," and in doing so set aside his own passions to practice law and play music. I now understood why, when I tell him one wacko idea after another of what I wanted to do at various times in my life, he wouldn't judge, but just ask, "Michael, does it make you happy?" That was his criteria. As Joseph Campbell was fond of saying, "Follow your bliss." I always thought that Dad's measure of life's purpose was some kind of cliché, when in fact he meant it deeply as it was something he was never able to pursue for himself. But now, goddam it, he's going for it!

Now he surprises us by telling us that he has a "girlfriend." Like a smitten teen-ager, he stealthily drives us by her house but doesn't slow down or stop. When we finally meet her, we discover she is the polar opposite of my mother. My mother was always well-dressed, coiffed, tidy, cared about appearances and social standing. Dad met his girlfriend, Dorothea, on a bus ride to Branson (home of the country music stars). A real fireball, she drives a truck, rarely wears dresses, and is deeply involved with the University. Her devil-may-care attitude matches his own and they have a lot of fun together. Dad stops socializing with many of his old crowd of friends that he shared with my mother and takes Dorothea on cross-country excursions, driving from Champaign to Florida, where he has a condo.

CASHING IN

One day Geraldine gets a call from Dad. He is in Florida with Dorothea. He's in trouble. He'd had radiation for prostate cancer and it has caused bleeding. The doctors in Florida refuse to give him any more blood transfusions because it's wasteful and leaks out. There is nothing more the doctors can do for him. So he and Dorothea drive back to Champaign. I tell him I am on my way. He tells me adamantly that if he needs me he will call me and not to come. Geraldine, Julia, and I go anyway. When I see him he is pencil thin and weak, skin and bones. When I hug him I hide my tears. After a few days in the hospital and more blood transfusions, the Champaign doctors also say they can't do any more and will stop the transfusions. He is told he will be moved into hospice. He thinks hospice means he will be going to another hospital. When they explain it to him, he says, "Oh... well, I guess it's time to cash in my chips."

I sit with him for a couple of days. Julia has just learned the alphabet, which she dances, making every letter by angling her tiny body, arms and legs. She's so beautiful, a ray of light in a dark hospital room. Granddad smiles, applauds weakly, and falls back to sleep.

Geraldine and I bathe him, give him ice to suck to keep him from getting dehy-drated, and watch as his body discolors, indicating the imminent. Except for brief meal breaks, we wait. He breathes slowly, letting himself go. He struggles ever so slightly and adjusts to a new inner reality with each breath. I am caught between two very different states of being: not wanting him to die, and wanting it to happen fast because it's so painful to watch him slipping away. But I realize this isn't about me and that if I just hold the space for him, not wanting anything, I will be of more service to him. I do just that.

It's strange what comes to you in these moments... I remember when Dad would go on vacations, he would always return with a small stone on which he would write where it was from. After a while, he had an extensive collection of these souvenir stones lined up on a bookshelf in the family room. "Barcelona," "Paris," "Fort Lauderdale," "Miami," "Yokohama"... Maybe he did this to save money, or as his own private joke, or because he just liked doing it. I'll never know. Maybe he just wanted to have a piece of the earth to take with him.

When Geraldine and I arrive at my aunt's house where we have arranged for Julia to spend the night, we discover that Dad had died just as we left the hospital.

He looks elegant; parchment skin, like an Egyptian pharaoh. I touch his face and say goodbye. My brother Jeff arrives. He is mortified to see me touching Dad.

We arrange a New Orleans style "second line" jazz band for his memorial service celebration. Like some kind of musical snake, the swinging and sassy band sweeps the congregation outside and into the parking lot. My trumpet-playing Dad is surely looking down on us and smiling. Love ya, Dad!

Enjoying
Cornwall

1988  *2006*

"Think contentment the greatest wealth."

— George Shelley

. . . .

The Cove at St. Loy, Cornwall. Geraldine Overton

FIRST YEAR IN CORNWALL

The most amazing thing I've witnessed in our marriage is that when our intention is aligned it feels as if we can do anything. We created a wonderful home and life of travel. We started a family and embarked on another new adventure, one that would fulfill many dreams together. Intention is that powerful.

When we met, Geraldine and I agreed that each year we would alternate holidays in Cornwall and Bali. This year it's Paris, London, Cornwall, and Wales.

Julia loves London. Why wouldn't she? Geraldine dresses her in the most charming little outfits: pilot jackets, berets, suspenders, and colorful wellies. She gets her face painted as a lion in the London Zoo. She waves a flag as warplanes fly overhead on the 50th Anniversary of D-Day. The Queen watches from her balcony.

In the Welsh countryside we rent horses and ride through the moors. Julia is by far the best rider as she can get her horse to keep moving while ours stop to eat the flowers in the hedgerows. Every day there is something great for her to do, whether it's running through the fields, walking the coastal footpaths, or discovering secret beach coves. One night she joins in a barn dance that is kind of like an American square dance. She's the youngest one there and loves every do-see-do.

Back in Studio City, Julia enters kindergarten at the Roscomare Road Elementary School. Geraldine chauffeurs her in a little red Miata and makes up stories inspired by the rise and fall of classical music playing on the radio. A few years later these stories come true, but I am getting ahead of myself.

Ever since the earthquake, the overcrowding, the traffic jams and pollution, we have been trying to leave L.A. We visit and consider the San Juan Islands, Seattle, Bolinas, Santa Fe, Taos, Champaign, and even Bali, but decide Bali is too politically unstable at the time. None of these places are quite right for us.

Back in Studio City, Geraldine and I sit in our library and look out into the tiny garden. "Now that Granddad is gone, we could live in that little stone cottage in Cornwall!" we muse. "Yes, we actually could!"

By the afternoon, using an old ad from a saved issue of Geraldine's English magazine, *Lady*, I phone the owner of D.H. Lawrence's cottage in Zennor, Cornwall
(the number is still good!). I book two weeks. By June, we are in the cottage.
Geraldine loves it. This is the cottage where, during WWI, Lawrence and Frieda
were discovered singing German folk songs by the spying Cornish and conse-
quently kicked out of Cornwall!

From the kitchen window, Geraldine looks out over the fields stretching to the
ocean cliffs. Julia and I kick a red soccer ball around the field, or all three of us
walk the short mile or so to Zennor, taking the "coffin path" through the fields.
Horses and cows take a great interest and follow Julia. She has something of that
"horse whisperer" thing going.

We spend several months staying a week or two here and there all over Penwith
peninsula in Cornwall to get the lay of the land.

Cornwall is about five hours from London by train and is at the most south-west-
erly tip of Great Britain. On the north and west is the Celtic sea and Ireland, to
the south the English Channel and France and Spain. If you sail Southwest, like
the pilgrims from Plymouth (which is on the border of Cornwall and Devon),
you pass the Scilly Isles and eventually arrive in New England.

We love it because it's blustery, elemental, and very powerful, with granite cliffs
above crashing seas, somewhat like California's Big Sur. It was first inhabited in
Palaeolithic times. The stone walls dividing the fields are 5,000 years old and
are the oldest megalithic structures still in use. Cornwall, like Wales, Ireland,
and Brittany, is one of the Celtic nations. The Cornish are resourceful in the
most difficult of times, and are quite proud of their cultural heritage. Until the
1990s, tin mining was a major industry in Cornwall, but now all the mines are
closed and abandoned leaving stark silhouetted reminders of a more prosperous
time. There is a fishing community in Newlyn (near Penzance), but that is now
diminished due to foreign competition and restrictive quotas. Cornwall is one
of the most beautiful, but poorest, counties in the United Kingdom, with high
unemployment and a dependence on tourism.

We love the unbelievable natural beauty inhabited by an unpretentious and fiercely independent people. We want to expose five-year-old Julia to a different environment from the mini-malls in Hollywood, so we take her to performances of male voice choirs, barn dances, hay gathering, picnics on the cliffs, swims off hidden beaches, local fetes, and have a most magical time.

By the end of August, and with first grade approaching for Julia back in the States, we have to decide whether to extend our time in Cornwall, perhaps as long as a year, or hurry her back to Los Angeles for school.

We contact our previous landlady and she agrees that we can stay another year at D.H. Lawrence's cottage until the August 1999 total solar eclipse, at which time she wants to rent the cottage to tourists who are expected to flock to Cornwall and pay outrageous rents for this once-in-a-lifetime viewing. Cornwall is the first place on the planet where you can see this eclipse.

We enroll Julia in the delightful Bolitho School in Penzance, which is a quintessential English school, set in a huge old house, with a headmaster, uniforms and all.

Meanwhile, I let Ken Lee know that for at least a few months more, we will stay in Cornwall and try things out. My "office" is a red phone booth off the Zennor road. The length of my meetings is determined by the number of pound coins I have in my pockets. We are now primarily publishing filmmaking and screenwriting books. We are releasing about seven books per year and have a dozen in development. *The Writer's Journey, Film Directing Shot by Shot, Directing Actors*, and my *Independent Film and Videomaker's Guide* were all recently published and are on their way to becoming bestsellers for the company. Ken is developing the foreign sales market and occasionally a German or French publisher will buy the foreign translation rights to one of our titles. After our "meeting," I walk or cycle the mile back to the cottage down a one-lane dirt road.

Cornwall is terrific. The people are not immediately open to us, but over time we make many friends among the locals and the "up country" parents among Julia's school friends. I start organizing, teaching, and working with the burgeoning community of filmmakers. We live on Penwith peninsula, which juts out into the Atlantic. The weather is very changeable and a powerful warm Gulf Stream makes for extraordinary light in the clouds. It's this light that has given rise to the painting communities of Newlyn, Lamorna, and St. Ives (which boasts a Tate Museum).

I want to improve my storyboard skills and for five years I take life-drawing classes from painter Colin Scott. While it does little for my storyboarding, it does teach me to look very deeply and honestly portray what I see. Drawing becomes a meditation that I look forward to once or twice a week. Out of hundreds of drawings, only a handful are any good. As I discover, drawing is about process, not result.

During our first year in Cornwall we become friends with Mark and Marga Thomas, the proprietors of a small literary bookshop near Penzance quay. We share and exchange books every time we meet. They live in Gurnard's Head, and during hot summer days Julia, Mark, and I swim in the chilly waters off the rocks while Marga and Geraldine talk about great literature.

Geraldine's mom, Gerrye, visits us often from California and sees Julia's performance as the Angel Gabriel in the Bolitho School Christmas play. Grammy also gets to see Julia ride her bike for the first time without trainer wheels. Ken Lee, who is used to traveling to big international cities, visits. When he sees our small hamlet, not even a village, he exclaims, "That's Zennor?" Greg White, my old typing friend and band mate from Uni High also visits. We go late to a Cornish party where most people are already drunk. A woman I know from art class comes up. I introduce Greg as "one of my oldest and dearest friends." She squints at him and slurs, "But he's black!" Greg smiles warmly, "It happens."

Julia and I like to throw the Frisbee in the field behind our cottage. Sometimes, in the late afternoon, when it's breezy and getting dark, we like to scare ourselves by exploring the old ruins of a chapel with most of its roof caved in. There is ivy growing all over it. We hold each other's hand as we creep silently inside, trying not to wake up the ghosts.

BROTHER JEFF

I receive a long-distance call from my cousin, Bill Youngerman, who is a doctor in Champaign. My brother has had another stroke and things are not looking good. I immediately fly to Champaign. I find him in a critical care unit. His big body is hooked up to life support machines. He is completely paralyzed except for his eyes. The nurse describes him as being "locked in." She claims she can communicate with him by having him blink once for "yes" and twice for "no." For several days, I try this but don't find I can get any consistent response. Sometimes I think maybe he is responding. Other times he twitches or grimaces, but I can't tell if it's in response to my question or not. Probably not. I ask him if he's in pain and he just looks through me, or out into space. His eyes do not follow things in the room.

After a week, some other doctors come to see me. They say they can't keep him on machines forever. Jeff has developed serious infections that the doctors are fighting with intravenous drugs. Being next of kin, they want me to authorize discontinuing the life support. Bill and I discuss this. Bill feels he should be kept alive as long as possible, as we can't be sure of whether he is conscious or not. I sit with Jeff. I have, but don't want, the responsibility to decide on the continuation of my brother's life. I try to sense with all my heart if he's really there. I can't tell. I move the chair as close to him as I can. Calmly I tell him the situation he's in. I ask him if he is aware of this. I ask him if he wants us to pull the plug. He looks at me. Are his eyes tearing up more than usual or is it my eyes that are watering?

I give the doctors the okay to stop the machines. I sit with Jeff and hold his bloated, immobile hand. I tell him what a kind and generous brother he's always been. I tell him I am very sorry it turned out this way. Unable to bear it any longer, I say goodbye. I walk to the door. I turn around. He's still looking straight ahead, unable to move, the same position as always. I pray I am doing the right thing. I return to Cornwall. Why couldn't I sit with him until the end?

A few weeks later there is a memorial service for Jeff. Geraldine, Julia, and I fly to Champaign. He had a lot of friends, mostly from his construction jobs, who show up to honor him. Many kind things are said about him. Ever since he was young, Jeff had a hard time of it, as if a black cloud followed him. Something he could not shake. He was intelligent, but success in school, work, or relationships did not come to him. He was the one who stayed at home in Champaign while I charged around the world. We couldn't have been more dissimilar. When I go to clean out his apartment I discover an altar of cards, photos, and crayon drawings that Julia had given him. He adored her. Another altar displays my film posters, newspaper clippings, and photos of us together that he has saved from many years ago. I sit and remember....

PERMANENT RESIDENCE

After a year or so, we decide to live permanently in Cornwall and begin to look for a cottage to buy. At first we look on the north side of Penwith near Zennor, where it's primal and blustery. Trees grow sideways because of the gale-force winds, and sometimes at night it gets so foggy you can't see a foot in front of you.

Every so often I go back to the States to present seminars. I go to Dallas, where I give a filmmaking seminar for Kodak. We stage the seminar in a cowboy saloon in a ghost town. I present several other seminars in Madison Wisconsin for ITVA, Toronto for the Canadian Film Board, Washington, D.C., for Kodak (my largest audience yet at 250) and do several book signings at Barnes & Noble for the revised edition of my book *The Independent Film and Videomaker's Guide*. After nearly four weeks on the road, I want more than anything to return to the peace and quiet of Cornwall. When I return, Geraldine, her mom Gerrye, Julia, and I go to the little village of Mousehole for the lighting of the Christmas lights, which are strung out across many of the tiny boats in the little harbor. A magical event for children of all ages.

People seem to be fascinated that we moved to Cornwall. They can't imagine how we did it. I tell them that it didn't happen all at once. There were all kinds of logistical hoops to jump through to obtain a permanent residence visa, set up bank accounts, and even to get a phone. (You can't get a phone without a bank account, and you can't get a bank account without a residence, and you can't get a residence without a bank account — you get the idea.) The authorities also require financial statements to prove that we wouldn't go on the dole or become a burden on the public benefit system. They also don't want my work to take a job from an Englishman. Fortunately, I have the book business in the States that I can run from Cornwall.

Our search for a cottage continues, but we find nothing available on the North Coast. We drive a short 30 minutes over the moors to the South coast to look at a cottage in St. Loy that is described like this by the estate agent: "If the connoisseur's Cornwall is West Penwith, then the connoisseur's West Penwith is St. Loy." We park our car at a dairy farm and walk down a dirt lane marked "private" until it comes to the ocean. Then we follow the estate agent's map, which leads us 500 feet up a driveway through a dense forest to a cottage nestled in a small valley overlooking the ocean. Before we even see the cottage, it feels right. Geraldine says, "Let's put in an offer!" Even though it's January and there's nothing in bloom, there is something about this small valley, the smell in the air, the feel of the place.

The cottage is no great shakes. Actually, it's in dreadful condition. The water comes from a dilapidated reservoir that belongs to a man who lives up the hill in the manor house. He hasn't fixed the reservoir in years and doesn't plan to. When you turn on the water tap, all kinds of creatures come through the pipes, including newts.

So we decide to drill a borehole, but first we have to find water. A dowser comes out and walks the property with two metal rods looking for water. Geraldine gives it a go and the rods indicate a possible underwater stream under our driveway. The dowser confirms this. We contract with a drilling company who spends three days and as many drill bits drilling through layers of dense granite before locating an underground stream. A pump at the top of the borehole brings water to a large holding tank behind the house. The water then goes through several media filters and a UV light before being pumped into the house. Water and waste leaving the house go through another purification system to become pure water before entering the stream which runs through the garden and then into the ocean a few hundred yards later.

The cottage is dark because the Cornish don't value views. They value warmth, small windows, and protection from the blustery winter winds. We have 2.5 acres of land that is overgrown with weeds and an untended forest. Basically it's a mess.

We buy the cottage in January. Geraldine supervises the remodelling of each room. We equip the kitchen with an Aga, a Swedish stove that will cook your food, heat your water, and warm your house. It is the heart of the home. We tear some of the wallpaper and plaster, back to the original 200-year-old walls, and render everything, leaving some of the granite rocks showing around the windows. We lay down slate floor titles.

The cottage at St. Loy is very small for the three of us, with only four rooms: two small bedrooms, small kitchen, and small sitting room. I need an office, so we build an 8' x 10' wooden shed behind the cottage. In the beginning, I don't have anything but dial-up Internet. Reluctantly, I invest a small fortune on a huge satellite dish. The dish gives me a blazing speed of 2K for downloads when there is no rain, winds, or solar flares. After a year the company goes out of business and I have to pay someone to lug what looks like a crashed space vehicle to the dump. Even today we only have 2K broadband speeds because we live remotely and it's not cost-effective for the communication providers to deliver high speeds to a sparse rural population. Ironically, the trans-Atlantic fiber-optic cable carrying much of Europe's data to the States is buried just a mile away under our country road at the top of our lane. (And yes, I've thought about sneaking out under the cover of darkness, digging a hole and tapping in.)

Sheds are a cheap way to extend our space. We build one for Julia, where she can play with her friends, and one for Geraldine, where she strings necklaces with antique beads that we have collected from Tibet, Bali, Peru, and India. More recently we built another shed that is a tea and meditation room. It sits at the edge of the forest, facing the sunrise, and has a view down to the ocean and a point that jags out into the English Channel. When the weather is poor I go there to meditate and Geraldine uses it as a reading room.

Julia's room is too small for a bed, so we have a local craftsman build a beautiful bed where the closet had been. It looks like an antique sleeper berth on the Orient Express. She is tucked away safe and comfy. At the foot of the bed are Julia's books that we read to her before she goes to sleep.

By August most of the remodelling is done. The day before the total solar eclipse we move in. An auspicious beginning. Our first morning is glorious. It feels like the start of a new life. Geraldine, Julia, and I stand on the cliffs and wait. As the moon slowly covers the sun, the light begins to fade. Julia hides. Only her two eyes peek up from under a blanket. Then everything goes dark. The birds stop singing. It's silent and eerie. Nearly two and a half minutes later, it's light again.

Julia has written and storyboarded a short movie she wants to direct and star in. It's called *The Girls That Save the World* and co-stars her best friend Emily and Emily's older brother Christopher. Julia has been learning Tae Kwon Do, so naturally this is the skill that allows her to conquer the invading alien by knocking him into the stream, where he dissolves. It's a charming little film and very ambitious for an eight-year-old. It's invited to the Cornwall Film Festival, where it gets a great reception.

MWP

Two weeks later I fly to Vancouver to present another seminar for Kodak. In Los Angeles, Ken arranges an informal evening gathering of about two dozen of our film book authors. This is the beginning of an annual gathering of authors (with the grandiose name of The MWP Publishing Summit, and now totals nearly 200 authors). It's a real treat to see everyone in one place, from the old masters to the up-and-coming new voices. Moreover, there is great energy and networking among the authors themselves. We have a lot of power as a group, and I think about what we can do to expand our reach into the creative community.

When I return to Cornwall we audition hundreds of kids for the Witchey Eye Gang, who are the ensemble for *Field of Fish*, a short film I've been invited to make with Steve Tanner. I am delighted, because although in the last few years I've given a lot of seminars on filmmaking and published dozens of books about it, I haven't actually been able to get anything into production. We go over storyboards and search Mousehole village for locations. In early October we shoot the short film. It's finished in time for me to meet Ken at the Frankfurt Book Fair, where we sell the foreign translation rights to our books.

Every day I rise at 4:30 a.m. This gives me time to do an hour of meditation and exercise, take a shower, wake Julia and take her to school, or meet Emily's mom at the lay-by where we alternate who will drive the twenty minutes into Penzance. Julia is very active in gym, netball, horseback riding, swimming, life-guarding, and ballet. Following the school fete she is awarded Sports Girl of the Year. It's great to see her excel at something she loves.

DOLPHIN GIRL

In December the family flies to Bali and celebrates Christmas in Ubud. I visit friends in Pengosaken and film shaman Ketut Liyer healing the sick villagers in his compound. Julia watches attentively and then plays with Ketut's nephews. I like to hang out with the old men in the village. Julia likes Waterbom, the big water park in Kuta, where she takes countless "go's" on the biggest of the water slides. Geraldine searches for antique Javanese trading beads.

Bali is great, and living in Cornwall is even better. We love our beach that is a two-minute walk from our cottage. It's not a sandy beach, but is covered in very large, round, tide-washed stones, so tourists don't come to this beach. Julia and I leap from boulder to boulder and make our way down to a place where, if the waves are gentle enough and when it's high tide, we can slip into the water. On most days the sea is rough and it's too dangerous to go in. If you do, a wave could smash you into a rock. But today is a perfect day to go for a swim. We hurry to put on our wetsuits, flippers and masks, and adjust our snorkels.

We swim through a labyrinth of rocks and marvel at the world of seaweed, strange fish and lobsters below. When we swim in the shallow water above the stones, the water turns warm because the rocks have retained the heat they collected at low tide. We swim out 100 feet in what looks like mid-ocean and stand up on a submerged rock. Geraldine watches us. To her it looks as if we are walking on the water. Julia loves this. When the tide is lower we dive off this rock. A seal watches us and lets out an excited yelp every time we dive. When the sun goes behind a cloud, the water turns dark and the bottom black. Julia gets a little afraid, swims over and takes my hand. It feels great to be a Dad.

We try to expose Julia to every opportunity. Geraldine and I take her to Ireland to the Dingle Peninsula to see the friendly dolphin "Fungi." He is famous for his interest in humans and this is especially so with Julia. She is enchanted and screams with glee as Fungi surfaces on whatever side of the boat Julia is on. Not only does she have that "horse whisperer" thing, but now it has extended to dolphins! Later at an Irish pub, we celebrate our day of interspecies communication with rounds of Guinness. Julia likes the foam on top but thinks the beer tastes yucky.

Julia's young life is filled with adventure. The barn dances, the kid's parties, the exploration of the coastal paths, the village fetes, and magical stone circles are the manifestation of the stories that Geraldine used to put into Julia's little brain during their Miata ride along Mulholland Drive to Roscomare Road. Here she is, living her storybook fantasies.

As a little girl, Julia had always loved our *Dolphin* movie. She told me she wanted to swim with dolphins in the open oceans like we did. I promised her that when she was old enough and was a good swimmer we would go. Years passed. Little did I think she would one day be old enough and have accomplished several swimming awards, including a lifesaving certificate. I'll have to keep my promise.

I contact my old friend and former producing partner in the *Dolphin* film, Hardy Jones. He is now founder of BlueVoice.org, an ocean conservation organization. He arranges an expedition that we will join. We will visit the same location in the Bahamas to see if we can find the sons and daughters of the dolphin pod we had filmed in 1977 — so that I can introduce my daughter to them. I love the symmetry of that.

We meet up in Miami and set off for five days. We weren't out but a few hours when I get seasick. And not just a little! In my exuberance to take Julia to meet the dolphins, I forgot that I don't do well on boats. While I spend most of my time in the prone position, Julia has the time of her life swimming with the dolphins. They really like her, bringing their babies close for Julia to see.

ST. LOY TODAY

After fifteen years of living in St. Loy, the garden has evolved into an extraordinary paradise. Julia calls it a "Buddhist retreat." Each year is more magnificent than the last. We pinch ourselves every day wondering how we were lead, all the way from Los Angeles, to this heavenly place. A stream runs through the garden with several waterfalls. There is a memorial garden for Geraldine's aunt and mother with a beautiful white statue of the Hindu goddess of knowledge — Saraswati — that I shipped from Bali. She is the focal point on a little island in the pond whose overflow creates a small waterfall. Exquisite. After long hikes on the coastal paths I like to sit here to cool off.

The cottage had been a daffodil farm many years ago, and the daffodils still come up. Usually starting in late December we get thousands of yellow flowers which peek their heads up to greet us. Masses of yellow expressing pure joy and happiness.

I had expected to go back to L.A. twice a year on business, but have managed to do so about once a year when we have our Publishing Summit, where fifty or more authors gather together to exchange ideas and network. Several times we meet in Judith Weston's studio in Venice and we screen my latest films at the Landmark Theater in Westwood.

These meetings and social events bring us closer together. I encourage the authors to support each other's work, whether it be speaking engagements or book sales. Just because another author has written a book on a similar subject — say screenwriting — it doesn't mean that another facet of the diamond isn't valuable. Ken and I encourage authors to do book signings and workshops together. This eventually evolves into several large events that Ken produces called "The Future of Story" that features fifteen or twenty authors in one venue. We arrange the event so that the authors can not only interact with each other, but network afterwards with the audience. Other publishers don't want their authors to get together, probably because they don't want them sharing notes on whose book has been promoted more or is getting a higher royalty or who has more color pages. But it's our idea to make the whole publishing operation as transparent as possible so that everyone participates and contributes to the whole. This idea has been embraced by the authors and the whole company feels like a family of brothers and sisters, uncles and aunts, all pulling in the same direction. I learned this at Vestron: if people are having fun and growing, they will be much more productive. I am thrilled every time I meet with the authors to see how much admiration and respect they have for each other's work. And important work it is. It has influenced major studios, film students, and filmmakers around the world.

Over the years I've been on half a dozen trips to the Cannes Film Festival, where I pitch films, consult, and present independent filmmaking seminars for Kodak, and represent the book line. I went to the Berlin Film Festival, and go every other year to the London Book Fair, which is a five-hour train ride from Penzance; not as close as many people think. Four times I was invited to old friend Roger Ebert's Film Festival in Champaign to show films and speak. It's a treat to see my aunt, who is approaching 100 years of age, and visit the few old haunts that are still standing. But home is truly in Cornwall, where we prefer to be.

Living in the UK gives the family easy access to Europe. Besides many trips to Paris and Dublin, we also visit Vienna, Barcelona, Venice, Sienna, San Gimignano, Florence, Crete, Rhodes, Cyprus, Cairo, and Alexandria. Julia also has traveled on school trips to Germany, Austria, Italy, and France, and on her own to Hungary, South Africa, Namibia, Buenos Aires, Rio, Costa Rica, and Panama.

Cornwall is a tourist destination and boasts five of the top ten beaches in the UK. It's also a center for surfing, and so in the summer our tiny one-lane roads become treacherous with holiday drivers. We frequently go somewhere else during August, like the Maine Media Workshops where I lead a week-long workshop in producing or directing. Julia takes a Young Filmmakers class and has made some terrific shorts, including *Deliverance* (which can be seen on YouTube[*]). Geraldine combs the antique fairs and bookshops in the surrounding coastal towns near Camden Maine.

---

[*]View *Deliverance* at http://www.youtube.com/watch?v=Q1sjSnZ1vfk

BALI BROTHERS

It's truly amazing how long a project can be kept alive without ever getting onto a screen. I carried *Monkey*, *Inter Ice Age Four*, and *Bali Brothers* around for years, never getting them made. Unproduced screenplays and projects is a reality that every dreamer and filmmaker must face. Just because you want to make it doesn't mean it will be made. This arduous path (sometimes called "development hell") has the potential to ruin lives, break up marriages, and be detrimental to one's health. I know many who have been destroyed by disappointment or gone bankrupt. I've been scathed by it myself. It's something to think about when pursuing a creative career.

My solution is to not have all my eggs in one basket. Fortunately with the publishing company, month after month, year after year, we have books coming out. Some flop, some do well, and some are phenomenally successful. I have the satisfaction of always having something in development, in production, and in release. All the time cash flow is being generated and supporting everyone's efforts. Most books need to be profitable, but every so often we will publish a book just because it deserves to be published.

Bali Brothers consumed me for more than fifteen years. My seminal years in Bali were so magnificent, I felt a film just had to be made! Living with Larry Reed in what was then a remote village transformed me at the deepest level, and so it was natural to want to express this. Larry has been successful with Shadowlight Theater, a fantastic new form of shadow play, which is his expression of his transformation. I want to make my mark too, so I've returned to Bali more than twenty times.

In 1995, I published a novel called *On the Edge of A Dream: Magic and Madness in Bali,* that tells the story of that first year. Since then, more than forty years have passed. The world of Bali has changed dramatically. It is unrecognizable today. While it was not my intention at the time, the book is a valuable historical document for anyone wishing to learn about life in Bali before the tourist invasion.

The novel was the basis for a film script that has had thirty rewrites over fifteen years. I spent every cent I could to develop and package the project for financing, but was never able to do so. Year upon year this unmade film became a bigger and bigger disappointment.

Of course, more than anyone else, Geraldine has watched me twist and turn in the wind, getting up and dusting myself off after each rejection. Howard Suber, UCLA educator, author of *The Power of Film* and mentor to just about every major director and producer in Hollywood, told me the average film takes nine years to make. People don't realize this. They think a script is written, and then shot, then appears in the theaters.

Ultimately, I had to face the facts and know when to cut my losses. What happened next was a blessing in disguise that took me out of my head and into the present moment, freeing my creative energies once again.

SACRED SITES

Years ago, my good friend Steve Dancz, a musician and composer who composed the soundtracks for several of my films, including *Diet for a New America*, invited me to a Sacred Music Festival that would be held in India and sponsored by the Dalai Lama, who would also attend. I hemmed and hawed and felt that since I didn't play music anymore I would be a fifth wheel hanging out with Steve and other world-class musicians. So I passed. Turns out that it was my loss.

First, Japanese shakuhachi flute players came on and received a polite response. And next were chanting Tibetan monks. More modest response. But when Steve's jazz band came on, everyone leapt to their feet, clapping and dancing. The Dalai Lama was very impressed and invited Steve to a private audience that lasted for several hours. I could've been there! I kick myself.

So when Steve calls again in 2005 and invites me to join him on a pilgrimage to Tibet with his Buddhist teacher Glenn Mullin, I put the phone down and turn to Geraldine. "Say yes!"

A few months later, Steve and I along with several others are traveling over 1,200 kilometers with Glenn, a Tibetologist and former interpreter for the

Dalai Lama, to dozens of sacred sites all over Central Tibet. We visit many monasteries where the previous Dalai Lamas had meditated and taught. We meditate in caves where great masters like Milarepa achieved realization, or in the Potala where the remains of the Second Dalai Lama are kept. Every day my consciousness seems to expand and fill with the endless expansive landscapes of the Himalayas. It's very humbling to see the resilience of the Tibetans, who've endured so much since the Cultural Revolution and subsequent takeover by China. It's moving to talk to monks and abbots who welcome us into their monasteries with such warmth and appreciation. At one point we are meeting with some monks who thank us Americans for supporting the Tibetan cause. At this, many of us start to weep, feeling the enormous great gap between American humanitarian efforts and the state of affairs that the Tibetans have to endure, but who nevertheless thank us with the deepest gratitude. I'll never forget them.

The highpoint of the pilgrimage is a trek to Lhama Latso, or the Oracle Lake, where every Dalai Lama has had visions when looking into the lake. At 17,000 feet, I must stop every ten paces to catch my breath. Most people are unable to get to this lake high in the Himalayas because of ice and snowstorms, but remarkably for us, for a few hours there is a break in the weather. I have made it my spiritual "practice" to film every day of the pilgrimage. Now I have a conflict.

All the Western pilgrims in our group will meditate on the top of the mountain and look into the lake for visions. Glenn says that everyone will probably have visions. I want to have visions too! Maybe I won't film. But I'd made a commitment to film and so I will stick to the plan. After a few hours it starts to rain and hail hammers down on us. We have to get off the mountain.

Later, most people report vivid visions, and those who don't have lucid dreams. I have neither. Suddenly it occurs to me that the film I've been shooting — for the past three weeks — is my vision! It's called *The Sacred Sites of the Dalai Lamas*. The first person to view the film is the Dalai Lama himself. It's shown several times on his holiness' birthday by the Foundation for Tibet and the Office of Tibet, and plays the festival circuit. In 2011 we publish a companion book by Glenn and the photographers on the trip.

When I picked up the camera for *Sacred Sites,* I returned to a level of filmmaking and expression that was totally fulfilling. To shoot it I had to empty my brain of everything and simply be, watching what unfolds in front of me, like a cat staring at a mouse hole, waiting for the moment to turn on the camera. It was an awakening. It brought me back to the initial joy I had making films before I had to get a job.

I did not realize it at the time, but the *Sacred Sites* is a direct continuation of *Silver Box.* Another personal sacred journey. I make only one Hitchcock-style appearance in the entire Tibet film, but I wrote all of Steve's narration. It appears that it's his journey. Actually it's both our journeys, but I hide behind him. I am not yet the front man. This is still to come. The experience of making this simple one-man film reinvigorated my filmmaking. Of course Geraldine (she who knows all, sees all) had been telling me for years to make my little films and put the complex, actor-heavy *Bali Brothers* movie aside, which was becoming watered down with each rewrite and moving further from my own experience. *Sacred Sites* plugged me back into spiritual filmmaking, where I held the camera, had the experience, and passed that along to the audience. This was the beginning of a creative breakthrough.

THE EXTENSION

After several years of pleading and cajoling with the local authorities, we finally get permission to expand our tiny cottage. Geraldine is supervising the construction of our expansion with military precision. She is a perfectionist, whether it is arranging objects in the house, preparing a beautiful meal (both in taste and presentation), copyediting a book, or critiquing the cut of one of my films. She doesn't take any credit for this, but it is this remarkable skill that makes a good meal/book/film great.

Now, we are doubling the size of our cottage with a library that reaches up two stories for all our books that have been in storage since we got here. Julia, now a teenager, will move into our bedroom, as she's outgrown her tiny bed. We'll have a new bedroom and bathroom. Since we live on the side of a valley, there is not a single bit of level ground, so new landscaping creates several levels of

Michael Wiese

Geraldine Overton
She's even got a picture of Blind Lemon Jefferson on her refrigerator! I'm captivated.

Geraldine Overton

Geraldine dresses Julia in the most charming little outfits: pilot jackets, berets, suspenders, and colorful wellies. She gets her face painted as a lion in the London Zoo.

Geraldine Overton

We visit a balian, a Balinese healer, who tells us that Julia is sleeping poorly because we haven't told the spirits of the house who we are, what we are doing there or how long we will be staying. In Champaign, Julia celebrates the 4th of July.

Geraldine Overton

At the British Museum and Zennor.

Geraldine Overton

With Grandad, we pick and roast Illinois "super sweet" corn straight from a farmer's field. Julia attends Big Chief Al's Indian Day Camp (just like I did), and fearlessly jumps off the high dive at the Country Club which she calls the "crunchy club."

Geraldine Overton

Julia and I kick a red soccer ball around the field, or all three of us walk the short mile or so to Zennor, taking the "coffin path" through the fields. Horses and cows take a great interest and follow Julia. She has something of that "horse whisperer" thing going.

Geraldine Overton

Geraldine Overton

The barn dances, the kid's parties, the exploration of the coastal paths, the village fetes,
and magical stone circles are the manifestation of the stories that Geraldine used to put
into Julia's little brain during their Miata ride along Mulholland Drive.

Geraldine Overton

A Cornish childhood. When it's breezy and getting dark, we like to scare ourselves by exploring the ruins of a chapel with most of its roof caved in. There is ivy growing all over it. We hold each other's hand as we creep inside trying not to wake up the ghosts.

Geraldine Overton

Michael in Egypt, in an Irish pub with Julia, swimming off the rocks at Gurnard's Head, and during an annual visit to Los Angeles.

Geraldine Overton

Steve Dancz & Michael Wiese

*Glenn Mullin takes us to meditate in caves where great masters like Milarepa achieved
realization, or in the Potala where the remains of the 2nd Dalai Lama are kept. Every day
my consciousness seems to expand in the endless landscapes of the Himalayas.*

Steve Dancz & Michael Wiese

When Steve Dancz's jazz band came on the monks leapt to their feet, clapping and dancing.
The Dalai Lama was very impressed and invited Steve to a private audience.

Pablo Amaringo

Don José and painter Pablo Amaringo tell us how experienced shamans can travel inside the earth, underwater and into the cosmos, and of their extraordinary healing powers.

Geraldine Overton

Geraldine Overton

Don José Campos is recorded for his book, The Shaman & Ayahuasca, *by translator Alberto Roman. Plant medicines are plentiful in the Iquitos market.*

This small man went into trance and transformed himself into a giant.

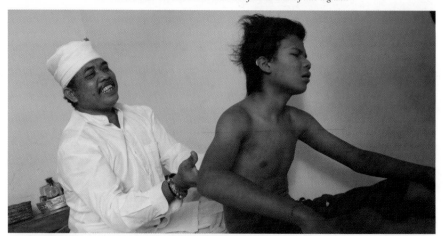

Allowing spirits to work through him, this healer helps a boy who was injured in a motorcycle accident.

Madé Roberto

At midnight, the entire village takes this mask to the graveyard for activation.

My dear friends and hosts during the first trip to Bali over 40 years ago, village head Dewa Nyoman Batuan and his wife Desak Nyoman Cana.

Madé Roberto

Long time friend, teacher and shadow puppet master I. Nyoman Sumandhi.

Michael Wiese

The Bali film crew: Photographer Madé Roberto (Sumandi's son), Simon Olszewski, and Alberto Roman at Batur volcano.

217

Julia in Paris in 2010.

Geraldine in Cyprus in 2012. Photo by Michael.

Michael in Lima in 2011. Photo by Geraldine.

Mediterranean-like terraces. Removing some of the scraggy Sycamore trees gives us a spectacular view down the valley to the crashing waves below.

It's a very difficult location for construction projects because it's hard to get building materials to the site. All large, golden, granite stones for the walls come from digging into the ground because Cornwall is one big heap of granite. The cottage extension is designed by architect Barry Brisco and built by Nick Hellyer and Richard Boekee. It takes three years. The disruption is massive. The old garden has been decimated and there is mud everywhere. I dread walking through the mud pit between the cottage and my office shed.

Inside the cottage everything is in boxes and every day we find a new layer of dust. They've had to take down the chimney and break two doorways through the granite wall upstairs and downstairs to connect the extension with the main cottage. A forty-foot tree is rolled down a farmer's field behind the cottage that will hold the roof up. Somehow Nick and Richard erect it. I give them a sacred clay pot that was given to me by Tibetan monks to protect the cottage, which they bury under the tree.

Geraldine enjoys bringing every detail to her high standard of perfectionism. Whether it's how the tiles are laid, the walls painted, or the flow of the stone staircase, her eagle eyes don't miss anything. And while this occasionally means that something has to be redone, it brings the cottage extension to a very high level.

After yet another full year of work, Nick, on his own, builds a cascade of steps leading down to the lower garden, which winds through several levels of terraces. It's like one of the Seven Wonders of the World. They are both meticulous artists and their work is extraordinary.

It took me many years to realize that beauty is an expression of the divine. You can tell when your consciousness expands because beauty rushes in and every-thing around you is transformed. You begin to see that everything created is perfect. This is what Geraldine has manifested in my life by striving to be impec-cable in everything she does. The beauty in our life — both seen and unseen — didn't just happen. It was earned, step by step.

MY NEW BEST FRIEND

It starts in my thumb. I have a funny feeling, a twitching. Something isn't quite right. For a year or two I notice how it sometimes affects my handwriting, making tiny, almost illegible letters. In December 2007 I go to our local doctor, who refers me to a neurologist who does some tests. He says it's early Parkinson's, which is a degenerative disorder of the central nervous system. It's caused by the death of dopamine-generating cells in the midbrain. First signs are slowness of movement, shaking, and rigidity. Later, more serious problems occur.

I am shocked by the diagnosis and over the next six months get some other opinions that confirm it. No one, of course, will say what the future may bring, or how fast, and I try not to dwell on it.

After a couple of years the symptoms get more pronounced. My right hand and leg shake as if the expanding muscles and the contracting muscles can't get synchronized. When I walk with Geraldine, I find that I can't keep up with her, and sometimes I can't quite get my feet to move forward. My voice weakens and my face starts to take on the typical frozen mask that is common to Parkinson's.

I resist going on medications, with their side effects, but finally succumb to Co-Carledopa, which gives the brain the dopamine it needs. The medication helps smooth out my movements.

I read and research. I radically change my diet. I go on a massive vitamin and nutrient regime. I do chelation to detoxify and flush out metals (a possible cause of Parkinson's) from my system. Intravenously, I take lipid fats. I exercise more, meditate more, do Tai Chi, acupuncture, physical therapy, and learn the Alexander Technique, a kind of body mindfulness training. I lay on a special mat to stimulate cellular activity. These things I believe help slow the progression of Parkinson's. Some of the symptoms show improvement.

STEM CELL ADVENTURE

The fight against Parkinson's continues. I am looking through a blog on Parkinson's and stumble across a link to the XCell-Center in Düsseldorf,

Germany. They are the only place in the world where you can receive stem cell treatment using your own cells for the treatment of Parkinson's.

I call them up and learn that only thirty to forty people with Parkinson's have had this treatment. It's very controversial, and different aspects of it had been banned and reinstated and then banned again in Germany depending on what political party is in power.

Of those taking the treatment the anecdotal reports claim that about 50%–60% found some depletion in their symptoms. No clinical surveys have been done — because the population taking the treatment is so low. Nevertheless, with good faith, I sign up.

Geraldine and I arrive at the XCell-Center in Düsseldorf ready to begin the process. I am a bit anxious and nervous. I hope I am making the right decision to have this treatment. People with Parkinson's are very vulnerable and will try almost anything which claims to alleviate the symptoms.

Day one is the diagnostic day. I am shuttled through a high-tech facility and given an MRI, a CAT scan, and sonographs. The MRI is a huge tunnel. I am strapped into a kind of plastic sled like a high-tech Egyptian sarcophagus. A Hannibal Lecter-like mask is put over my face. It's getting pretty weird already.

A CT showed moderate narrowing of the bilateral internal jugular veins under the thyroid glands. All other arteries were fine. The MRI is normal. No decrease in the bilateral *substantia nigra*. No hemorrhage, everything else is fine. Doppler (sonography) showed a mild stenosis of the jugular veins. Therefore they will perform an angioplasty to allow more oxygen to get to the brain.

We are shown a series of black and white images of my brain on a computer screen, which gives the impression of traveling through 3D-like layers. The doctor — a small, no-nonsense woman — seems overjoyed by the results. There are no lesions, nothing to indicate strokes, no shrinkage of the brain. She says she'd seen 7,000 scans and my brain is in the best condition she'd ever seen.

Sitting in front of a large computer screen, the doctor takes us on a trip through my brain — top to bottom, side to side — each view revealing a different area. This is me?! I can only recognize myself in the faint profile. The rest of "me" is a gelatinous mass of brain. Usually we think of ourselves as what we see in the mirror or in a home movie. Here, I see and feel myself as this amazing creature with a myriad of processes going on quite unconsciously and on their own, my skin being the layer that holds it all together. It changes my image of myself.

I am given a whole battery of tests both physical and cognitive that will act as a baseline. I am given points for awareness, balance, agility, muscle grading, and isometric strength. I rank very high in most tasks with the exception of agility, where I get a 68%.

Day two is bone marrow collection day. I go into a small room with a doctor and one assistant. I ask Geraldine to take some photos, but they won't let her — something about "trade secrets." She stays with me during the procedure, which is probably harder on her when I struggle with the pain.

They give me a local anesthesia, which does little for the stabbing pain when the doctor sticks a huge needle in my hipbone. It's supposed to take twenty minutes, but it takes an hour and a half. For a long time he couldn't find the sweet spot where stem cells reside in the bone marrow. Then, once he does, he can't get the cap off the needle. So two other doctors come in and struggle with it (while the needle is still in me, sending out electrical bursts of pain). Finally, he finds the sweet spot and draws out twenty test tube vials of fluid.

But that's not all. He rolls me over on the other side and goes into my left hipbone. This time he strikes gold instantly and withdraws another twenty-two vials of stem cells and blood. The forty-two vials are sent off for processing.

Day three is return of the stem cells. I lie down as they put Mannitol via an IV into me, which opens the blood-brain barrier for about an hour. Half of the collected stem cells (two million of those puppies) are fed into me through the IV. The whole procedure takes a couple of hours as the stem cells go into the brain and hopefully replace any damaged dopamine-producing cells.

Day four is angioplasty. Squinting from the bright pin lights in the ceiling, I lay flat on a thin plank. My arms hang over the sides, so I have to hold them together. This is difficult, so they strap them in. From either anxiety about the upcoming procedure or because I didn't take my dopamine medicine (because I thought it might interfere with the other medications), I start shaking like crazy. They give me an injection and after about two minutes the shaking stops completely.

They puncture my groin, which doesn't hurt at all, and run a tube up the jugular vein in the right side of my neck. They have given me a contrast media so that we can all see a video monitor as the tube progresses. The screen is tilted so I can just about see, but every time I try to look they shout "Don't move ze head," so the curious videomaker in me has to miss the show. When the end of the tube gets to the place in the vein where there is an obstruction, they pump up a little balloon that opens up the obstruction that is keeping the blood from flowing freely. They hold the balloon in place for about ten minutes. It's a very weird feeling to feel something alien expanding in my neck.

Then they repeat the procedure in the artery or vein on the other side of my neck. After this, they inject the second batch (another million-plus stem cells) that is carried by my blood to the brain.

They wheel me on a gurney out into the hallway and I'm left alone with Geraldine. I try telling Geraldine something, but halfway through I forget what I am trying to say. It's as if a giant eraser wipes out my memory, leaving me blank at mid-sentence. I find this short-term memory loss funny, strange.

They roll me to a recovery room where I am to wait for two hours before being released to return to the hotel. When the doctors come to release me, I try to talk to them, but the more I talk, the more I can see the doctors looking at me as if I am completely incoherent. I am quickly losing all credibility and must sound like a babbling idiot.

Geraldine tells me that it was worse than that. I was asking such things as, "What's the population of that bottle of water?" or "How many countries do you have in your purse?" She is horrified! My brain is completely fried!

The doctors have never seen this before. Geraldine refuses to let me leave and demands that we spend the night in the hospital under observation. By the next morning, I am pretty much back to clear thinking. What surprises us all is that the sedative had a very strong and very rare side effect. I am glad to be back.

The angioplasty gives me 20% more blood flow to and from the brain immediately after the procedure. I don't notice any physical differences then, but it's probably because I am emotionally and physically depleted. The next day, however, I notice that in doing my morning exercise, my limbs ache less and I have greater upper body movement. This is quite exciting.

Usually when I wake up I have strong, violent shaking for ten to twenty seconds in my arms. I don't know why this happens, but for the first five days after the procedure I don't have any "start up" shaking, but then it returns.

I find that I can floss with no trouble whatsoever, a function that usually leaves me in frustration. For a week the flossing had been easier and now it's a hit-or-miss thing.

In Düsseldorf, after the procedure I walk a couple of blocks with Geraldine. I have a long gait and walk at top speed. I haven't been able to do this for years. So this is another indicator to watch.

I am told that it will take four to eight weeks to start seeing results from the stem cell treatment. But perhaps what I am seeing are hints of results from the angioplasty.

For the last six months it's been very difficult to get in and out of bed. It can take me twenty or thirty small moves. It seems easier for a short time, but it's difficult again.

A few weeks later, when I pass the flowers on our terrace I notice their beautiful scent. This is a delightful change.

[Note: As of this writing it has been fifteen months since the stem cell therapy. There have been no dramatic changes of any one symptom that I can attribute to the therapy. Some things seem slightly better and some things worse. But then

I've continued with other therapies to keep body and mind together. I imagine everything helps. The thing that helps the most is giving gratitude for my life, my work, my family, my friends, and finding humor in life as much as possible. Sometimes I think of myself as having a disability and then realize that by doing so I create my own reality. Or occasionally I can become depressed when I think of how the future may turn out. But no one really knows. The future is not certain for any of us. There are endless possibilities. I begin to think of the Parkinson's as my new best friend, someone who is always with me, asking me to slow down and smell the roses. I am changing and, like the caterpillar, have an unpredictable new life form to look forward to.]*

---

*The XCell-Center had some bad publicity over its controversial procedure and has, as of mid-2011, been shut down by the current German government.

Knowing
Other Realms

2007 *2010*

"The universe (which others calls the Library) is composed
of an indefinite number of hexagonal galleries."
— Jorge Luis Borges

....

Michael Wiese

This period in my life has been monumentally rich. I give gratitude daily. I can't believe my reality. I get to participate in the life of my wife and daughter and to see them bloom and flourish. We've created a miracle paradise in which to live. We enjoy deep friendships with people in many different lands around the world. Geraldine had it right about what kind of movies I should be making, and if I have a regret it's that I was a slow learner holding on to *Bali Brothers* and not letting go. *Silver Box* was the template for my new work, but I had been so devastated by one negative review that I refused to look in that direction and it was under my nose all the time. This period also made it vividly clear that life is not a dress rehearsal. If you want something, go for it. The passing of my parents, Greg White, Steven Arnold, Teiji Ito, Cherel, and many other dear ones made this very clear. Parkinson's constantly reminds me that we are in a process of change. Enormous energies are pulsing through our bodies, the oceans, the forests, the weather, and between the planets and stars. This is the energy of creativity, of life and death. The doors of perception are opening.

MOTHER AYAHUASCA

In my search for a cure, I learn that in the 1920s an Amazonian vine called *Banisteriopsis caapi* had been used successfully to treat Parkinson's but had been discontinued because the drug companies couldn't figure out how to patent the plant profitably. I learn that the plant, when mixed with a psychoactive leaf called *Psychotria viridis*, creates a powerful jungle medicine called Ayahuasca, which, some say, has been used by the indigenous people of South America for 70,000 years. Individually the vine and leaf do nothing, but when combined they produce an extremely powerful brew providing healing and insight into the nature of reality and our place in the cosmos.

Ayahuasca has a reputation for healing all kinds of physical, psychological, emotional, and spiritual ailments, and for many people brings vivid visions. It's gaining a lot of attention in the West and a kind of psychedelic tourism has emerged throughout South America among serious and not-so-serious explorers. In the past, it has been forced underground during periods of oppression and is again rising and coming into the awareness of the Western world. Although illegal in the U.S. and Europe, it is a national treasure in Peru and widely used for healing by men, women, and families.

The first thing Ayahuasca teaches is that plants have consciousness. It seems so obvious now, but before my Ayahuasca experience I could never have believed it. My worldview has completely changed.

It's impossible to describe the inner experience of an Ayahuasca ceremony. It is a very powerful teacher. It heals. It is an earth spirit that shows us our true nature.

Sadly, we are culturally conditioned to question this — but the experience is undeniable. Trying to get someone to understand who hasn't done it is like a fish trying to explain life on land.

Through a friend who has been working with Don José Campos, a Peruvian *curandero*, Geraldine and I make arrangements to go to Peru to meet him and take Ayahuasca. To prepare our bodies for the medicine we must give up salt, sugar, oil, red meat (which I don't eat anyway), spices, coffee, and sex for three weeks before drinking Ayahuasca. I also have to go off all my medication for three days before and three days after. Things could get a little shaky.

We arrive in Pucallpa, Peru, and are met by Don José. We are immediately struck by his good humor and welcoming spirit. Here is a man we can trust. Alberto Roman, a shamanic musician and a man with enormous heart, will serve as translator. A day later we are all in the jungle in a *maloca*, drinking the most vile-tasting substance on Earth. I hadn't planned to take a camera because the purpose of the trip was for Geraldine to collect material for a book called *The Shaman & Ayahuasca*, but it occurred to me that there might be some fantastic things we could also shoot for a companion film. This turns out to be very true. One of the first things Don José does before giving his own interviews over the next two weeks is to introduce us to his friend, Pablo Amaringo, the legendary visionary shaman and painter whose work reveals the many realms and entities encountered with Ayahuasca. What Picasso was to cubism, Amaringo is to visionary states. These paintings are not fantasies, but documentaries! This small, unassuming man is tremendously generous as he unrolls canvas after canvas and narrates the fantastic depictions of these otherworldly realms and their inhabitants. He shows us how and where experienced shamans can travel — inside the earth, underwater, and into the cosmos — and tells us of their extraordinary healing powers when working with the spirits of the plants and animals.

When I return home I write this to friends:

First, I must express my thanks to everyone who has supported me on this psycho-nautic exploration, directing me to the literature, leading physicians, shamans, and adventurers, and particularly to those friends who can best be described as "temple guard dogs" who protected me and looked after me during the Journey itself. It was, hands down, both the most exhilarating and most horrendous inner journey of my life.

The Ayahuasca journey happens outside of our common experiences expressed through language. Nevertheless, I write something, stumble along, use the best words I can find that pale in comparison to the teachings bestowed from the awe-inspiring, sometimes terrifying, Great Mother Ayahuasca. Here we go....

FIRST JOURNEY

Don José and musician Artur Mena cram into one *motocarro* and the rest of us cram into another. We are taken outside of Pucallpa to an isolated maloca in the jungle.

One by one Geraldine, Alberto, and I (and a dozen others) go up to a little altar and Don José pours each of us a shot glass of the dark molasses. When it is my turn I go up, kneel, accept the cup, honor it by holding it up above my head, and force it down. It's truly the most vile thing I've ever had to swallow. Imagine mixing putrid thick syrup, a dead animal, and chunks of root into a blender and you might have a hint at how foul this stuff tastes. I am getting nauseated and can taste bile in the back of my throat as I write about it. It's all I can do to keep it down long enough to feel its effects. Before I say more, this is not some psyche-delic joy-ride that you try alone at home or at a disco, it's only for the courageous, serious-minded, high-intentioned explorer who has a damn good reason to be taking the two-by-four of Amazon medicine. You're about to see why.

My first journey is filled with so much energy I cannot stay balanced. It has the force of a tsunami washing over me and goes on for hours. It starts with a beautiful landscape of jewels and a woven electronic blanket of undulating snakes with extremely garish orange and green colors. Nothing subtle about Ayahuasca's taste in art! The detail is incredible and there is too much to watch.

When I first see the landscape, I think "how beautiful." Suddenly the relationship of separateness between me and my vision shifts. Subject and object merge. Duality is gone. There is no "other." I am the vision. I <u>am</u> the mesh of energy and jewels and snakes that I am seeing. The sacred verse "I am that I am" best describes it. I am part of... no... I <u>am</u> the Divine Matrix.

Then the scanning begins. It's as if the plant medicine has a hi-tech medical team of entities working for it, and although I can't see them, their presence is all around me as my body is scanned and sliced and diced in every direction as if I am being pushed through a giant electronic cheese grater. Later I realize what I am describing sounds an awful lot like alien abduction literature.

It's not frightening, but it's overwhelming. I certainly hope they know what they are doing. My DNA, my entire operating system, seems to have been reprogrammed — and fast. I feel it. Billions of terabytes of information are being flushed through me and are shuttling through every cell.

Suddenly, Mother Ayahuasca is present. I feel my inner mind opening. As instructed, I form my question. I ask her to show me the spirit world. As I make the request, infinite dimensions and lands appear... Amazing animals and beings come to me. As many as atoms in an ocean of worlds. I can't believe it!

I remember Don José's instructions to breathe consciously, in and out, to stay centered. Miraculously, I can ask the plant questions and get immediate answers either verbally, or visually, or telepathically.

But there is so much energy that for much of the time it is all I can do to surf the energy, let alone try to further a master-student relationship. I am not sure — but I may have lost consciousness, as there is a vast amount I do not remember.

Sometime later I see other images of organic green and flesh-colored entities. I guess they are life forms, but more alien than anything we might see even on the deep floor of the ocean. At first the light is beautiful, but when I look deeper into the shadows there is real evil and it's terrifying. I try not to look. Wrong move. The lesson being taught is that good and evil are part of the same thing and, like it or not, they come in the world of duality as a packaged deal. I try to accept this and breathe through the realization that even though I don't like what I am learning — I see that it is true.

All around me and throughout the night are the unmistakable sounds of the other participants puking their guts out, growling and bellowing like beasts as they heave into their buckets. I try to give them love and compassion and just hold the space, as we were instructed to do, and not get caught up in their purges. I have my own healing to attend to and that is my responsibility. There are helpers watching the group to assist if anyone gets into trouble, and several do. Without staying focused on your breathing and intent, it's very easy to get disoriented.

At one point I'm doing okay. I am centered. I feel I can hold the space for the circle and want help out the others. Fine. I can take on their suffering. Then I wonder if I can hold the space for the world. I try. For about two seconds, and even this is too much, I feel the suffering of millions in wars, starving, dying. It practically annihilates me. Suddenly, I understand what all those enlightened masters meditating in caves have been doing. They are holding space for all humanity. I am immediately plunged back into pure experience, too fast for thought.

Energy pours into and through me with a fire hose intensity, pummeling me. So much so that I feel that my life force will be completely drained very soon and I will be annihilated. I try to sit up in half-lotus and breathe in and out. I am nauseated and vomit several times over the next five hours.

As waves of nausea hit me, I prop my head over the bucket as bright-colored pearls — like pop beads — come tumbling out of my mouth. The torrent of energy continues to hammer me. Occasionally there is a break in the songs that

Don José sings, but then once he starts shaking his rattle, the snake-like coiling and uncoiling of energy is reinvigorated. Don José conducts the spirits, inviting them in while at the same time protecting us with his *icaros*. There is no resisting these forces, which are both Creative and Destructive. Everything is constantly being born and dying. This force brings everything into being and recycles it in death. I am tapped in directly to the main fuse box of the Universe. All Powerful does not describe it, and it's surging through me constantly.

I am on a Möbius strip, dying and being born again and again and again and again and again and again. It's painful, and frightening, and dizzying, and like an out-of-control roller coaster. I beg the carnival operator to let me off, and vow to never do this again, but there is no one with a hand on the lever to stop the onslaught. What a nightmare.

I am sure I won't make it. I have nothing left. Still, I fight to hang on to my last drop of energy, but in the face of Ayahuasca, resistance is futile.

Hours after the ceremony ends, I am back in our room. I lay on a bed unable to move. I am still heavily intoxicated, shaking, weaving, and dizzy. But the visions continue and I am hammered for another seven hours. I realize it was foolish to have eaten so little before the session because I have no fuel and no reserves. I am dehydrated but am too weak and sick to reach the few inches to the water bottle at the bedside. I feel that if I don't nurse myself back to life, I'll be dead by dawn. After many tries, it takes enormous strength to reach the water and suck a few drops.

My thoughts go to insane paranoia. Ayahuasca has now reprogrammed my entire DNA. I feel the hard drive of my brain has been erased and I have a whole new operating system that has been installed by alien beings. I convince myself that the whole thing is a vast conspiracy — all my friends had a secret plan, they introduced me to the shaman, the literature is all propaganda, and now my previous life-slate has been wiped clean. I am now transformed and one of them! Worse yet, so is my wife, who is asleep beside me!

At 7 a.m. the visions stop. The journey has lasted twelve brutal hours in Earth time — an eternity in experiential time.

I take the tiniest nibble of a pear and the taste blasts through my body. The Quintessential Pear is showing off its flavor. Throughout the day I am weak and I swear to everyone over and over, "I will never, ever, ever do this again."

I have a delicious vegetarian meal and rest for a day. I tell Don José what has happened and that I am not going to do it again. I don't have the strength. I am in a mind space of weakness, of feeling myself small and incapable. Geraldine points out to me that I did, in fact, survive. The spiritual warrior did return home with the elixir of knowledge. I am indeed changed. I have had countless insights, which decimated and smashed old beliefs, habits, negative and limited ways of thinking. These treasures are indeed worth the horrific struggles. I went to the Underworld, Experienced the Supreme Ordeal, was Resurrected and Returned with the Elixir. I even had "The Dark Night of the Soul." The Joseph Campbell "Hero's Journey" paradigm resonates because it describes the shamanic initiation that I just received.

I have survived, so I must have had the strength. But it was a terrifying journey and the most difficult thing I'd ever done in my life. Only a fool would sign up again. My theory is, because I'd stayed on a raw vegetable diet for two or three weeks prior to ingesting the plant medicine, the Ayahuasca worked intensively and quickly through my empty stomach, hence little came up during the purging.

Don José suggests I take a lesser dose if I want to do it again. But I don't want to do it again! Never! I already have enough insights to process and integrate for a lifetime.

But as I regain strength and energy from my first real meal in weeks, my confidence is restored. It's a great privilege to be allowed even a glimpse of this multi-dimensional universe peopled with gods, demons, fairies, spirits, ancestors, and mythological beasts. These creatures that I saw are only a small sliver of the inhabitants who share the Universe in infinite parallel dimensions but have been described in our myths and legends. I realize that my ordinary consciousness consists mostly of being asleep, unaware, caught up in addictive and habitual patterns, that gives "me" the illusion of separateness where really there is no "me." Ayahuasca blew the top off that and with cosmic tough love took me on an express train to the true nature of reality.

In the ceremony, I die and am reborn... over and over again. I am terrified, but as this is endlessly repeated I notice that my consciousness is still intact. There is a vast space in which I can travel. I have no need of a body. I am free. I discover that there is no death.

Ayahuasca is demanding that I "up my game," inherit my birthright, and become all that I can in sharing my own sacred and divine nature. Isn't that what we're all looking to do? She has given me a dress rehearsal of my own death and shown me there is no death. She has shown me that I can have a life with no fear of death.

Working with Ayahuasca is not easy and requires enormous strength, stamina, and courage. We discover that we are not separate beings. We are all connected. We are multi-dimensional, able to travel into subatomic as well as cosmic realms, through the past, the future, and through multiple universes. We can converse with our departed friends and great minds of the past. A vast store of knowledge through direct experience is available to us.

Ayahuasca is the greatest teacher I've ever had. Am I going to walk away from more teachings? As my friend, Steve Dancz, says, "I don't want to die stupid." I will meet the challenge and ingest the healing medicine once again. Besides, as I am told, if you've had a difficult journey and return again, Mother Ayahuasca may reward you with a gentler journey. I sure hope so. I commit to drinking another cupful.

THE SECOND JOURNEY

Don José shakes his rattle. He whistles, breathlessly. His seductive voice weaves through me with his beautiful and eerie *icaros*, which create openings in my brain. I remember to focus on my intention. I am here to learn. To go deeper. I breathe slowly in and out. I feel the gritty, molasses-thick medicine of Mother Ayahuasca ripple through my belly, my liver and kidneys, and then jet up my spine to my brain. She is present. It's time to ask. "Show me Divine Love."

Faintly at first, with hardly any color saturation, geometric images appear. It brightens and I see peach-colored gauze. I feel there is something behind it. Slowly Mother Ayahuasca pulls back the veil to reveal a soft yellow room. I realize it's a nursery. Curiosity draws me nearer as I try to focus on this vision.

As I look more closely, I see a womb-like room, secure and comforting. How strange. Why would She show me a nursery? And like any nursery, which may display the A-B-C letters of the alphabet or a fanciful mobile for the new arrival, this too has pre-school teachings. Everywhere, in this room, is the support and love of all the child's previous ancestors going back to pre-history.

I move into the room. The designers of this nursery have prepared the most fantastic and elaborate carvings — too vast for the eye to take in except in short gasps — for the being who will arrive shortly. The carvings are perfect and stretch on as far as I can see. It's as if ten thousand craftsmen have been commanded by a great King to carve for ten thousand years. It's as if generations of the universe's most accomplished artisans have been told a Divine Child is coming and to get the room ready. And they have done so.

These intricate carvings — far more advanced than the Taj Mahal, the Potala, the Great Pyramid, or anything in the Forbidden City — are sacred scriptures in Sanskrit, Egyptian, Hebrew, Arabic, Sumerian, and from thousands of other ancient civilizations I don't recognize. The walls are filled with knowledge that the child will absorb in its life. I am trying to take it all in and remember it because it's the most extraordinary place I've ever been.

As I move around the room I can feel the breathing presence of two huge black boas that encircle and protect the room. I can't see them, but I can feel their warm, deep electric hum. I think to myself, "Oh great, giant snakes." I don't want to see them because I might be afraid. But as I breathe out again I find I am not. "The Giant Snakes are here to protect the Child."

"So who is the Child?" I ask.

"You are the Child. This room is for you."

I am overwhelmed with emotion, I try to take it all in.

Then, a second wave of realization comes over me. All humans are Divine Children. She provides for us all. We are already living in her Paradise! This isn't just a lesson for me, it's a lesson for us all.

Hours later, the vision is wearing off. I look into the emerald green jungle — I see every fern a masterpiece. Like the carved detail in the room, Mother Ayahuasca has poured the same love and creativity into providing food and beauty for all human life. We live in an exquisite paradise. I fall to my knees in gratitude for our sacred Earth.

During the weeks we spend around the shaman there is an incredible feeling of love and acceptance. My mind is usually filled with judgments — judging everything in some way — separating myself from others. The main teaching seems to be that we are all part of the same thing. It's ironic that as I experience Parkinson's and its limitations, I recognize that my body does not end at my skin, it extends throughout the cosmos. I do not live on the earth, I am the earth, and you, and that animal and that tree over there. We are not separate and we will suffer until we realize this, at which time our healing will begin.

A remarkable thing about Ayahuasca is that the teachings, visions, and insights may continue days, weeks, or months after a journey. Or as Don José says, "Once you take Ayahuasca, She will always be with you."

Two weeks after our Ayahuasca journey with Don José we return to our hotel in Iquitos. In the street, Geraldine is immediately surrounded by a dozen Shipibo women, stretching out their textiles, creating a protective space around her. At that moment, I get an international call from Ken Lee. He tells me that Geraldine's mother isn't expected to live beyond 48 hours. I break the news to Geraldine as we climb the stairs.

In the room, Geraldine feels her heart constrict. It is frightening to watch. She can barely breathe in or out. She makes gasping sounds. She lies down on the bed, and closes her eyes. It's then that she has a rush of visions. It's like a movie strip playing out before her: scenes of her mother reading to her on the swing, carrying her up the hill, and hanging a pink *piñata* on the olive tree. As Don José enters the room he begins to shake his rattle and sing his *icaros*, trying to settle her energies. Ken calls me again. He says, "I'm sorry, Geraldine's mother has just died." I say, "Yes, thank you, we know." It is then that Geraldine realizes she has been participating in her mother's death.

Ayahuasca teaches that there is a very thin membrane between realities, between me and you, between us and others. Maybe there is no membrane at all and it is our senses that delude us into thinking we are separate beings. This profound experience of Geraldine's demonstrates the depths of which we are part of each other's lives. She entered her mother's mind and shared the moment of her passing!

It's a very deep spirit world that we dip into. We realize that living with spirits is part of the nature of reality. That "spirit" is a dimension that interacts with the physical world. Very powerfully. And that's what the Ayahuasca journey is about. It's about going into that spirit realm where there are entities of all kinds willing to help and teach. The Ayahuasca experience redefines who we think we are and shows us that as human beings we are far more complex than we ever imagined.

Geraldine's mother's death was an extraordinary teaching experience for us all. What better way to illustrate our ability to navigate multiple realms? This is exactly the kind of psychic space I'd wanted to explore in film. Thanks to Ayahuasca, the reality is sinking in.

TALKING WITH SPIRITS

Back home, I repeated something to myself that I say to students in my seminars. "There are three budgets you can have for your film: the one you'd like to have, the one that won't buy you everything but that you'll accept, and the one that will force you to make it in your garage."

I re-examine what I really want to say with *Bali Brothers*, and decide to "make it in my garage." I will shoot a very low-budget, self-funded documentary and do it pretty much all myself! Would I be able to film all the things I'd seen which fascinated me about Bali?

Since Julia is still in school, Geraldine must remain in England, so she suggests that I invite Alberto Roman, who had been so helpful on our last film, *The Shaman & Ayahuasca,* to join me. I throw a camera in my bag, and we set off to Bali. Before we shoot anything we have a high priest make offerings to the Balinese gods on our behalf. Once done, the doors of Bali's unseen worlds are thrown open to us as spirit healers, trance dancers, priests, and spirits come forth to reveal themselves. A small farmer transforms himself to a giant, a manifestation of Hanuman. A woman who runs a market stall by day gathers her devotees for trance channeling at night, when she is inhabited by powerful deities. A mask of the protector, Barong, is taken to a graveyard at midnight and "activated" as its spirit descends and "seats" itself in the mask. These and many other remarkable demonstrations show the convergence of the spiritual world with the physical world.

I believe the success of this filming was due to our expanded awareness given to us by Ayahuasca and the reverential approach we took in every moment of filming. I'd been going to Bali over the last forty years, perhaps some twenty or more times, but never had she shown me her mysteries in such a deep way.

Thus was born *Talking with Spirits*, a 90-minute documentary that I finished in 2011 and had its world premiere in Bali at the Global Social Change Film Festival and a U.S. premiere at San Francisco's Asian Museum. ("Premiere" does not mean klieg lights and stars walking down red carpets, but merely the first public showing in a territory; U.S., Europe, World.) The film is just now being offered to specialized venues as part of the *Sacred Journeys* festival.

I found that I can be creatively fulfilled making one or two self-contained, very small-scale documentaries a year. Something Geraldine has been suggesting for years! These films cost very little to make. I need only to sell a thousand DVDs and make a few TV licensing deals to break even. Besides, these days with Parkinson's, I no longer have the stamina required to direct a cast and crew through long 14-hour days for six or seven weeks. I have, instead, found a solution that suits me perfectly. I am making very specialized films for a very small but appreciative audience.

THE BIRTH OF DIVINE ARTS

A day after our first Ayahuasca ceremony, Geraldine has another set of visions. It happens at night. She wakes me up and says, "Michael, I have just been told by Mother Ayahuasca that we will publish a range of books to share what we are learning." I say "okay" and roll over and go back to sleep.

In 2010, we launched Divine Arts, which has published thirteen books and presently has another eight in the pipeline. The people, ideas, and funding seem to show up when needed. Manny Otto, who has worked with a number of spiritual luminaries and the Joseph Campbell Foundation, comes on board as associate publisher. Geraldine joins the imprint as founder and co-publisher.

Naturally, the first book and film that starts it all is Don José Campos' *The Shaman & Ayahuasca*. First, Geraldine researches and prepares hundreds of questions for Don José. Then Alberto Roman translates Don Jose's Spanish responses and stories into English in real time onto an audio recorder. The audio files are transcribed in India and sent to Geraldine, who compiles our many weeks of interviews and conversations with Don José. Geraldine then edits and weaves them into a beautiful book (including a few dozen of her photographs). The book gently gives readers a real feeling for the Ayahuasca experience through the life experience of shaman Don José. It is the only book available from a practicing Peruvian shaman and is Divine Arts' best-selling book.

GERALDINE

A life without a wife is not a life. This book has been all about me, but I don't end where my skin contacts the air. Geraldine begins where I leave off. She expands me. She has so permeated my consciousness that I think her thoughts are mine. Her thoughts and feelings are often indistinguishable from mine. We often catch ourselves thinking what the other was thinking at that moment. We laugh, "I am you and you are me."

When we set our intentions on something, it has the power of planets lining up. We can accomplish anything. Designing a life of beauty, having a daughter, moving to and starting a life in Cornwall, enhancing a dream cottage by the sea, making sacred journey films and starting the Divine Arts book imprint. All this has come about through our profound partnership.

These are things that can be seen by others as evidence of our union. But for me, it's the private memorable moments that I cherish the most. For many years, on Geraldine's birthday, Mother's Day, or our anniversary, I add little drawings in a special book for her. Ten years ago I started the book which begins, "Had we never met, I would have missed a lot..." and then is followed by sketches of the "moments." These drawings do not translate well by being described. After years of additions, this tiny book has grown into a treasure trove of small moments that reveal a huge and fulfilling life. If I were to be sent to a desert island and could only take one thing, it would be this little book.

Transforming
Self

2011  2012

"You are the traveler,
You are the path,
And you are the destination.

Be careful,
Never
To lose
The way to yourself."

Shihab Al-din Yahya Suhrawardi

....

Geraldine Overton

243

THE QUEST CONTINUES

Last month Geraldine and I joined the "Esoteric Quest to Ancient Alexandria," a conference presented by Ralph White and The New York's Open Center. We explored Egyptian magic and religion, Greek philosophers, and the confluence of ideas streaming into the ancient library at Alexandria. We attended a poetry reading at Constantine Cavafy's house, saw Sufi dancing, and joined the people in the street and squares where Egypt's revolution is taking place. The study of ancient civilizations — Egypt, Mesopotamia, Assyria, and Sumer all are new areas of interest for me. It's a time of celebration and appreciation, opened up by Ayahuasca and a return to my creative source. That inquisitive, searching, testing Michael is still looking upward.

We have launched a traveling Sacred Journeys Film Festival to show my recent films in many cities in the U.S. Hopefully, it will develop into an annual event and next year will include the spiritual films of other filmmakers. The intention is not only to show films, but to build communities and cross-pollinate sacred teachings.

I couldn't be more pleased with the publishing company. We enjoy a good reputation with the book trade, our vendors and our stable of beloved authors. We are putting out great books and the company has a small, but steady, growth rate. Our film book line, MWP, increased its yearly production from 14 books in 2010 to 22 books in 2011 for a combined MWP/Divine Arts output of 29 books. This year we will publish another 24 books. MWP also launched a series of radio blogs and hosted several "The Future of Story" screenwriting conferences. Geraldine, Julia, and I just returned from UFVA, a film educator's conference in Chicago. It was thrilling to join 20+ authors in presenting a number of panels and seeing them support each other's work in the MWP book booth. Of all the exhibitors, the MWP booth had the energy of a 24-hour party. It was always packed and we sold well over 600 books to film educators from all over the world. Many of them will make our books a mandatory text in their next classes.

I realize that we've created a cooperative creative community, something few other publishers have achieved. I am so grateful to be able to participate with these magnificent people, who are our authors, friends, almost family.

Julia, now 19, has finished high school (in the UK high school goes through year 13, so it's kind of like finishing junior college). She's been taking her gap year. So far she's worked in Capetown, South Africa, teaching English to young children in an orphanage; in Namibia, tracking elephants in a conservation program; in Buenos Aires, getting a TEFL certificate; and in Guatemala, working on a village community project. Now she's interning at London's Raindance Film Festival. We're very proud of her. I learned more from traveling than from my school years and it seems she is too. When she goes to university or film school she will enter as a much more evolved human being.

Creativity and productivity make me feel useful and I believe contribute to my healing, and there are benefits that go beyond this. There is clearly a "before" Ayahuasca and "after." Afterwards, life is more intense, more rich, more magical and mysterious than ever. My spiritual practices have deepened and throughout the day greater moments of lucidity occur, revealing beauty all around me. I've come to cherish our garden and the forest as a living library, and the plants as friends and teachers that enrich and enliven our lives. I am remembering to accept joy and love into my life, moment to moment.

The Parkinson's remains and yet changes. The constellation of symptoms change, like clouds in the sky, sometimes worsening, more times improving. Strange as it sounds, I have to give thanks to Parkinson's, because it has brought me to a deeper understanding of myself and my life.

Geraldine and Julia are bright beacons of light and a radiant source of joy. Many times when I see them cooking together or just sitting together talking, I think to myself, "It doesn't get any better than this." My network of friends, colleagues, and authors span the globe, with clusters in San Francisco, New York, Los Angeles, Bali, Peru, and England. I have had, and continue to have, many teachers to whom I am very grateful and hold in the highest esteem. I've had many lives, infinite lives, within this lifetime. And I feel this is just the beginning.

As Geraldine and I go through thousands of family photographs to select the ones for this book, I have conflicting emotions. First, there is a sadness; a feeling of loss. Couldn't I have just one more moment with baby Julia, feeling the curls on the back of her neck? At the same time, there is an enormous gratitude for the life I've been given and for the life Geraldine and I have created together. It is filled with an abundance of beauty. The life in Los Angeles and then in Cornwall that Geraldine has created for Julia is extraordinary. Our art is a personal art. It is a gift of life to ourselves. It's not a movie or a photograph or a book. It's what we surround ourselves with. It's a gift of friends, of visions, of quests in foreign lands, of mystery.

Today I walked onto the Cornish coastal path that borders our garden. I climbed up the cliffs and looked down upon a sparkling sea. It's a perfect moment. Around me are daffodils, bluebells, campion, yellow gorse and wild flowers in full bloom. I am still questing. I am still on the journey. The spirits of the forest, sea, and sky surround me. I am grateful to be alive.

Onward and Upward!

FILMS AND BOOKS FROM MICHAEL WIESE
MENTIONED IN THIS BOOK

THE SACRED SITES OF THE DALAI LAMAS
by Glenn H. Mullin

"As this most beautiful book reveals, the Dalai Lamas continue to teach us that there are, indeed, other ways of thinking, other ways of being, other ways of orienting ourselves in social, spiritual, and ecological space."

— Wade Davis, Explorer-in-Residence, National Geographic Society

$29.95 • 182 PAGES • ORDER NUMBER: TIBETBK
ISBN: 9781611250060

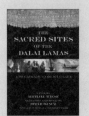

THE SACRED SITES OF THE DALAI LAMAS: A Pilgrimage to Oracle Lake
a film by Michael Wiese

This remarkable film visits the sacred sites of the Dalai Lamas in Tibet, tracing a pilgrimage with translator and author Glenn Mullin. This fascinating journey explores the caves where the early Buddhist masters meditated, enters the monasteries where the Dalai Lamas and others taught, and — at an altitude of over 16,000 feet — looks down into the famous Oracle Lake of Lhamo Lhatso where every Dalai Lama has had prophetic visions.

DVD ALL REGIONS: $24.95 • ORDER NUMBER: TIBET
ISBN: 1932907211 • 2 HOURS

THE SHAMAN & AYAHUASCA: Journeys to Sacred Realms
by Don José Campos

"This remarkable and beautiful book suggests a path back to understanding the profound healing and spiritual powers that are here for us in the plant world. This extraordinary book shows a way toward reawakening our respect for the natural world, and thus for ourselves."

— John Robbins, author, *The Food Revolution* and
Diet for a New America

$16.95 • 144 PAGES • ORDER NUMBER: SHAMANBK
ISBN: 9781611250039

THE SHAMAN & AYAHUASCA: Journeys to Sacred Realms
a film by Michael Wiese

"This is a gem of a movie — contemplatively paced, beautifully photographed, and filled with insights into the practice of Ayahuasca shamanism in the Upper Amazon. Poignant and moving, the film is enriched with an evocative soundtrack by Peruvian recording artist Artur Mena Salas."

— Steve Beyer, author, *Singing to the Plants*

DVD ALL REGIONS: $24.95 • ORDER NUMBER: SHAMAN
ISBN: 9781932907834 • 72 MINUTES

DOLPHIN ADVENTURES
a film by Michael Wiese and Hardy Jones
appearance by Buckminster Fuller

Jacques Cousteau tried. Pioneer dolphin researcher John Lilly said it couldn't be done. But in 1978 a ship of fools set out to swim in the open oceans with wild dolphins. Taking a cue from Aristotle, who said, "dolphins care for man and enjoy his music," the filmmakers played an 'underwater piano' and for three days interacted with a school of wild dolphins. A "close encounter of the aquatic kind," this classic film documents the first recorded human-wild dolphin encounter in modern times. With Ric O'Barry (*The Cove*).

DVD ALL REGIONS: $24.95 • ORDER NUMBER: DOLPHDVD
ISBN: 9781932907599 • 75 MINUTES

HARDWARE WARS: *Collector's Edition DVD*
written and directed by Ernie Fosselius
produced by Michael Wiese

This is the acknowledged granddaddy of all *Star Wars* parodies — and George Lucas' favorite, the sprawling space saga of romance, rebellion, steam-iron spaceships, flying toasters, and Digi-Redo 8.0 sound! It's time you were reunited with your old friends and fiends like Fluke Starbucker, Augie Ben Doggie, Princess Anne-Droid, Ham Salad, and the evil Darth Nader!

DVD REGION 0: $14.95 • ORDER NUMBER: HARD DVD
ISBN: 0941188477 • 1 HOUR

TALKING WITH SPIRITS: *Journeys into Balinese Spirit Worlds*
a film by Michael Wiese

"Opens the door to a new level of cultural and spiritual experience. This film breathes life into those who view it, giving us a journey that's unforgettable. Color, music, dance, sound and wonder abound and draw us in."

— Kathie Fong Yoneda, studio executive

DVD ALL REGIONS: $24.95 • ORDER NUMBER: TALKING
ISBN: 9781932907988 • 90 MINUTES

LIVING WITH SPIRITS: *10 Days in the Jungle with Ayahuasca*
a film by Michael Wiese

Under the auspices of Peruvian shaman Don José Campos, filmmaker Michael Wiese undertook a ten-day "dieta," during which he ate a special diet and drank plant medicines. *Living with Spirits*, a diary-style film, documents this extraordinary once-in-a-lifetime experience.

DVD ALL REGIONS: $24.95 • ORDER NUMBER: LIVING
ISBN: 9781615931347 • 60 MINUTES

MANDALAS OF BALI: *Our Place in the World*
by Dewa Nyoman Batuan   introduction by Lawrence Blair (*Ring of Fire*)

This powerful book is filled with images encapsulating physical and spiritual worlds of the most extraordinary island culture in the world.

$39.95 • 160 PAGES • ORDER NUMBER: 134RLS
ISBN: 9781932907650

1.800.833.5738 • 25% discount on books available online • www.divineartsmedia.com

{ THE MYTH OF MWP }

In a dark time, a light bringer came along, leading the curious and the frustrated to clarity and empowerment. It took the well-guarded secrets out of the hands of the few and made them available to all. It spread a spirit of openness and creative freedom, and built a storehouse of knowledge dedicated to the betterment of the arts.

The essence of the Michael Wiese Productions (MWP) is empowering people who have the burning desire to express themselves creatively. We help them realize their dreams by putting the tools in their hands. We demystify the sometimes secretive worlds of screenwriting, directing, acting, producing, film financing, and other media crafts.

By doing so, we hope to bring forth a realization of 'conscious media' which we define as being positively charged, emphasizing hope and affirming positive values like trust, cooperation, self-empowerment, freedom, and love. Grounded in the deep roots of myth, it aims to be healing both for those who make the art and those who encounter it. It hopes to be transformative for people, opening doors to new possibilities and pulling back veils to reveal hidden worlds.

MWP has built a storehouse of knowledge unequaled in the world, for no other publisher has so many titles on the media arts. Please visit www.mwp.com where you will find many free resources and a 25% discount on our books. Sign up and become part of the wider creative community!

Onward and upward,

Michael Wiese
Publisher/Filmmaker